PRENTICE HALL MATHEMATICS

ALGEBRA 2

Study Guide & Practice Workbook

PEARSON

Prentice Hall

Needham, Massachusetts
Upper Saddle River, New Jersey

ISBN: 0-13-125452-9
5 6 7 8 9 10 07 06 05

Study Guide & Practice Workbook

Contents

Answers appear in the back of each Grab & Go File.

Contents (cont.)

Name _____ Class _____ Date _____

Reteaching 1-1

OBJECTIVE: Finding additive and multiplicative inverses	**MATERIALS:** None

The *additive inverse* of a number a is $-a$. The number $-a$ is also called the *opposite* of a. The sum of a number and its opposite, $a + (-a)$, is always 0.

The *multiplicative inverse* of a nonzero number a is $\frac{1}{a}$. The number $\frac{1}{a}$ is also called the reciprocal of a. The product of a nonzero number and its reciprocal, $a \cdot \frac{1}{a}$, is always 1. The number 0 does not have a multiplicative inverse.

Examples

Find the opposite and reciprocal of each number.

a. -7.4 **b.** $3\frac{1}{2}$

a. Opposite: $-(-7.4) = 7.4$

Reciprocal: $\frac{1}{-7.4} = \frac{10}{-74} = -\frac{10}{74} = -\frac{5}{37}$

b. Opposite: $-\left(3\frac{1}{2}\right) = -3\frac{1}{2}$

Reciprocal: $\frac{1}{3\frac{1}{2}} = \frac{1}{\frac{7}{2}} = \frac{2}{7}$

Exercises

Find the opposite and reciprocal of each number.

1. 3 **2.** -2 **3.** $-\frac{1}{6}$ **4.** $\frac{3}{5}$

5. -2.4 **6.** 0.6 **7.** $-5\frac{2}{3}$ **8.** $2\frac{1}{4}$

9. $\frac{\pi}{2}$ **10.** $-\frac{1}{\pi}$ **11.** -0.25 **12.** 1.3

13. $1\frac{2}{5}$ **14.** $-\sqrt{2}$ **15.** $\pi + 2$ **16.** $-\frac{9}{10}$

Name _____ Class _____ Date _____

Practice 1-1

Properties of Real Numbers

Simplify.

1. $-|4.2|$

2. $|12 - 16|$

3. $\left|-\dfrac{7}{6}\right|$

4. $|3| - |-2|$

5. $\left|\dfrac{2}{3}\right|$

6. $0.3|-6|$

7. $|14 - 8|$

8. $|-0.01|$

Replace each \$ with the symbol <, >, or = to make the sentence true.

9. $-\sqrt{6}\ \$\ \sqrt{10}$

10. $\dfrac{3}{2}\ \$\ 1.5$

11. $0.06\ \$\ 0.6$

12. $4\ \$\ |-4|$

13. $-0.4\ \$\ 0$

14. $-|-7|\ \$\ |-7|$

15. $0.9\ \$\ \dfrac{2}{3}$

16. $\sqrt{2}\ \$\ \sqrt{5}$

Name all the sets of numbers to which each number belongs.

17. -5

18. 0

19. $\sqrt{5}$

20. $2.\overline{7}$

21. 9

22. $\dfrac{10}{7}$

23. $1.2345267831\ldots$

24. $-\dfrac{4}{2}$

Name the property of real numbers illustrated by each equation.

25. $\pi + 3 = 3 + \pi$

26. $\sqrt{2} + 0 = \sqrt{2}$

27. $(2 + x) + 3 = 2 + (x + 3)$

28. $\dfrac{5}{9} \cdot \dfrac{9}{5} = 1$

29. $16(3t + 4v) = 48t + 64v$

30. $\sqrt{2} \cdot 3 = 3 \cdot \sqrt{2}$

31. $0.01 \cdot 1 = 0.01$

32. $\dfrac{3}{2} \cdot \dfrac{2}{3} = 1$

33. $7 + (-7) = 0$

34. $2(xy) = (2x)y$

Graph the number on the following number line. Estimate if necessary.

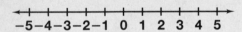

35. $-\sqrt{2}$

36. $\dfrac{3}{2}$

37. 0.5

38. -1

Find the opposite and the reciprocal of each number.

39. $-2\dfrac{1}{2}$

40. 3

41. $\dfrac{5}{9}$

42. -4

Which set of numbers best describes the values of each variable?

43. the number of stops N a commuter train makes on a certain day

44. the high H and low L for a certain stock during a period of n weeks

45. the average time per lap t it takes a race car to complete n laps

Algebra 2 Chapter 1

Name _____ Class _____ Date _____

Reteaching 1-2

OBJECTIVE: Simplifying and evaluating algebraic expressions   **MATERIALS:** None

To simplify an algebraic expression, combine like terms using the basic properties of real numbers. Like terms have the same variables raised to the same powers.

To evaluate an algebraic expression, replace the variables in the expression with numbers and follow the order of operations.

Example

Simplify the algebraic expression $3(4x + 5y) - 2(3x - 7y)$. Then evaluate the simplified expression for $x = 3$ and $y = -2$.

Simplify the algebraic expression using the basic properties of real numbers.

$$3(4x + 5y) - 2(3x - 7y) = 3(4x + 5y) + (-2)(3x + (-7)y) \longleftarrow \textbf{definition of subtraction}$$
$$= 12x + 15y + (-6)x + 14y \longleftarrow \textbf{Distributive Property}$$
$$= 12x + (-6)x + 15y + 14y \longleftarrow \textbf{Commutative Property of Addition}$$
$$= (12 + (-6))x + (15 + 14)y \longleftarrow \textbf{Distributive Property}$$
$$= 6x + 29y$$

Now replace x with 3 and y with -2 in the simplified expression.

$$6(3) + 29(-2) = 18 - 58 = -40$$

Exercises

Simplify the algebraic expression. Then evaluate the simplified expression for the given values of the variable.

1. $(4x + 1) + 2x; x = 3$

2. $7(t + 3) - 11; t = 4$

3. $3y + 4z + 6y - 9z; y = 2, z = 1$

4. $2(u + v) - (u - v); u = 8, v = -3$

5. $5a^2 + 5a + a + 1; a = -2$

6. $6p^2 - (3p^2 + 2q^2); p = 1, q = 5$

7. $\frac{3}{4}(m + n) - \frac{1}{4}(m - n); m = 6, n = 2$

8. $\frac{r}{2} + \frac{s}{3} - \frac{r}{4} + \frac{1}{5}; r = -1, s = 0$

Practice 1-2

Simplify by combining like terms.

1. $6x + x$

2. $11t + 3t - 5$

3. $-6a - 5a + b - 1$

4. $5i + 7j - 3i$

5. $16xy - 4xy$

6. $5x - 3x^2 + 16x^2$

7. $3(m - 2) + m$

8. $\frac{3(a - b)}{9} + \frac{4}{9}b$

9. $t + \frac{t^2}{2} + t^2 + t$

10. $4a - 5(a + 1)$

11. $2(m - n^2) - 6(n^2 + 3m)$

12. $x(x - y) + y(y - x)$

13. The expression $6s^2$ represents the surface area of a cube with edges of length s. Find the surface area of a cube with each edge length.

   a. 3 inches

   b. 1.5 meters

14. The expression $4.95 + 0.07x$ models a household's monthly long-distance charges, where x represents the number of minutes of long-distance calls during the month. Find the monthly charges for 73 minutes.

Evaluate each expression for the given value of the variable.

15. $5y^2 + y + 1; y = 4$

16. $a + 6 + 3a; a = 5$

17. $-t^2 - (3t + 2); t = 5$

18. $i^2 - 5(i^3 - i^2); i = 7$

19. $k + 2 - 4k - 1; k = -3$

20. $6a - 3a^2 - 2a^3; a = 1$

21. $-m(2m + m^2); m = -4$

22. $3 - 2n - 5 + n^2; n = -3$

23. $12b - 3 + b^2; b = 9$

24. $a^2 + b^2; a = 3, b = 4$

25. $c(3 - a) - c^2; a = 4, c = -1$

26. $-a^2 + 3(d - 2a); a = 2, d = -3$

27. Write an expression for the perimeter of the figure as the sum of the lengths of its sides. Then simplify your answer.

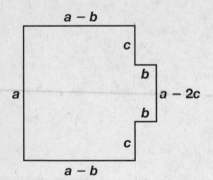

Name _____ Class _____ Date _____

Reteaching 1-3   Solving Equations

OBJECTIVE: Solving an equation for one of its variables

MATERIALS: None

To solve an equation for one of its variables, rewrite the equation as an equivalent equation with the specified variable on one side of the equation by itself and an expression not containing that variable on the other side.

Example

Solve the equation $\frac{ax - b}{2} = x + 2b$ for x.

Use the properties of equality and the properties of real numbers to rewrite the equation as a sequence of equivalent equations.

$$\frac{ax - b}{2} = x + 2b$$

$$2\left(\frac{ax - b}{2}\right) = 2(x + 2b) \quad \longleftarrow \textbf{Multiply each side by 2.}$$

$$ax - b = 2(x + 2b) \quad \longleftarrow \textbf{Simplify.}$$

$$ax - b = 2x + 4b \quad \longleftarrow \textbf{Distributive Property}$$

$$ax - 2x = 4b + b \quad \longleftarrow \textbf{Add and subtract to get terms with } x \textbf{ on one side and terms without } x \textbf{ on the other side.}$$

$$ax - 2x = 5b \quad \longleftarrow \textbf{Simplify.}$$

$$x(a - 2) = 5b \quad \longleftarrow \textbf{Distributive Property}$$

$$x = \frac{5b}{a - 2} \quad \longleftarrow \textbf{Divide each side by } a - 2.$$

The final form of the equation has x on the left side by itself and an expression not containing x on the right side.

Exercises

Solve each equation for the indicated variable.

1. $3m - n = 2m + n$, for m

2. $2(u + 3v) = w - 5u$, for u

3. $ax + b = cx + d$, for x

4. $k(y + 3z) = 4(y - 5)$, for y

5. $\frac{1}{2}r + 3s = 1$, for r

6. $\frac{2}{3}f + \frac{5}{12}g = 1 - fg$, for f

7. $\frac{x + k}{j} = \frac{3}{4}$, for x

8. $\frac{a - 3y}{b} + 4 = a + y$, for y

Practice 1-3

Solving Equations

Solve each formula for the indicated variable.

1. $V = \frac{\pi}{3} r^2 h$, for h

2. $S = L(1 - r)$, for r

3. $S = \ell w + wh + \ell h$, for w

Solve for x. State any restrictions on the variables.

4. $\frac{4}{9}(x + 3) = g$

5. $a(x + c) = b(x - c)$

6. $\frac{x + 3}{t} = t^2$

7. Two brothers are saving money to buy tickets to a concert. Their combined savings is $55. One brother has $15 more than the other. How much has each saved?

8. The sides of a triangle are in the ratio 5 : 12 : 13. What is the length of each side of the triangle if the perimeter of the triangle is 15 in.?

9. Find three consecutive numbers whose sum is 126.

Solve each equation.

10. $\frac{1}{2}(x - 3) + \left(\frac{3}{2} - x\right) = 5x$

11. $5w + 8 - 12w = 16 - 15w$

12. $7y + 5 = 6y + 11$

13. $1.2(x + 5) = 1.6(2x + 5)$

14. $t - 3\left(t + \frac{4}{3}\right) = 2t + 3$

15. $0.5(c + 2.8) - c = 0.6c + 0.3$

16. $3(x + 1) = 2(x + 11)$

17. $\frac{u}{5} + \frac{u}{10} - \frac{u}{6} = 1$

18. Mike and Adam left a bus terminal at the same time and traveled in opposite directions. Mike's bus was in heavy traffic and had to travel 20 mi/h slower than Adam's bus. After 3 hours, their buses were 270 miles apart. How fast was each bus going?

19. Two trains left a station at the same time. One traveled north at a certain speed and the other traveled south at twice the speed. After 4 hours, the trains were 600 miles apart. How fast was each train traveling?

20. Find four consecutive odd integers whose sum is 336.

21. The length of a rectangle is 5 cm greater than its width. The perimeter is 58 cm. Find the dimensions of the rectangle.

Reteaching 1-4

Solving Inequalities

• •

OBJECTIVE: Solving and graphing inequalities   **MATERIALS:** None

To solve an inequality, use the techniques used to solve an equation with one difference: when multiplying or dividing each side by a negative number, reverse the inequality.

Examples

Solve each inequality. Graph the solutions.

a. $2x - 5 \geq 13$ **b.** $4 + 3(1 - 2x) > 37$

Use the properties of real numbers and the properties of inequalities to rewrite each inequality in equivalent forms.

a. When dividing each side by a positive number, do not reverse the inequality.

$$2x - 5 \geq 13$$

$\qquad 2x \geq 18$ ⟵ **Add 5 to each side.**

$\qquad x \geq 9$ ⟵ **Divide each side by 2.**

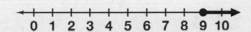

b. When dividing each side by a negative number, reverse the inequality.

$$4 + 3(1 - 2x) > 37$$

$\qquad 4 + 3 - 6x > 37$ ⟵ **Distributive Property**

$\qquad 7 - 6x > 37$ ⟵ **Simplify.**

$\qquad -6x > 30$ ⟵ **Subtract 7 from each side.**

$\qquad x < -5$ ⟵ **Divide each side by –6 and reverse the inequality.**

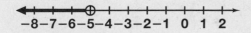

Exercises

Solve each inequality. Graph the solutions.

1. $3(y - 5) \leq 6$ **2.** $-4t > 2$ **3.** $3 - 4m < 11$ **4.** $7d \leq 2(d + 5)$

5. $-2(3 - h) + 2h \geq 0$ **6.** $3k - (1 - 2k) > 1$ **7.** $5p + 12 \leq 9p - 20$ **8.** $3 - 2r < 7 - r$

• •

Practice 1-4

Solving Inequalities

Solve each inequality. Graph the solutions.

1. $16 - 4t \leq 36$

2. $2(m + 3) + 1 > 23$

3. $7 + 13(x + 1) \leq 3x$

4. $-6a < 21$

5. $\frac{2}{3}(4x + 5) > \frac{9}{4}x$

6. $2[5x - (3x - 4)] < 3(2x + 3)$

7. $8(x - 5) \geq 56$

8. $6 - x \leq 7x + 3$

9. $10 - x \geq -2(3 + x)$

Solve each compound inequality. Graph the solutions.

10. $-9 \leq 4x + 3 \leq 11$

11. $16x \leq 32$ or $-5x < -40$

12. $9x < 54$ and $-4x < 12$

13. $6(x + 2) \geq 24$ or $5x + 10 \leq 15$

14. $14 > 3x - 1 \geq -10$

15. $4 < 1 - 3x < 7$

16. $2(x - 1) < -4$ or $2(x - 1) > 4$

17. $3x - 5 \geq -8$ and $3x - 5 \leq 1$

Solve each problem by writing an inequality.

18. A salesperson earns $350 per week plus 10% of her weekly sales. Find the sales necessary for the salesperson to earn at least $800 in one week.

19. The length of a rectangular yard is 50 ft, and its perimeter is less than 170 ft. Describe the width of the yard.

20. Xul is two years older than his sister Maria. The sum of their ages is greater than 32. Describe Maria's age.

21. A research team estimates that 30% of their questionnaires will not be returned. How many questionnaires should they mail out in order to be reasonably certain that at least 750 will be returned?

Solve each problem by writing a compound inequality.

22. Watermelons cost $.39 per pound at a local market. Kent's watermelon cost between $4.00 and $5.00. What are the possible weights of his watermelon?

23. How much must a carpenter cut off a 48-inch board if the length must be 40 ± 0.25 inches?

24. A concrete slab requires between 10 and 12 yd^3 of concrete. If 2.5 yd^3 of concrete can be poured each hour, how long will it take to pour the slab?

Reteaching 1-5

Absolute Value Equations and Inequalities

| **OBJECTIVE:** Solving absolute value equations | **MATERIALS:** None |

For every positive real number a, both a and $-a$ satisfy the equation $|x| = a$.

To solve an absolute value equation, first rewrite the equation as an equivalent equation with the absolute value expression on the left side by itself. Then rewrite this equation as a compound equality using the rule that if $|x| = a$ then $x = a$ or $x = -a$.

Example

Solve the equation $2|x - 3| + 1 = 6x + 7$. Check for extraneous solutions.

Use the properties of equality to rewrite the equation as an equivalent equation with the absolute value expression on one side by itself. Then write that equation as a compound equality and solve each resulting equation.

$$2|x - 3| + 1 = 6x + 7$$
$$2|x - 3| = 6x + 6 \qquad \longleftarrow \textbf{Subtract 1 from each side.}$$
$$|x - 3| = 3x + 3 \qquad \longleftarrow \textbf{Divide each side by 2.}$$

$$x - 3 = 3x + 3 \text{ or } x - 3 = -(3x + 3) \qquad \longleftarrow \textbf{Rewrite as a compound equality.}$$
$$-2x = 6 \qquad \text{or} \quad x - 3 = -3x - 3 \qquad \longleftarrow \textbf{Solve each equation.}$$
$$x = -3 \qquad \text{or} \qquad 4x = 0$$
$$x = -3 \qquad \text{or} \qquad x = 0$$

To check for extraneous solutions, substitute each value for x in the original absolute value equation. Any value that does not satisfy the original equation must be discarded.

Check $2|-3 - 3| + 1 \stackrel{?}{=} 6(-3) + 7 \qquad 2|0 - 3| + 1 \stackrel{?}{=} 6(0) + 7$

$\qquad\qquad 2|-6| + 1 \stackrel{?}{=} -18 + 7 \qquad\qquad 2|-3| + 1 \stackrel{?}{=} 0 + 7$

$\qquad\qquad\quad 2(6) + 1 \stackrel{?}{=} -11 \qquad\qquad\qquad 2(3) + 1 \stackrel{?}{=} 7$

$\qquad\qquad\qquad\quad 13 \neq -11 \qquad\qquad\qquad\qquad\quad 7 = 7$

The only solution is 0; -3 is an extraneous solution.

Exercises

Solve each equation. Check for extraneous solutions.

1. $|2x + 7| = 5$ **2.** $|x - 3| = -1$ **3.** $|x + 7| = 2x + 8$ **4.** $|x - 0.5| + 0.3 = 1$

5. $3|2x + 5| = 15$ **6.** $|5x - 1| + 7 = 3x$ **7.** $2|x + 1| + x = 1$ **8.** $|x + 1| = 2x$

Practice 1-5

Absolute Value Equations and Inequalities

Write each specification as an absolute value inequality.

1. $6.3 \leq h \leq 10.3$ **2.** $-2.5 \leq a \leq 2.5$ **3.** $22 \leq x \leq 33$

Solve each inequality. Graph the solutions.

4. $|x + 5| > 12$ **5.** $|k - 3| \leq 19$ **6.** $|x + 2| \geq 0$

7. $2|t - 5| < 14$ **8.** $|3x - 2| + 7 \geq 11$ **9.** $5|2b + 1| - 3 \leq 7$

10. $|2 - 3w| \geq 4$ **11.** $-3|7m - 8| < 5$ **12.** $|2u| > 6$

Solve each equation. Check for extraneous solutions.

13. $|4x| = 28$ **14.** $|3x + 6| = -12$ **15.** $|z - 1| = 7z - 13$

16. $|s + 12| = 15$ **17.** $|-3x| = 63$ **18.** $2|5x + 3| = 16$

19. $|6x + 7| = 5x + 2$ **20.** $|7r - 4| = 24$ **21.** $|3c| + 2 = 11$

22. $5|x + 1| + 6 = 21$ **23.** $|3x + 5| - 2x = 3x + 4$ **24.** $-|d + 2| = 7$

Write an absolute value inequality and a compound inequality for each length x with the given tolerance.

25. a length of 4.2 cm with a tolerance of 0.01 cm

26. a length of 3.5 m with a tolerance of 0.2 cm

27. a length of 10 ft with a tolerance of 1 in.

28. Write an absolute value inequality and a compound inequality for the temperature T that was recorded to be as low as 65°F and as high as 87°F on a certain day.

29. The weight of a 40-lb bag of fertilizer varies as much as 4 oz from the stated weight. Write an absolute value inequality and a compound inequality for the weight w of a bag of fertilizer.

30. The duration of a telephone call to a software company's help desk is at least 2.5 minutes and at most 25 minutes. Write an absolute value inequality and a compound inequality for the duration d of a telephone call.

Reteaching 1-6

Probability

OBJECTIVE: Finding theoretical probability	**MATERIALS:** None

The possible results of an experiment are **outcomes.** If you want to find the theoretical probability of a particular event, or a **favorable outcome,** you use this formula:

$$P(\text{event}) = \frac{\text{number of outcomes in the event}}{\text{number of possible outcomes}}$$

Example

Find the theoretical probability of rolling a number cube and having an outcome of either 2 or 4.

$$P(2 \text{ or } 4) = \frac{(\text{number of times 2 or 4 are outcomes})}{(\text{total possible numbers on cube})} = \frac{2}{6}$$

$$= \frac{1}{3}$$

Exercises

Use the spinner at the right to determine the theoretical probability for each event.

1. P(the number is even)

2. $P(5)$

3. P(the number is prime)

4. P(the number is less than 6)

5. P(an odd number)

6. P(a number divisible by 2)

7. P(a multiple of 3)

8. P(an 11 or 15)

9. P(a composite number)

10. P(the number represents your age)

11. P(a perfect square)

12. P(the number represents your grade)

13. P(not a 5 or 7)

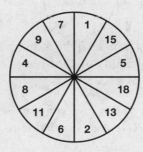

Practice 1-6

1. You select a number at random from the sample space {1, 2, 3, 4, 5}.
   Find each theoretical probability.

   a. P(the number is 2)   **b.** P(the number is even)

   c. P(the number is prime)   **d.** P(the number is less than 5)

2. In a class of 19 students, 10 study Spanish, 7 study French, and 2 study
   both French and Spanish. One student is picked at random. Find each
   probability.

   a. P(studying Spanish but not French)   **b.** P(studying neither Spanish nor French)

   c. P(studying both Spanish and French)   **d.** P(studying French)

3. In a telephone survey of 150 households, 75 respondents answered
   "Yes" to a particular question, 50 answered "No," and 25 were "Not
   sure." Find each experimental probability.

   a. P(answer was "Yes")   **b.** P(answer was "No")

   c. P(answer was "Not sure")   **d.** P(answer was not "Not sure")

4. A wallet contains four bills with denominations of $1, $5, $10, and $20.
   You choose two of the four bills from the wallet at random and add the
   dollar amounts.

   a. What is the sample space? How many outcomes are there?

   b. What is the probability of getting $15?

   c. What is the probability of getting $50?

   d. What is the probability of getting at least $25?

5. A basketball player has attempted 24 shots and made 13. Find the
   experimental probability that the player will make the next shot that
   she attempts.

6. A baseball player attempted to steal a base 70 times and was successful
   47 times. Find the experimental probability that the player will be
   successful on his next attempt to steal a base.

**For Exercises 7–8, define a simulation by telling how you represent correct
answers, incorrect answers, and the quiz. Use your simulation to find each
experimental probability.**

7. If you guess the answers at random, what is the probability of getting at
   least three correct answers on a four-question true-false quiz?

8. A five-question multiple-choice quiz has four choices for each answer.
   If you guess the answers at random, what is the probability of getting
   at least four correct answers?

9. A circular pool of radius 12 ft is enclosed within a rectangular yard
   measuring 50 ft by 100 ft. If a ball from an adjacent golf course lands at
   a random point within the yard, what is the probability that the ball
   lands in the pool?

10. Five people each flip a coin. What is the theoretical probability that all
    five will get heads?

Reteaching 2-1

OBJECTIVE: Determining whether a relation is a function

MATERIALS: Number cube

- A **relation** is a set of ordered pairs.

- The **domain** is the set of the first numbers in each pair, or the *x*-values.

- The **range** is the set of the second numbers in each pair, or the *y*-values.

- A relation is a **function** if each input value *x* corresponds to exactly one output value *y*. In a set of ordered pairs for a function, an *x*-value cannot be repeated with two or more different *y*-values.

Example

Roll a number cube six times to get the *x*-values of six ordered pairs in a relation. Roll it six more times to get the *y*-values of the ordered pairs. Decide whether the relation is a function. Find the domain and the range of the relation.

$\{(6, 1), (2, 1), (5, 4), (2, 2), (1, 4), (4, 2)\}$ ⟵ **Write the ordered pairs.**

$\{(6, 1), (②, 1), (5, 4), (②, 2), (1, 4), (4, 2)\}$ ⟵ **Circle any *x*-values that repeat to determine whether the relation is a function.**

The *x*-value 2 is repeated with two different *y*-values so the relation is not a function.

The domain is the set of first numbers in each pair: $\{6, 2, 5, 1, 4\}$.
The range is the set of second numbers in each pair: $\{1, 4, 2\}$.

Exercises

Roll a number cube to find the indicated number of ordered pairs. Determine whether each set of ordered pairs is a function. Find the domain and range of each relation.

1. 5 ordered pairs **2.** 4 ordered pairs **3.** 6 ordered pairs **4.** 8 ordered pairs

Determine whether each relation is a function. Explain your answer. Find the domain and range of each relation.

5. $\{(1, 2), (1, 3), (1, 4), (1, 5), (1, 6)\}$ **6.** $\{(0, -1), (1, 2), (-1, -1), (-2, 5), (2, 9)\}$

7. $\{(A, B), (C, D), (E, F), (G, H)\}$ **8.** $\{(I, M), (N, P), (I, T), (I, P)\}$

9. $\{(0, 0)\}$ **10.** $\left\{\left(\frac{1}{2}, 3\right), (0.5, 4), (2, 1)\right\}$

Practice 2-1

Relations and Functions

For each function, find $f(-2)$, $f\left(-\frac{1}{2}\right)$, $f(3)$, and $f(7)$.

1. $f(x) = 5x + 2$

2. $f(x) = -\frac{1}{3}x + 1$

3. $f(x) = -3x + 1.8$

Use the vertical line test to determine whether each graph represents a function.

4.

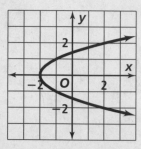

5.

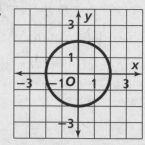

6.

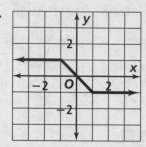

Graph each relation. Find the domain and range.

7. $\left\{ (1, -2), \left(2, \frac{3}{4}\right), \left(3, 3\frac{1}{2}\right), (5, 9) \right\}$

8. $\{(-3, 5), (0, -2), (0, 4), (1, -2)\}$

9. $\{(-1, 2), (2, 2), (3, 2)\}$

10. $\{(0.5, -1), (0.5, 0). (0.5, 1), (0.5, 3)\}$

Determine whether each graph represents y as a function of x.

11.

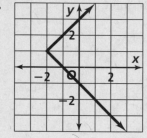

12.

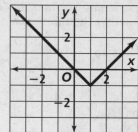

13.

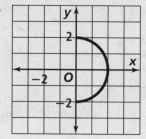

Make a mapping diagram for each relation, and determine whether it is a function.

14. $\{(1, 2), (2, 3), (2, 4), (3, 5)\}$

15. $\{(-1, 1), (0, 0), (1, 1), (2, 4), (3, 9)\}$

Suppose $f(x) = -3x + 2$ and $g(x) = \frac{1}{2}x - 1$. Find each value.

16. $f\left(\frac{1}{3}\right)$

17. $3g(4)$

18. $\dfrac{g(-2)}{f(3)}$

19. $\dfrac{f(-1)}{g(5)}$

Reteaching 2-2

OBJECTIVE: Using the slope-intercept form to write equations of lines	**MATERIALS:** None

- The slope-intercept formula is $y = mx + b$, where m represents the slope of the line, and b represents its y-intercept. The y-intercept is the point at which the line crosses the y-axis.

- The slope of a horizontal line is always zero, and the slope of a vertical line is always undefined.

Example

Find the equation of the line that contains the point $(3, -1)$ and has a slope of $-\frac{4}{3}$.

$-1 = \left(-\frac{4}{3}\right)(3) + b$ ⟵ **To find b, substitute the values $-\frac{4}{3}$ for m, 3 for x, and -1 for y into the slope-intercept formula.**

$-1 = -4 + b$

$3 = b$

$y = -\frac{4}{3}x + 3$ ⟵ **Substitute $-\frac{4}{3}$ for m and 3 for b into the slope-intercept formula.**

Exercises

Write the equation of each line.

1. $m = 4$; contains $(3, 2)$ **2.** $m = -2$; contains $(4, 7)$ **3.** $m = 0$; contains $(3, 0)$

4. $m = -1$; contains $(-5, -2)$ **5.** $m = 3$; contains $(-2, -4)$ **6.** $m = 0$; contains $(0, -7)$

7. $m = 8$; contains $(5, 0)$ **8.** $m = -1$; contains $(0, 7)$ **9.** $m = 0$; contains $(3, 8)$

10. $m = 4$; contains $(2, 5)$ **11.** $m = 7$; contains $(3, 2)$ **12.** $m = -1$; contains $(2, -6)$

Write the equation of each line.

13.
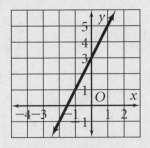

14.
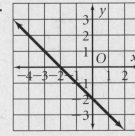

15.
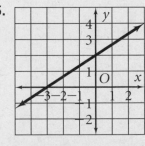

Practice 2-2

Linear Equations

Find the slope of each line.

1. $2x - 5y = 0$

2. $5x - y = -7$

3. $x - \frac{2}{3}y = \frac{1}{4}$

4.
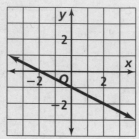

5.
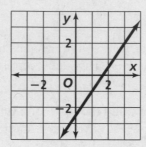

6.
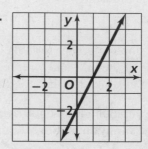

7. through $(4, -1)$ and $(-2, -3)$

8. through $(3, -5)$ and $(1, 2)$

Write in point-slope form the equation of the line through each pair of points.

9. $(0, 1)$ and $(3, 0)$

10. $\left(\frac{1}{2}, \frac{2}{3}\right)$ and $\left(-\frac{3}{2}, \frac{5}{3}\right)$

11. $(-3, -2)$ and $(1, 6)$

Graph each equation.

12. $4x + 3y = 12$

13. $\frac{x}{3} - \frac{y}{6} = 1$

14. $y = -\frac{3}{2}x + \frac{1}{2}$

Write in standard form an equation of the line with the given slope through the given point.

15. slope $= -4; (2, 2)$

16. slope $= \frac{2}{5}; (-1, 3)$

17. slope $= 0; (3, -4)$

Find the slope and the intercepts of each line.

18. $3x - 4y = 12$

19. $y = -2$

20. $f(x) = \frac{4}{5}x + 7$

21. $x = 5$

Write an equation for each line. Then graph the line.

22. through $(-1, 3)$ and parallel to $y = 2x + 1$

23. through $(2, 2)$ and perpendicular to $y = -\frac{3}{5}x + 2$

24. through $(-3, 4)$ and vertical

25. through $(4, 1)$ and horizontal

Reteaching 2-3

OBJECTIVE: Writing and interpreting direct variation equations	**MATERIALS:** None

A linear function defined by an equation of the form $y = kx$, where $k \neq 0$, represents *direct variation*. The constant k, the slope of the line, is called the *constant of variation*.

Given the value of y corresponding to a specific value of x, you can find the constant of variation k by substituting the given values of x and y into the equation $k = \frac{y}{x}$.

The equation $y = kx$ can be used to find the values of y that correspond to other values of x or vice versa.

Examples

Find the missing value for each direct variation.

a. If $y = 5$ when $x = 2$, find y when $x = 7$.

$$k = \frac{y}{x} = \frac{5}{2}$$ ⟵ **Use $y = 5$, $x = 2$, and $k = \frac{y}{x}$ to find the value of k.**

$$y = \frac{5}{2}x$$ ⟵ **Now use the form $y = kx$ and $k = \frac{5}{2}$ to write the equation of the direct variation.**

$$y = \frac{5}{2}x = \frac{5}{2}(7) = \frac{35}{2} = 17\frac{1}{2}$$ ⟵ **To find the value of y when $x = 7$, replace x with 7 in the direct variation equation and simplify to find y.**

b. If $y = 6$ when $x = -3$, find x when $y = -4$.

$$k = \frac{y}{x} = \frac{6}{-3} = -2$$ ⟵ **Use $y = 6$, $x = -3$, and $k = \frac{y}{x}$ to find the value of k.**

$$y = -2x$$ ⟵ **Now use the form $y = kx$ and $k = -2$ to write the equation of the direct variation.**

$$-4 = -2x$$
$$2 = x$$ ⟵ **To find the value of x when $y = -4$, replace y with -4 in the direct variation equation and solve for x.**

Exercises

Find the missing value for each direct variation.

1. If $y = 8$ when $x = 4$, find y when $x = 6$.

2. If $y = 12$ when $x = 3$, find y when $x = 5$.

3. If $y = 9$ when $x = 3$, find x when $y = 7$.

4. If $y = -6$ when $x = 2$, find x when $y = 9$.

5. If $y = \frac{3}{2}$ when $x = \frac{1}{4}$, find y when $x = \frac{2}{3}$.

6. If $y = 7$ when $x = 2$, find x when $y = 3$.

7. The height of an object varies directly with the length of its shadow.
A person 6 ft tall casts an $8\frac{1}{2}$ ft shadow, while a tree casts a 38 ft shadow.
How tall is the tree?

Practice 2-3

Direct Variation

For each direct variation, find the constant of variation. Then find the value of y when x = 3.

1. $y = 3$ when $x = -2$ **2.** $y = \frac{3}{4}$ when $x = \frac{1}{8}$ **3.** $y = -\frac{3}{8}$ when $x = -\frac{2}{3}$

Determine whether y varies directly with x. If so, find the constant of variation.

4. $y = \frac{4}{9}x$ **5.** $y = -1.2x$ **6.** $y + 4x = 0$ **7.** $y - 3x = 1$

8. $y = 3x$ **9.** $y + 2 = x$ **10.** $y - \frac{3}{5}x = 0$ **11.** $y = -3.5x + 7$

For each function, determine whether y varies directly with x. If so, find the constant of variation and write the equation.

12.

x	y
1	1
2	4
3	9

13.

x	y
-1	-3
1	3
3	9

14.

x	y
-2	-1
2	1
5	$\frac{5}{2}$

15.

x	y
-2	-3
0	1
1	3

Write an equation for a direct variation with a graph that passes through each point.

16. $(6, 2)$ **17.** $(-1.5, 9)$ **18.** $(-5, 90)$ **19.** $(7, 3)$

20. $\left(-1, -\frac{2}{3}\right)$ **21.** $\left(\frac{3}{5}, -\frac{7}{2}\right)$ **22.** $(10, 25)$ **23.** $(3, 165)$

In Exercises 24–27, y varies directly with x.

24. If $y = 3$ when $x = 2$, find x when $y = 5$.

25. If $y = -4$ when $x = \frac{1}{2}$, find y when $x = \frac{2}{3}$.

26. If $y = -14$ when $x = -7$, find x when $y = 22$.

27. If $y = \frac{5}{17}$ when $x = 10$, find y when $x = 5$.

28. A 15-minute long-distance telephone call costs $.90. The cost varies directly with the length of the call. Write an equation that relates the cost to the length of the call. How long is a call that costs $1.32?

29. The distance a spring stretches varies directly with the amount of weight that is hanging on it. A weight of 2.5 pounds stretches a spring 18 inches. Find the stretch of the spring when a weight of 6.4 pounds is hanging on it.

Reteaching 2-4

OBJECTIVE: Representing data graphically   **MATERIALS:** Graph paper, ruler

---

- A trend line is a mathematical model that shows the relationship between two sets of data.

- A trend line can be used to make predictions.

Example

Use the data in the table to draw a scatter plot and a trend line. Then predict the expenditures on drugs and other medical nondurables in 2001.

**U.S. Health Expenditures
Drug and Other Medical
Nondurables**

Year	Expenditures (billions of dollars)
1995	8.9
1996	9.4
1997	10.0
1998	10.6

Source: *The World Almanac and Book of Facts, 2001*

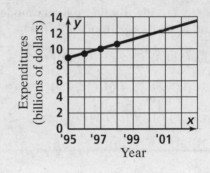

The model predicts expenditures of approximately 12.3 billion dollars in 2001.

Exercises

Use the data in the table.

**Percent of U.S. Population
Enrolled in HMOs**

Year	Percent	Year	Percent
1992	14.3	1996	22.3
1993	15.1	1997	25.2
1994	17.3	1998	28.6
1995	19.4	1999	30.1

Source: *The World Almanac and Book of Facts, 2001*

1. Draw a scatter plot.   **2.** Draw a trend line and write its equation.

3. Use your model to predict the percent of the U.S. population enrolled in HMOs in 2006.

Practice 2-4

Write an equation for each line.

1. y-intercept of -2.1, x-intercept of 3.5

2. through $(1.2, 5.1)$, x-intercept of 3.7

For each situation, find a linear model and use it to make a prediction.

3. The cost of producing 4 units is \$204.80. The cost of producing 8 units is \$209.60. How much does it cost to produce 12 units?

4. There were 174 words typed in 3 minutes. There were 348 words typed in 6 minutes. How many words will be typed in 8 minutes?

5. After 5 months the number of subscribers to a newspaper was 5730. After 7 months the number of subscribers to the newspaper was 6022. How many subscribers to the newspaper will there be after 10 months?

Graph each set of data. Decide whether a linear model is reasonable. If so, draw a trend line and write its equation.

6. $\{(1, 2.1), (3, 3.1), (5, 4.0), (7, 5.2), (9, 5.9)\}$

7. $\{(2, 3.5), (4, 4.9), (6, 6.3), (8, 4.6), (10, 2.9)\}$

8. $\{(-2, -3.9), (-1, -1.8), (0, 0.1), (1, 1.9), (2, 3.8)\}$

9. $\{(0.3, 0), (0.8, 3), (1.1, 5), (2.0, 6), (2.5, 6)\}$

10. The table shows the percentage of the population not covered by health insurance in selected states for the years 1990 and 1999.

State	Idaho	Illinois	Michigan	Montana	New York
1990	15.1	10.9	9.4	14.0	12.1
1999	19.1	14.1	11.2	18.6	16.4

Source: *The World Almanac and Book of Facts, 2001*

a. Draw a scatter plot showing the relationship between the percentage not covered by health insurance in 1990 and the percentage not covered in 1999. Use the 1990 percentage as the independent variable.

b. Use your scatter plot to develop a model relating the 1990 percentage to the 1999 percentage.

c. In Wyoming, 12.5% of the population were not covered by health insurance in 1990. Use your model to estimate the percentage who were not covered in 1999.

d. The actual percentage for Wyoming in 1999 was 16.1. Is your model reasonable?

Name _____ Class _____ Date _____

Reteaching 2-5

Absolute Value Functions and Graphs

●●

OBJECTIVE: Graphing absolute value functions   **MATERIALS:** Graph paper, ruler

A function of the form $f(x) = |mx + b|$ is an *absolute value function.*

The graph of $f(x) = |mx + b|$ looks like an angle; its vertex is located at

the point $\left(-\dfrac{b}{m}, 0\right)$.

Example

Graph $f(x) = |2x + 3|$.

First find the vertex. Using the form $\left(-\dfrac{b}{m}, 0\right)$ where $b = 3$ and $m = 2$, we obtain the

vertex $\left(-\dfrac{3}{2}, 0\right)$.

Now find several points on the graph of $f(x) = |2x + 3|$. Choose values of
x on both sides of the vertex.

x	-3	-2	-1	0	1
y	3	1	1	3	5

Plot the vertex and the points from the table in a rectangular coordinate
system. Finish the graph by drawing two rays emanating from the vertex
and passing through the other points.

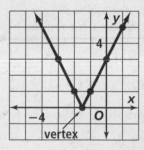

Exercises

Find the vertex of each absolute value function.

1. $f(x) = |5x|$

2. $f(x) = |x + 3|$

3. $f(x) = |x - 4|$

4. $f(x) = |3x + 1|$

5. $f(x) = \left|\dfrac{1}{2}x - 3\right|$

6. $f(x) = \left|\dfrac{1}{4}x + 2\right|$

**Find the vertex of each absolute value function. Then graph the function by
plotting several other points.**

7. $f(x) = |2x - 1|$

8. $f(x) = |3x - 1|$

9. $f(x) = |2x + 4|$

10. $f(x) = |x + 1|$

11. $f(x) = |x - 2|$

12. $f(x) = \left|2x - \dfrac{3}{2}\right|$

13. $f(x) = |3x|$

14. $f(x) = \left|\dfrac{1}{2}x + 1\right|$

15. $f(x) = \left|\dfrac{2}{3}x + 2\right|$

●●

Practice 2-5

Absolute Value Functions and Graphs

Match each equation with its graph.

1. $y = |x - 1|$　　　　**2.** $y = 2|x - 1|$　　　　**3.** $y = |2x| - 1$

4. $y = |x| - 1$　　　　**5.** $y = |2x - 1|$　　　　**6.** $y = |2x| - 2$

A. 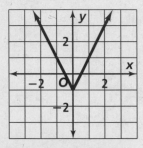　　　　**B.** 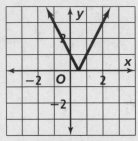　　　　**C.**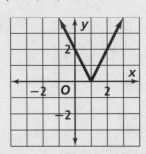

D. 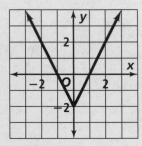　　　　**E.** 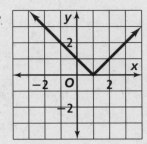　　　　**F.**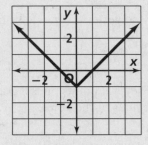

Graph each equation by writing two linear equations.

7. $y = |x - 3|$　　　　**8.** $y = |2x - 5|$　　　　**9.** $y = 2|x + 2|$

10. $y = |x + 3| - 1$　　　　**11.** $y = -|3x + 4|$　　　　**12.** $y = \left|\frac{1}{2}x - 2\right| + 1$

Graph each absolute value equation.

13. $y = |3 - x|$　　　　**14.** $y = -\frac{2}{3}\left|\frac{1}{3}x\right|$　　　　**15.** $y = 3 - |x + 1|$

16. $y = -|-x - 2|$　　　　**17.** $3y = |2x - 9|$　　　　**18.** $y = -|x| + 2$

19. $\frac{1}{2}y = |3x - 1| - 2$　　　　**20.** $y + 3 = |x + 1|$　　　　**21.** $-2y = |2x - 4|$

Reteaching 2-6

OBJECTIVE: Analyzing vertical, horizontal, and diagonal translations of the absolute value function

MATERIALS: Graph paper

If h and k are positive numbers, then

$g(x) = |x| + k$ shifts the graph of $f(x) = |x|$ up k units;

$g(x) = |x| - k$ shifts the graph of $f(x) = |x|$ down k units;

$g(x) = |x + h|$ shifts the graph of $f(x) = |x|$ left h units;

$g(x) = |x - h|$ shifts the graph of $f(x) = |x|$ right h units.

Examples

Graph each translation of $f(x) = |x|$.

1. a. $g(x) = |x| - 2$ ⟵ **Shift the graph of $f(x) = |x|$ down 2 units.**

b. $h(x) = |x + 1|$ ⟵ **Shift the graph of $f(x) = |x|$ left 1 unit.**

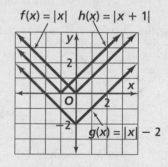

2. a. $g(x) = |x - 3| + 1$ ⟵ **Shift the graph of $f(x) = |x|$ right 3 units and up 1 unit.**

b. $h(x) = |x + 2| - 3$ ⟵ **Shift the graph of $f(x) = |x|$ left 2 units and down 3 units.**

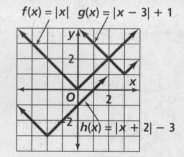

Exercises

Complete each sentence. Then graph the translation of $f(x) = |x|$.

1. $g(x) = |x - 2|$ ⟵ Shift the graph of $f(x) = |x|$ _____ 2 units.

2. $g(x) = |x| + 1$ ⟵ Shift the graph of $f(x) = |x|$ _____ 1 unit.

3. $g(x) = |x| - 3$ ⟵ Shift the graph of $f(x) = |x|$ _____ 3 units.

4. $g(x) = |x + 3|$ ⟵ Shift the graph of $f(x) = |x|$ _____ 3 units.

5. $g(x) = |x - 1| - 5$ ⟵ Shift the graph of $f(x) = |x|$ _____ 1 unit and _____ 5 units.

6. $g(x) = |x + 4| + 2$ ⟵ Shift the graph of $f(x) = |x|$ _____ 4 units and _____ 2 units.

Practice 2-6

Describe each translation of $f(x) = |x|$ as vertical, horizontal, or diagonal. Then graph each translation.

1. $f(x) = |x + 2|$

2. $f(x) = |x + 4|$

3. $f(x) = |x| - 5$

4. $f(x) = |x + 1| - 1$

5. $f(x) = |x - 2| + 1$

6. $f(x) = \left| x - \frac{3}{2} \right|$

7. $f(x) = |x| - \frac{1}{3}$

8. $f(x) = \left| x - \frac{5}{2} \right|$

9. $f(x) = \left| x + \frac{1}{2} \right| + \frac{3}{2}$

Write an equation for each translation.

10. $y = |x|$, 1 unit up, 2 units left

11. $y = |x|$, 4 units right

12. $y = -|x|$, 3 units up, 1 unit right

13. $y = -|x|$, $\frac{3}{2}$ units down, $\frac{1}{2}$ unit right

14. $y = |x|$, 2 units down, 3 units left

15. $y = -|x|$, $\frac{3}{5}$ unit up

Write the equation of each translation of $y = x$ or $y = |x|$.

16.

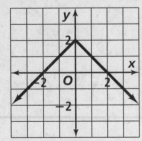

17.

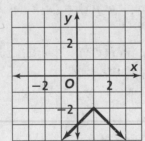

18.

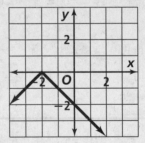

Each graph shows a translation of $y = -|x|$. State the values of h and k.

19.

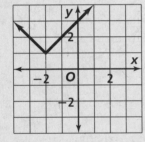

20.

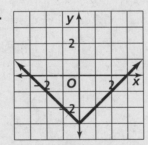

21.

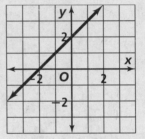

Graph each equation.

22. $y = |x - 1| + 2$

23. $y = -\left| x + \frac{1}{2} \right|$

24. $y = -|x + 3| - 1$

25. $y = |-x - 1|$

26. $y = -|x - 2| + 4$

27. $y = |x + 2| - 1$

Reteaching 2-7

OBJECTIVE: Graphing inequalities with two variables

MATERIALS: Highlighting marker

Example

Graph the inequality $6x - 2y \leq 12$.

$6x - 2y \leq 12$

$y \geq 3x - 6$ ← To graph the boundary line, write the inequality in slope-intercept form as if it were an equation.

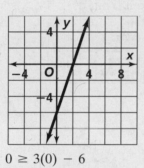

← The boundary line is solid if the inequality contains $\leq$ or $\geq$. The boundary line is dashed if the inequality contains $<$ or $>$. Graph the boundary line $y = 3x - 6$ as a solid line.

$0 \geq 3(0) - 6$ ← Since the boundary line does not contain the origin, substitute the point $(0, 0)$ into the inequality.

$0 \geq -6$ ← Simplify. The resulting inequality is true.

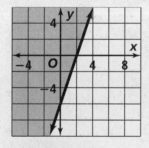

← Use your highlighting marker to shade the region that contains the origin. If the resulting inequality were false, then you would shade the region that does not contain the origin.

Exercises

Graph each inequality.

1. $y > 2x$ **2.** $x + y < 4$ **3.** $y < x + 1$

4. $y > x - 2$ **5.** $3x + 4y \leq 12$ **6.** $2y - 3x > 6$

7. $3x - 2 \leq 5x + y$ **8.** $x < -4$ **9.** $y \geq 5$

10. $x + 2y \geq 4$ **11.** $x + y < x + 2$ **12.** $3x - 3y < 3$

13. $x - 1 \geq 0$ **14.** $2y \leq 3$ **15.** $3x > 2 + y$

Practice 2-7

Two-Variable Inequalities

Write an inequality for each graph. In each case, the equation for the
boundary line is given.

1. $y = x - 2$

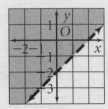

2. $x - 2y = 4$

3. $y - 2x = 4$

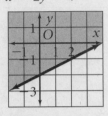

4. $y = -2$

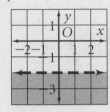

5. $x = 2$

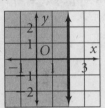

6. $-2x - 3y = 6$

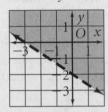

7. $3x - y = 3$

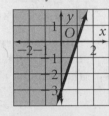

8. $y - 3x = 3$

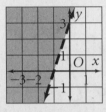

Graph each inequality on a coordinate plane.

9. $y < x$ **10.** $y \geq x$ **11.** $y > 2$ **12.** $y < 2$

13. $x \leq 2$ **14.** $x > 2$ **15.** $y \geq |x|$ **16.** $y > -2x + 1$

17. $y \geq 3x - 4$ **18.** $4x + 2y \leq 8$ **19.** $4x - 2y \leq 4$ **20.** $4y - 2x \geq 4$

21. $y > |x + 2|$ **22.** $y \leq |x - 2|$ **23.** $y > |x| + 2$ **24.** $y < |x| - 2$

25. $y \leq |4x| + 1$ **26.** $y \geq \left|\frac{1}{6}x\right| - 3$ **27.** $y > -\frac{1}{6}x - 1$ **28.** $3x \leq 5y$

29. You need to make at least 150 sandwiches for a picnic. You are making
tuna sandwiches and ham sandwiches.

  a. Write an inequality for the number of sandwiches you can make.

  b. Graph the inequality.

  c. Does the point $(90, 80)$ satisfy the inequality? Explain.

30. A salesperson sells two models of vacuum cleaners. One brand sells for
$150 each, and the other sells for $200 each. The salesperson has a
weekly sales goal of at least $1800.

  a. Write an inequality relating the revenue from the vacuum cleaners
to the sales goal.

  b. Graph the inequality.

  c. If the salesperson sold exactly six $200 models last week, how many
$150 models did she have to sell to make her sales goal?

Name _____ Class _____ Date _____

Reteaching 3-1

Graphing Systems of Equations

OBJECTIVE: Solving a system by graphing

MATERIALS: One blue and one yellow highlighter

As you solve a system of equations, remember the following ideas.

- Lines that have the same slopes but different y-intercepts are parallel and will never intersect. These systems are *inconsistent*.
- Lines that have both the same slope and the same y-intercept are the same line and will intersect at every point. These systems are *dependent*.
- Lines that have different slopes will intersect, and the system will have one solution. These systems are *independent*.

Example

Solve the system of equations by graphing. $\begin{cases} 2x + y = 8 \\ y - x = 2 \end{cases}$

$y = -2x + 8$ ⟵ **Write both equations in $y = mx + b$ form.**
$y = x + 2$

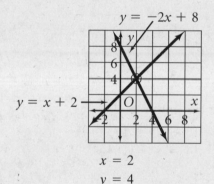

⟵ **Graph the line $y = -2x + 8$ with a blue highlighter. Graph the line $y = x + 2$ with a yellow highlighter. The point of intersection will be green. Circle it.**

$x = 2$ ⟵ **Determine the x- and y-coordinates of the point of intersection.**
$y = 4$

The solution is the ordered pair $(2, 4)$.

$2(2) + 4 \stackrel{?}{=} 8$ ⟵ **Check by substituting the solution into both equations.**

$4 + 4 \stackrel{?}{=} 8$

$8 = 8$ ✔

$4 - 2 \stackrel{?}{=} 2$

$2 = 2$ ✔

Exercises

Use colored highlighters to solve each system of equations by graphing.

1. $\begin{cases} 3x + y = 6 \\ y = 3 \end{cases}$

2. $\begin{cases} -2x + y + 3 = 0 \\ x - 1 = y \end{cases}$

3. $\begin{cases} x + y = 3 \\ y = 3x - 1 \end{cases}$

4. $\begin{cases} y = 1 - x \\ 2x + y = 4 \end{cases}$

5. $\begin{cases} -x + 2y = 2 \\ 3x + 2y = -6 \end{cases}$

6. $\begin{cases} -x + y = -2 \\ -2x + 3y = -3 \end{cases}$

Practice 3-1

Classify each system without graphing.

1. $\begin{cases} x + y = 3 \\ y = 2x - 3 \end{cases}$

2. $\begin{cases} 2x + y = 3 \\ y = -2x - 1 \end{cases}$

3. $\begin{cases} x + 3y = 9 \\ -2x - 6y = -18 \end{cases}$

4. $\begin{cases} x + y = 4 \\ y = 2x + 1 \end{cases}$

5. $\begin{cases} x + 3y = 9 \\ 9y + 3x = 27 \end{cases}$

6. $\begin{cases} x + 2y = 5 \\ 2x + 3y = 9 \end{cases}$

7. $\begin{cases} 3x + 2y = 7 \\ 3x - 15 = -6y \end{cases}$

8. $\begin{cases} x + y = 6 \\ 3x + 3y = 3 \end{cases}$

9. $\begin{cases} x + y = 11 \\ y = x - 5 \end{cases}$

10. $\begin{cases} x + 2y = 13 \\ 2y = 7 - x \end{cases}$

11. $\begin{cases} y = 12 - 5x \\ x - 4y = -6 \end{cases}$

12. $\begin{cases} 25x - 10y = 0 \\ 2y = 5x \end{cases}$

13. The spreadsheet below shows the monthly income and expenses for a new business.

   a. Find a linear model for monthly income and a linear model for monthly expenses.

   b. Use the models to estimate the month in which income will equal expenses.

	A	B	C
	Month	**Income**	**Expenses**
1	May	$1500	$21,400
2	June	$3500	$18,800
3	July	$5500	$16,200
4	August	$7500	$13,600

Solve each system by graphing. Check your answers.

14. $\begin{cases} y = x - 2 \\ x + y = 10 \end{cases}$

15. $\begin{cases} y = 7 - x \\ x + 3y = 11 \end{cases}$

16. $\begin{cases} x - 2y = 10 \\ y = x - 11 \end{cases}$

17. $\begin{cases} 5x + y = 11 \\ x - y = 1 \end{cases}$

18. $\begin{cases} x + y = -1 \\ x - y = 3 \end{cases}$

19. $\begin{cases} x - y = -1 \\ 2x + 2y = 10 \end{cases}$

20. $\begin{cases} 4x + 3y = -16 \\ -x + y = 4 \end{cases}$

21. $\begin{cases} y = -3x \\ x + y = 2 \end{cases}$

22. $\begin{cases} y = \frac{2}{3}x - 5 \\ y = -\frac{2}{3}x - 3 \end{cases}$

23. $\begin{cases} y = \frac{1}{2}x + 3 \\ y = -\frac{1}{4}x - 3 \end{cases}$

24. $\begin{cases} 2x - 4y = -4 \\ 3x - y = 4 \end{cases}$

25. $\begin{cases} x + y = 6 \\ x - y = 4 \end{cases}$

Algebra 2 Chapter 3

Reteaching 3-2

OBJECTIVE: Using elimination to solve a system	**MATERIALS:** Graphing calculator (optional)

Follow these steps when using elimination to solve systems.

Step 1: Arrange the equations with like terms in columns.

Step 2: Circle the like terms for which you want to obtain coefficients that are opposites.

Step 3: Multiply each term of one or both equations by an appropriate number.

Step 4: Add the equations.

Step 5: Solve for the remaining variable.

Step 6: Substitute the value obtained in step 5 into either of the original equations, and solve for the other variable.

Step 7: Check the solution in the other original equation.

Example

Solve the system using the elimination method. $\begin{cases} 2x + 5y = 11 \\ 3x - 2y = -12 \end{cases}$

$$\boxed{2x} + 5y = 11 \qquad \longleftarrow \textbf{Circle the terms that you want to make opposite.}$$
$$\boxed{3x} - 2y = -12$$

$$6x + 15y = 33 \qquad \longleftarrow \textbf{Multiply each term of first equation by 3.}$$
$$-6x + 4y = 24 \qquad \longleftarrow \textbf{Multiply each term of second equation by} -2.$$

$$19y = 57 \qquad \longleftarrow \textbf{Add the equations.}$$
$$y = 3 \qquad \longleftarrow \textbf{Solve for the remaining variable.}$$

$$3x - 2(3) = -12 \qquad \longleftarrow \textbf{Substitute 3 for } y \textbf{ to solve for } x.$$
$$x = -2$$

$$2(-2) + 5(3) \overset{?}{=} 11 \qquad \longleftarrow \textbf{Check using the other equation.}$$
$$-4 + 15 \overset{?}{=} 11$$
$$11 = 11 ✔$$

The solution is $(-2, 3)$. You can also check the solution by using a graphing calculator.

Exercises

Solve each system of equations using elimination.

1. $\begin{cases} 3x + 2y = -17 \\ x - 3y = 9 \end{cases}$
2. $\begin{cases} 5f + 4m = 6 \\ -2f - 3m = -1 \end{cases}$
3. $\begin{cases} 3x - 2y = 5 \\ -6x + 4y = 7 \end{cases}$
4. $\begin{cases} -2x - 4y = 2 \\ 10x + 20y = -10 \end{cases}$

Practice 3-2

Solving Systems Algebraically

• •

Solve each system by elimination.

1. $\begin{cases} x + y = 10 \\ x - y = 2 \end{cases}$

2. $\begin{cases} -x + 3y = -1 \\ x - 2y = 2 \end{cases}$

3. $\begin{cases} x + y = 7 \\ x + 3y = 11 \end{cases}$

4. $\begin{cases} 4x - 3y = -2 \\ 4x + 5y = 14 \end{cases}$

5. $\begin{cases} x + 2y = 10 \\ 3x - y = 9 \end{cases}$

6. $\begin{cases} 2x - 5y = 11 \\ 4x + 10y = 18 \end{cases}$

7. $\begin{cases} x - y = 0 \\ x + y = 2 \end{cases}$

8. $\begin{cases} x + 3y = -4 \\ y + x = 0 \end{cases}$

9. $\begin{cases} 3x - y = 17 \\ y + 2x = 8 \end{cases}$

10. Suppose your drama club is planning a production that will cost
    $525 for the set and $150 per performance. A sold-out performance
    will bring in $325. Write an equation for the cost C and an equation for
    the income I for p sold-out performances. Find how many sold-out
    performances will make the cost equal to the income.

Solve each system by substitution. Check your answers.

11. $\begin{cases} y = x + 1 \\ 2x + y = 7 \end{cases}$

12. $\begin{cases} x = y - 2 \\ 3x - y = 6 \end{cases}$

13. $\begin{cases} y = 2x + 3 \\ 5x - y = -3 \end{cases}$

14. $\begin{cases} 6x - 3y = -33 \\ 2x + y = -1 \end{cases}$

15. $\begin{cases} 2x - y = 7 \\ 3x - 2y = 10 \end{cases}$

16. $\begin{cases} 4x = 8y \\ 2x + 5y = 27 \end{cases}$

17. $\begin{cases} x + 3y = -4 \\ y + x = 0 \end{cases}$

18. $\begin{cases} 3x + 2y = 9 \\ x + y = 3 \end{cases}$

19. $\begin{cases} 2y - 3x = 4 \\ x = -4 \end{cases}$

20. Suppose you bought eight oranges and one grapefruit for a total of
    $4.60. Later that day, you bought six oranges and three grapefruits for
    a total of $4.80. Now you want to find the price of each orange and of
    each grapefruit. Write an equation for each purchase. Solve the system
    of equations.

Solve each system.

21. $\begin{cases} y = x + 3 \\ 5x + y = 9 \end{cases}$

22. $\begin{cases} 5x + 4y = 2 \\ -5x - 2y = 4 \end{cases}$

23. $\begin{cases} y = 2x + 3 \\ 5x - y = -3 \end{cases}$

24. $\begin{cases} 14x + 2y = 10 \\ x - 5y = 11 \end{cases}$

25. $\begin{cases} x + 5y = 1 \\ 2x = 2 - 10y \end{cases}$

26. $\begin{cases} 0.3x + 0.4y = 0.8 \\ 0.7x - 0.8y = -6.8 \end{cases}$

27. $\begin{cases} 4x + 3y = -6 \\ 5x - 6y = -27 \end{cases}$

28. $\begin{cases} 2y = -4x \\ 4x + 2y = -11 \end{cases}$

29. $\begin{cases} 1.2x + 1.4y = 2.7 \\ 0.4x - 0.3y = 0.9 \end{cases}$

Reteaching 3-3

Solving Systems of Inequalities

OBJECTIVE: Solving systems of inequalities	MATERIALS: Graph paper and a graphing calculator (optional)

Example

Solve the system $\begin{cases} 2x - y > 1 \\ x + y \geq 3 \end{cases}$ by graphing.

Step 1
Solve each inequality for y.
$$2x - y > 1$$
$$-y > -2x + 1$$
$$y < 2x - 1$$
and
$$x + y \geq 3$$
$$y \geq -x + 3$$

Step 2
Graph the boundary lines. Use a solid line for $\geq$ or $\leq$ inequalities. Use a dotted line for $>$ and $<$ inequalities.

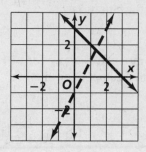

Step 3
Then shade on the appropriate side of each boundary line.

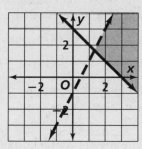

Exercises

Solve each system of inequalities by graphing.

1. $\begin{cases} y \leq x \\ y \geq 3x - 1 \end{cases}$

2. $\begin{cases} 2x + y > 3 \\ x - y < 2 \end{cases}$

3. $\begin{cases} x > 1 \\ y < x + 1 \end{cases}$

4. $\begin{cases} x + 3y \leq 9 \\ 2x - y > 1 \end{cases}$

5. $\begin{cases} y < -\frac{1}{3}x - 1 \\ y \geq 3x + 1 \end{cases}$

6. $\begin{cases} 4x + y \leq 1 \\ x + 2y \leq -1 \end{cases}$

7. $\begin{cases} y \leq 3 \\ y > 4x - 3 \end{cases}$

8. $\begin{cases} 2x + y < 3 \\ 3x - y < 2 \end{cases}$

9. $\begin{cases} y \geq -2 \\ 3x + y \leq 2 \end{cases}$

Practice 3-3

Solving Systems of Inequalities

Solve each system of inequalities by graphing.

1. $\begin{cases} y > x + 2 \\ y \le -x + 1 \end{cases}$

2. $\begin{cases} y \le x + 3 \\ y \ge x + 2 \end{cases}$

3. $\begin{cases} x + y < 5 \\ y < 3x - 2 \end{cases}$

4. $\begin{cases} x - 2y < 3 \\ 2x + y > 8 \end{cases}$

5. $\begin{cases} -3x + y < 3 \\ x + y > -1 \end{cases}$

6. $\begin{cases} x + 2y > 4 \\ 2x - y > 6 \end{cases}$

7. $\begin{cases} 2x \ge y + 3 \\ x < 3 - 2y \end{cases}$

8. $\begin{cases} 3 < 2x - y \\ x - 3y \le 4 \end{cases}$

9. $\begin{cases} y \ge 2 \\ y \ge |x| \end{cases}$

10. $\begin{cases} y < x - 3 \\ y \ge |x - 4| \end{cases}$

11. $\begin{cases} -2x + y > 1 \\ y > |x| \end{cases}$

12. $\begin{cases} y < -3 \\ y < -|x| \end{cases}$

13. Suppose you are buying two kinds of notebooks for school. A spiral notebook costs $2, and a three-ring notebook costs $5. You must have at least six notebooks. The cost of the notebooks can be no more than $20.

    a. Write a system of inequalities to model the situation.

    b. Graph and solve the system.

14. A camp counselor needs no more than 30 campers to sign up for two mountain hikes. The counselor needs at least 10 campers on the low trail and at least 5 campers on the high trail.

    a. Write a system of inequalities to model the situation.

    b. Graph and solve the system.

Solve each system of inequalities by graphing.

15. $\begin{cases} 2x + y > 2 \\ x - y \ge 3 \end{cases}$

16. $\begin{cases} y \le 3x \\ y \ge -2x + 2 \end{cases}$

17. $\begin{cases} y < 5x - 1 \\ y \ge 7 - 3x \end{cases}$

18. $\begin{cases} y \ge -2x + 2 \\ y \le 3x \end{cases}$

19. $\begin{cases} x + y > 2 \\ 2x - y < 1 \end{cases}$

20. $\begin{cases} y > 3x + 2 \\ y \le -2x + 1 \end{cases}$

21. $\begin{cases} y \ge -2 \\ y \le -|x + 3| \end{cases}$

22. $\begin{cases} y < x + 3 \\ y > |x - 1| \end{cases}$

23. $\begin{cases} y > x \\ y < |x + 2| \end{cases}$

Reteaching 3-4

OBJECTIVE: Solving linear programming problems	**MATERIALS:** Graph paper

Example

Use linear programming. Find the values of x and y that maximize and minimize the objective function $P = 10x + 15y$.

Restrictions $\begin{cases} x + y \leq 16 \\ 3x + 6y \leq 60 \\ x \geq 0 \\ y \geq 0 \end{cases}$

Step 1
Graph the restrictions.

Step 2
Find coordinates of each vertex of the region.

VERTEX

$A\,(0, 0)$

$B\,(16, 0)$

$C\,(12, 4)$

$D\,(0, 10)$

Step 3
Evaluate P at each vertex.

$P = 10x + 15y$

$P = 10(0) + 15(0) - 0$

$P = 10(16) + 15(0) = 160$

$P = 10(12) + 15(4) = 180$

$P = 10(0) + 15(10) = 150$

The maximum value of the objective function is 180. It occurs when $x = 12$ and $y = 4$.

The minimum value of the objective function is 0. It occurs when $x = 0$ and $y = 0$.

Exercises

Use linear programming. Find the values of x and y that maximize and minimize each objective function.

1. $\begin{cases} 5y + 4x \leq 35 \\ 5y + \ x \geq 20 \\ y \leq 6 \\ x \geq 1 \end{cases}$

$P = 8x + 2y$

2. $\begin{cases} x + y \geq 2 \\ x \geq y \\ x \leq 4 \\ y \geq 0 \end{cases}$

$P = x + 3y$

3. $\begin{cases} 3x + 4y \geq 12 \\ 5x + 6y \leq 30 \\ 1 \leq x \leq 3 \end{cases}$

$P = x - 2y$

Practice 3-4

Linear Programming

Graph each system of constraints. Name all vertices. Then find the
values of *x* and *y* that maximize or minimize the objective function.

1. $\begin{cases} x + 2y \leq 6 \\ x \geq 2 \\ y \geq 1 \end{cases}$

Minimum for
$C = 3x + 4y$

2. $\begin{cases} x + y \leq 5 \\ x + 2y \leq 8 \\ x \geq 0, y \geq 0 \end{cases}$

Maximum for
$P = x + 3y$

3. $\begin{cases} x + y \leq 6 \\ 2x + y \leq 10 \\ x \geq 0, y \geq 0 \end{cases}$

Maximum for
$P = 4x + y$

4. $\begin{cases} 3x + 2y \leq 6 \\ 2x + 3y \leq 6 \\ x \geq 0, y \geq 0 \end{cases}$

Maximum for
$P = 4x + y$

5. $\begin{cases} 4x + 2y \leq 4 \\ 2x + 4y \leq 4 \\ x \geq 0, y \geq 0 \end{cases}$

Maximum for
$P = 3x + y$

6. $\begin{cases} x + y \leq 5 \\ 4x + y \leq 8 \\ x \geq 0, y \geq 0 \end{cases}$

Minimum for
$C = x + 3y$

Find the values of *x* and *y* that maximize or minimize the objective
function for each graph. Then find the maximum or minimum value.

7.

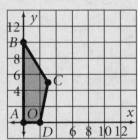

Maximize for $P = 2x + 3y$

8.

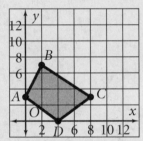

Minimize for $C = x + 2y$

9.

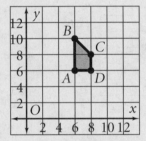

Maximize for $P = 3x + y$

10. You are going to make and sell bread. A loaf of Irish soda bread is
made with 2 c flour and $\frac{1}{4}$ c sugar. Kugelhopf cake is made with 4 c flour
and 1 c sugar. You will make a profit of $1.50 on each loaf of Irish soda
bread and a profit of $4 on each Kugelhopf cake. You have 16 c flour
and 3 c sugar.

a. How many of each kind of bread should you make to maximize
the profit?

b. What is the maximum profit?

11. Suppose you make and sell skin lotion. A quart of regular skin lotion
contains 2 c oil and 1 c cocoa butter. A quart of extra-rich skin lotion
contains 1 c oil and 2 c cocoa butter. You will make a profit of $10/qt
on regular lotion and a profit of $8/qt on extra-rich lotion. You have
24 c oil and 18 c cocoa butter.

a. How many quarts of each type of lotion should you make to
maximize your profit?

b. What is the maximum profit?

Reteaching 3-5

Graphs in Three Dimensions

OBJECTIVE: Graphing points in three dimensions

MATERIALS: Cardboard box

Use the inside corner of a cardboard box to model a three-dimensional coordinate system in which x, y, and z are all greater than 0.

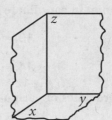

- First label the bottom (or horizontal) edges of the box as the x-axis and the y-axis.

- Then the z-axis will be the vertical edge that passes through the origin or corner where the three edges meet.

Example

Graph $(3, 4, 5)$ in three dimensions. First, locate the point using the cardboard box. Start at the back left corner of the box. Move forward three units. Move right four units. Move up five units.

Then graph the point.

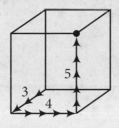

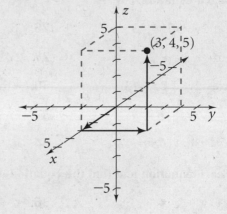

Exercises

Locate and graph each point in three dimensions by following the steps in the example.

1. $(1, 2, 0)$	**2.** $(3, 2, 3)$	**3.** $(4, 0, 3)$	**4.** $(5, 1, 2)$
5. $(2, 5, 1)$	**6.** $(0, 0, 4)$	**7.** $(3, -1, -1)$	**8.** $(-3, -3, -3)$
9. $(5, 0, 1)$	**10.** $(0, 1, 3)$	**11.** $(1, 2, -5)$	**12.** $(5, 3, -4)$
13. $(2, 4, 6)$	**14.** $(-2, -2, -2)$	**15.** $(-1, -2, 5)$	**16.** $(1, 2, 8)$
17. $(-4, -5, 1)$	**18.** $(0, 0, 2)$	**19.** $(1, -4, -5)$	**20.** $(-6, 2, -4)$

Practice 3-5

Graphs in Three Dimensions

Describe the location of each point in coordinate space.

1. $(3, 0, 0)$ **2.** $(0, 2, 0)$ **3.** $(3, -2, -4)$ **4.** $(-6, -4, -1)$

5. $(0, 0, 4)$ **6.** $(1, 2, 3)$ **7.** $(3, -1, 6)$ **8.** $(0, 4, -1)$

Graph each point in coordinate space.

9. $(0, 3, 0)$ **10.** $(2, 0, 0)$ **11.** $(0, 0, 5)$ **12.** $(-1, -4, -2)$

13. $(2, 3, 1)$ **14.** $(-1, -2, -3)$ **15.** $(6, -1, 0)$ **16.** $(4, -2, 3)$

Write the coordinates of each point in the diagram.

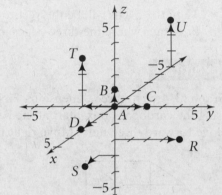

17. A **18.** B

19. C **20.** D

21. R **22.** T

23. U **24.** S

Graph each equation.

25. $x + 2y + 3z = 3$ **26.** $3x - 2y + z = 6$

27. $-6x - 3y + 2z = 6$ **28.** $2x - 3y + 3z = 6$

29. $8x - 2y - 2z = 8$ **30.** $-6x - 12y - 12z = 12$

31. $9x - 3y + z = 9$ **32.** $7x - 1y + 7z = 7$

33. $4x + 3y + 6z = 12$ **34.** $x - y + 2z = 6$

Graph each equation and find the equation of each trace.

35. $x + y + z = 3$ **36.** $x + 2y + 3z = 6$ **37.** $x + 3y + 2z = 6$

38. $2x + 3y + z = 6$ **39.** $-4x + 2y - 4z = 8$ **40.** $4x - 2y + 6z = 12$

41. $6x - 3y + z = 6$ **42.** $7x - 3y + 7z = 21$ **43.** $4x - 3y + 6z = -12$

Reteaching 3-6

Systems with Three Variables

OBJECTIVE: Using elimination to solve systems with three variables

MATERIALS: Pink, yellow, and green highlighting markers

Example

Solve the system using elimination.

$$\begin{cases} x + y + z = 6 \\ 2x - y + 3z = 9 \\ -x + 2y + 2z = 9 \end{cases}$$

⟵ **Use pink to highlight the first equation, yellow to highlight the second, and green to highlight the third.**

$$\begin{array}{rrrrr} x & + y & + z & = & 6 \\ -x & + 2y & + 2z & = & 9 \\ \hline & 3y & + 3z & = & 15 \end{array}$$

⟵ **Add the pink and green to eliminate x. Circle the resulting sum.**

$$\begin{array}{rrrrr} 2x & - y & + 3z & = & 6 \\ -x & + 2y & + 2z & = & 9 \end{array}$$

⟵ **Pair the yellow and green.**

$$\begin{array}{rrrrr} 2x & - y & + 3z & = & 9 \\ -2x & + 4y & + 4z & = & 18 \\ \hline & 3y & + 7z & = & 27 \end{array}$$

⟵ **Multiply the green equation by 2 to eliminate x and add the two equations. Circle the resulting sum.**

$$\begin{array}{rrrrr} 3y & + 3z & = & 15 \\ -3y & + (-7z) & = & -27 \\ \hline & -4z & = & -12 \\ & z & = & 3 \end{array}$$

⟵ **Pair the two circled equations. Subtract the second from the first to eliminate y and solve for z.**

$$\begin{aligned} 3y + 3(3) &= 15 \\ 3y &= 6 \\ y &= 2 \end{aligned}$$

⟵ **Substitute the value of z into either of the circled equations.**
⟵ **Solve for y.**

$$\begin{aligned} x + 2 + 3 &= 6 \\ x &= 1 \end{aligned}$$

⟵ **Substitute the values of y and z into any of the original equations. Solve for x.**

The solution is $(1, 2, 3)$.

Exercises

Solve each system using elimination.

1. $\begin{cases} 2x - y + 2z = 10 \\ 4x + 2y - 5z = 10 \\ x - 3y + 5z = 8 \end{cases}$

2. $\begin{cases} x - y + z = 6 \\ 2x + 3y + 2z = 2 \\ 3x + 5y + 4z = 4 \end{cases}$

3. $\begin{cases} 6x - 4y + 5z = 31 \\ 5x + 2y + 2z = 13 \\ x + y + z = 2 \end{cases}$

4. $\begin{cases} 3x + y + z = 2 \\ 4x - 2y + 3z = -4 \\ 2x + 2y + 2z = 8 \end{cases}$

5. $\begin{cases} 5x + 2y + z = 5 \\ 3x - 3y - 3z = 9 \\ x + 2y + 4z = 6 \end{cases}$

6. $\begin{cases} x + y + z = -1 \\ 4x + 3y + 2z = -10 \\ 2x - 4y - 2z = -6 \end{cases}$

Practice 3-6

Systems with Three Variables

Solve each system.

1. $\begin{cases} x + y + z = -1 \\ 2x - y + 2z = -5 \\ -x + 2y - z = 4 \end{cases}$

2. $\begin{cases} x + y + z = 3 \\ 2x - y + 2z = 6 \\ 3x + 2y - z = 13 \end{cases}$

3. $\begin{cases} 2x + y = 9 \\ x - 2z = -3 \\ 2y + 3z = 15 \end{cases}$

4. $\begin{cases} x - y + 2z = 10 \\ -x + y - 2z = 5 \\ 3x - 3y + 6z = -2 \end{cases}$

5. $\begin{cases} 2x - y + z = -4 \\ 3x + y - 2z = 0 \\ 3x - y = -4 \end{cases}$

6. $\begin{cases} 2x - y - z = 4 \\ -x + 2y + z = 1 \\ 3x + y + z = 16 \end{cases}$

7. $\begin{cases} x + 5y + 5z = -10 \\ x + y + z = 2 \\ x + 2y + 3z = -3 \end{cases}$

8. $\begin{cases} x - y - z = 0 \\ x - 2y - 2z = 3 \\ -2x + 2y - z = 3 \end{cases}$

9. $\begin{cases} 3x + y + z = 6 \\ 3x - 2y + 2z = 14 \\ 3x + 3y - 3z = -6 \end{cases}$

10. $\begin{cases} x + y + z = -2 \\ 2x + 2y - 3z = 11 \\ 3x - y + z = 4 \end{cases}$

11. $\begin{cases} x - 5y + z = 3 \\ x + 2y - 2z = -12 \\ 2x + 2z = 6 \end{cases}$

12. $\begin{cases} 2x + 3z = 2 \\ 3x + 6y = 6 \\ x - 2z = 8 \end{cases}$

13. $\begin{cases} x + y - z = 0 \\ 3x - y + z = 4 \\ 5x + z = 7 \end{cases}$

14. $\begin{cases} x - 2y = 1 \\ x + 3y + z = 0 \\ 2x - 2z = 18 \end{cases}$

15. $\begin{cases} x + y + 4z = 5 \\ -2x + 2z = 3 \\ 3x + y - 2z = 0 \end{cases}$

16. $\begin{cases} 3x + 2y + 2z = 4 \\ -6x + 4y - 2z = -9 \\ 9x - 2y + 2z = 10 \end{cases}$

17. $\begin{cases} 2x - 3y + z = -3 \\ x - 5y + 7z = -11 \\ -10x + 4y - 6z = 28 \end{cases}$

18. $\begin{cases} x + y + z = -8 \\ x - y - z = 6 \\ 2x - 3y + 2z = -1 \end{cases}$

19. $\begin{cases} 14x - 3y + 5z = -15 \\ 3x + 2y - 6z = 10 \\ 7x - y + 4z = -5 \end{cases}$

20. $\begin{cases} 5x - 3y + 2z = 39 \\ 4x + 4y - 3z = 34 \\ 3x - 2y + 6z = 14 \end{cases}$

21. $\begin{cases} x + y + z = 6 \\ 2x - y + 2z = 6 \\ -x + y + 3z = 10 \end{cases}$

22. $\begin{cases} 2x + y - z = 3 \\ 3x - y + 3z = 3 \\ -x - 3y + 2z = 3 \end{cases}$

23. $\begin{cases} 2x - 3y + z = 4 \\ -2x + 3y - z = -4 \\ 6x - 9y + 3z = 12 \end{cases}$

24. $\begin{cases} x + y - z = 1 \\ x + 2z = 3 \\ 2x + 2y = 4 \end{cases}$

Write and solve a system of equations for each problem.

25. The sum of three numbers is −2. The sum of three times the first number, twice the second number, and the third number is 9. The difference between the second number and half the third number is 10. Find the numbers.

26. Monica has $1, $5, and $10 bills in her wallet that are worth $96. If she had one more $1 bill, she would have just as many $1 bills as $5 and $10 bills combined. She has 23 bills total. How many of each denomination does she have?

Reteaching 4-1

Organizing Data into Matrices

OBJECTIVE: Organize data into matrices   **MATERIALS:** Number cube

---

- The size, or order, of a matrix is specified by its dimensions.
  A 4 × 9 matrix has 4 rows and 9 columns.

Example

Roll the number cube to set up a 4 × 2 matrix. Each time, roll twice to produce a two-digit number. Use the left hand first, then the right.

	Left	Right
Trial 1	36	
Trial 2		
Trial 3		
Trial 4		

← **Roll the cube twice with your left hand. Suppose these rolls generate a 3 and a 6; in this case, write 36 in row 1.**

	Left	Right
Trial 1	36	
Trial 2	24	
Trial 3	26	
Trial 4	55	

← **Repeat, rolling with your left hand to fill in the first column.**

	Left	Right
Trial 1	36	15
Trial 2	24	43
Trial 3	26	22
Trial 4	55	46

← **Fill the second column for trials 1–4 by rolling with your right hand.**

Exercises

Use a number cube to produce the following matrix.

1. Create a 6 × 3 matrix. Label your columns left hand, right hand, and both hands. Let your rows represent six trials.

2. Rewrite the Example matrix as a 2 × 4 matrix.

3. Rewrite the matrix in Exercise 1 as a 3 × 6 matrix.

Practice 4-1

Write the dimensions of each matrix. Identify the indicated element.

1. $\begin{bmatrix} 2 \\ -3 \\ -6 \end{bmatrix}; a_{21}$

2. $\begin{bmatrix} 5 & -7 & 23 & 10 \\ -9 & 3 & 5 & -2 \\ 1 & 9 & 0 & 2 \end{bmatrix}; a_{23}$

3. $\begin{bmatrix} 2 & 3 & -9 \\ 12 & -8 & 0 \end{bmatrix}; a_{21}$

4. $\begin{bmatrix} x & y & z \\ a & b & c \\ p & q & r \end{bmatrix}; a_{32}$

5. $\begin{bmatrix} 2 & -2 \\ 3 & -3 \\ 4 & -4 \end{bmatrix}; a_{31}$

6. $\begin{bmatrix} 5 & 8 & -7 & -4 \end{bmatrix}; a_{14}$

Use the table for Exercises 7–10.

7. Display the data in a matrix with the types of unemployment in the columns.

8. State the dimensions of the matrix.

9. Identify a_{21}, and tell what it represents.

10. Identify a_{16}, and tell what it represents.

Unemployment by Category

	June, 1992	June, 1996
Construction	17.6%	9.5%
Manufacturing	8.3%	5.1%
Transportation	5.4%	4.5%
Sales	8.7%	6.4%
Finance	4.0%	2.6%
Services	6.6%	5.1%
Government	3.5%	2.7%

Source: *U.S. News & World Report*

Use the table at the right for Exercises 11–14.

11. Write a matrix *M* to represent the data in the graph, with columns representing years.

12. What are the dimensions of this matrix?

13. What does the first row represent?

14. What does m_{32} represent?

Days Lost to Strikes per 1,000 Employees

Source: *U.S. News & World Report*

Reteaching 4-2

Adding and Subtracting Matrices

OBJECTIVE: Adding and subtracting matrices   **MATERIALS:** Colored pencils

• To add or subtract matrices of the same size, circle the corresponding entries and their results with the same color pencils.

Example

Add the two matrices. Use a different color for each set of corresponding entries.

$\begin{bmatrix} -3 & 5 \\ 9 & -2 \end{bmatrix} + \begin{bmatrix} 7 & -1 \\ 8 & -4 \end{bmatrix} =$ ← **Add the corresponding entries.**

$\begin{bmatrix} -3 & 5 \\ 9 & -2 \end{bmatrix} + \begin{bmatrix} 7 & -1 \\ 8 & -4 \end{bmatrix} = \begin{bmatrix} 4 & \\ & \end{bmatrix}$ ← **(−3) + 7 = 4**

$\begin{bmatrix} -3 & 5 \\ 9 & -2 \end{bmatrix} + \begin{bmatrix} 7 & -1 \\ 8 & -4 \end{bmatrix} = \begin{bmatrix} 4 & 4 \\ & \end{bmatrix}$ ← **5 + (−1) = 4**

$\begin{bmatrix} -3 & 5 \\ 9 & -2 \end{bmatrix} + \begin{bmatrix} 7 & -1 \\ 8 & -4 \end{bmatrix} = \begin{bmatrix} 4 & 4 \\ 17 & \end{bmatrix}$ ← **9 + 8 = 17**

$\begin{bmatrix} -3 & 5 \\ 9 & -2 \end{bmatrix} + \begin{bmatrix} 7 & -1 \\ 8 & -4 \end{bmatrix} = \begin{bmatrix} 4 & 4 \\ 17 & -6 \end{bmatrix}$ ← **(−2) + (−4) = (−6)**

Exercises

Circle the corresponding entries. Add or subtract the following matrices.

1. $\begin{bmatrix} -3 & 8 \\ 9 & -2 \end{bmatrix} + \begin{bmatrix} 1 & -5 \\ 5 & 0 \end{bmatrix}$

2. $\begin{bmatrix} 1 & -2 \\ 0 & -6 \end{bmatrix} - \begin{bmatrix} 6 & -3 \\ -1 & -8 \end{bmatrix}$

Add or subtract the following matrices.

3. $\begin{bmatrix} 1.5 & 0.5 \\ -2.5 & 2.5 \end{bmatrix} + \begin{bmatrix} -2.5 & -1.5 \\ 3.5 & -4.5 \end{bmatrix}$

4. $\begin{bmatrix} 3 & 1 & 4 \\ 0 & 2 & 1 \end{bmatrix} - \begin{bmatrix} 2 & 0 & 5 \\ 3 & 1 & 6 \end{bmatrix}$

5. $\begin{bmatrix} -9 & 2 & 0 \\ -1 & 0 & 3 \end{bmatrix} + \begin{bmatrix} -7 & -3 & -4 \\ 8 & -7 & -9 \end{bmatrix}$

6. $\begin{bmatrix} 7.5 & 4 \\ 3.5 & 5 \end{bmatrix} - \begin{bmatrix} 3 & -1.5 \\ 0.5 & -6.5 \end{bmatrix}$

7. $\begin{bmatrix} -1 & -4 \\ 0 & 5 \\ 9 & 0 \end{bmatrix} + \begin{bmatrix} -8 & -2 \\ 0 & -4 \\ -1 & 5 \end{bmatrix}$

8. $\begin{bmatrix} 0 & 1 \\ 5 & 2 \\ -9 & 0 \end{bmatrix} - \begin{bmatrix} -5 & -4 \\ -7 & -2 \\ 8 & 2 \end{bmatrix}$

9. $\begin{bmatrix} -2 & 5.5 \\ 9.5 & -4 \\ 0 & 3 \\ -7.5 & 6 \end{bmatrix} - \begin{bmatrix} 7 & -1.5 \\ 6 & 2.5 \\ -1.5 & 3 \\ -4 & 1 \end{bmatrix}$

10. $\begin{bmatrix} -4 & 0 & 2 \\ 1 & -7 & -5 \\ 2 & -4 & 9 \end{bmatrix} + \begin{bmatrix} -1 & -3 & 6 \\ 2 & 5 & 1 \\ 5 & -1 & -3 \end{bmatrix}$

Practice 4-2

Adding and Subtracting Matrices

Find the value of each variable.

1. $\begin{bmatrix} a & 2b \\ c-2 & d+3 \end{bmatrix} = \begin{bmatrix} 5 & -7 \\ 10 & 10 \end{bmatrix}$

2. $\begin{bmatrix} 3 & 5 & -y & x \\ z & 0 & 3a & b \end{bmatrix} = \begin{bmatrix} 3 & 3c & 7 & 4 \\ \frac{7}{2} & 0 & -9 & 3b \end{bmatrix}$

3. $\begin{bmatrix} 5 & 1 \\ 0 & 2 \end{bmatrix} + \begin{bmatrix} 2 & -13 \\ -10 & -10 \end{bmatrix} = \begin{bmatrix} 2x+1 & -4x \\ 5z & 2.5z-x \end{bmatrix}$

Use the information in the table.

4. Put the data in two matrices: one for males and one for females.

5. Use matrix subtraction to find the difference between the number of males and the number of females in each club each year.

Club Membership at TC High School

	1961–1962		2001–2002	
	Males	Females	Males	Females
Beta	37	23	56	58
Spanish	0	93	76	82
Chess	87	0	102	34
Library	6	18	27	29

Find each sum or difference.

6. $\begin{bmatrix} -1 & 2 \\ 3 & -1 \end{bmatrix} + \begin{bmatrix} -1 & 2 \\ -3 & 1 \end{bmatrix} + \begin{bmatrix} 0 & -1 \\ 2 & 0 \end{bmatrix}$

7. $\begin{bmatrix} 8 & -5 & -5 \\ 4 & -10 & 10 \\ 2 & -15 & -15 \end{bmatrix} - \begin{bmatrix} 0 & 0 & 1 \\ 1 & -2 & -2 \\ -2 & -3 & 3 \end{bmatrix}$

8. $\begin{bmatrix} -2 & -1 \\ -3 & 1 \\ -1 & -1 \end{bmatrix} - \begin{bmatrix} -2 & -2 \\ 3 & -1 \\ 0 & -2 \end{bmatrix} + \begin{bmatrix} -2 & 1 \\ 0 & 3 \\ -3 & -3 \end{bmatrix}$

9. $\begin{bmatrix} 1 \\ 1 \\ 1 \end{bmatrix} + \begin{bmatrix} -1 \\ -3 \\ 5 \end{bmatrix} + \begin{bmatrix} -10 \\ -7 \\ 11 \end{bmatrix} - \begin{bmatrix} -3 \\ -5 \\ -6 \end{bmatrix}$

Solve each matrix equation.

10. $X - \begin{bmatrix} 3 & 4 \\ 4 & 2 \\ 1 & 9 \end{bmatrix} = \begin{bmatrix} 5 & 7 \\ 9 & 12 \\ 3 & 2 \end{bmatrix}$

11. $X + \begin{bmatrix} 20 & -9 & -3 \\ 19 & -2 & -5 \\ -1 & 0 & -8 \end{bmatrix} = \begin{bmatrix} -7 & 92 & -5 \\ 0 & 91 & -6 \\ -9 & -1 & 12 \end{bmatrix}$

12. $\begin{bmatrix} -2 & -3 \\ 2 & 2 \end{bmatrix} = X - \begin{bmatrix} 1 & -1 \\ -2 & 2 \end{bmatrix}$

13. $\begin{bmatrix} 2 & 2 & 0 \\ 1 & -1 & -1 \end{bmatrix} = \begin{bmatrix} 2 & -2 & 3 \\ -3 & -3 & 4 \end{bmatrix} - X$

Determine whether the two matrices in each pair are equal. Justify your reasoning.

14. $\begin{bmatrix} 2 \\ \sqrt{9} \\ 16 \end{bmatrix}$; $\begin{bmatrix} \frac{4}{2} & 3 & 4^2 \end{bmatrix}$

15. $\begin{bmatrix} 2(3) & 3(1.5) \\ 7 & \frac{10}{2} \end{bmatrix}$; $\begin{bmatrix} 6 & 4.5 \\ 7 & 5 \end{bmatrix}$

Name _____ Class _____ Date _____

Reteaching 4-3

Matrix Multiplication

| **OBJECTIVE:** Multiplying matrices | **MATERIALS:** Two pencils |

- To multiply two matrices, the number of columns in the first matrix must be equal to the number of rows in the second matrix.

- The product matrix has the same number of rows as the first matrix and the same number of columns as the second matrix.

Example

Find the product AB.

$$AB = \begin{bmatrix} 3 & 1 & -1 \\ 2 & 0 & 3 \end{bmatrix} \begin{bmatrix} 1 & 4 \\ 3 & -1 \\ 2 & 5 \end{bmatrix}$$

Step 1: Check dimensions of matrices A and B to determine whether they can be multiplied. A has three columns and B has three rows.

$(3)(1) + (1)(3) + (-1)(2) = 4$

$\begin{bmatrix} 4 & \\ & \end{bmatrix}$

Step 2: Use two pencils to cover the second row of A and the second column of B so that only the first row of A and the first column of B can be seen. Multiply corresponding elements, and add the products. Place the result at $(AB)_{11}$.

$(3)(4) + (1)(-1) + (-1)(5) = 6$

$\begin{bmatrix} 4 & 6 \\ & \end{bmatrix}$

Step 3: Find $(AB)_{12}$ by multiplying the first row of A by the second column of B. Add the products, and enter the result. With your pencils, cover the rows and columns that you are not multiplying.

$(2)(1) + (0)(3) + (3)(2) = 8$

$\begin{bmatrix} 4 & 6 \\ 8 & \end{bmatrix}$

Step 4: Find $(AB)_{21}$ by multiplying the second row of A by the first column of B. Add the products, and enter the result.

$(2)(4) + (0)(-1) + (3)(5) = 23$

$\begin{bmatrix} 4 & 6 \\ 8 & 23 \end{bmatrix}$

Step 5: Find $(AB)_{22}$ by multiplying the second row of A by the second column of B. Add the products, and enter the result.

Exercises

Multiply the matrices.

1. $\begin{bmatrix} 1 & 2 \\ 4 & 3 \end{bmatrix} \begin{bmatrix} -3 & 5 \\ 2 & -1 \end{bmatrix}$

2. $\begin{bmatrix} 4 & 1 & 2 \\ -3 & 2 & 3 \\ 2 & 0 & 5 \\ 3 & 1 & 4 \end{bmatrix} \begin{bmatrix} 1 & 4 \\ 2 & 0 \\ -3 & 5 \end{bmatrix}$

3. $[4 \ 1 \ 0 \ 2] \begin{bmatrix} 1 & 0 & 1 \\ 2 & -1 & 0 \\ 3 & 5 & 1 \\ 1 & 3 & 0 \end{bmatrix}$

Practice 4-3

Matrix Multiplication

Use matrices *A*, *B*, *C*, *D*, and *E* to find each product, sum, or difference, if possible. If not possible, write *product undefined, sum undefined,* or *difference undefined.*

$$A = \begin{bmatrix} 1 & -1 \\ 3 & -2 \end{bmatrix} \qquad B = \begin{bmatrix} 0 & 2 \\ -2 & 1 \\ -1 & 0 \end{bmatrix} \qquad C = \begin{bmatrix} 3 & -3 & -1 \\ 2 & -2 & 4 \end{bmatrix} \qquad D = \begin{bmatrix} 1 & 0 \\ 0 & 1 \end{bmatrix} \qquad E = \begin{bmatrix} 3 \\ -3 \\ 2 \end{bmatrix}$$

1. $3AB$ **2.** $2A + 4D$ **3.** $5D - A$ **4.** $2C - E$ **5.** $3D + A$

6. DA **7.** AE **8.** BD **9.** DB **10.** CE

11. DC **12.** EB **13.** CB **14.** $2D$ **15.** BE

16. $0.2B$ **17.** $\frac{1}{4}C$ **18.** $0.5AC$ **19.** DE **20.** $-3DE$

Find the dimensions of the product matrix. Then find each product.

21. $\begin{bmatrix} 1 \\ 2 \\ 3 \end{bmatrix} \begin{bmatrix} 1 & 2 & 3 & 4 \end{bmatrix}$

22. $\begin{bmatrix} 1 & 2 & 12 \\ 12 & 2 & 1 \end{bmatrix} \begin{bmatrix} 3 & 4 \\ 4 & 3 \\ 5 & 2 \end{bmatrix}$

23. $\begin{bmatrix} 1 & 2 \\ 2 & 1 \end{bmatrix} \begin{bmatrix} 2 & 1 \\ 1 & 2 \end{bmatrix}$

Find each product if possible. If not possible, write *product undefined.*

24. $-12 \begin{bmatrix} -6 & -2 \\ -5 & -6 \\ 0 & 1 \end{bmatrix}$

25. $\begin{bmatrix} 3 & 2 \\ 4 & 6 \\ 1 & 1 \end{bmatrix} \begin{bmatrix} -3 & 3 & -2 \\ -2 & 5 & -1 \end{bmatrix}$

26. $\begin{bmatrix} 0 & 1 & 0 \\ 2 & 2 & 1 \end{bmatrix} \begin{bmatrix} -2 & 2 & 2 \\ -1 & 1 & 1 \\ 0 & -1 & -1 \end{bmatrix}$

27. $\begin{bmatrix} 1 & 1 & 1 \\ 1 & 1 & 1 \\ 1 & 1 & 1 \end{bmatrix} \begin{bmatrix} 2 & 3 \\ 4 & 1 \\ 5 & 6 \end{bmatrix}$

28. $\begin{bmatrix} 1 & 0 & 1 \\ 1 & 1 & 0 \\ 1 & 1 & 1 \end{bmatrix} \begin{bmatrix} 6 & 4 & 2 & 8 \\ 10 & 4 & 6 & 2 \\ 2 & 10 & 12 & 4 \end{bmatrix}$

29. $\begin{bmatrix} 4 & 3 \\ 9 & 7 \end{bmatrix} \begin{bmatrix} 6 & 3 \\ 9 & 4 \end{bmatrix}$

Solve each equation. Check your answers.

30. $2 \begin{bmatrix} 0 & 1 \\ 3 & -4 \end{bmatrix} - 3X = \begin{bmatrix} 9 & -6 \\ 1 & -2 \end{bmatrix}$

31. $\frac{1}{2}X + \begin{bmatrix} 5 & -1 \\ 0 & \frac{2}{3} \end{bmatrix} = 2 \begin{bmatrix} 3 & 0 \\ 1 & 2 \end{bmatrix}$

Reteaching 4-4

Geometric Transformations with Matrices

OBJECTIVE: Representing translations with matrices

MATERIALS: Graph paper and colored pencils

- A *translation* is a transformation that changes the location of a geometrical figure.

Example

A quadrilateral has vertices $A(0, 0)$, $B(-2, 3)$, $C(-5, 3)$, and $D(-5, 0)$. Use a matrix to translate the vertices 5 units right and 3 units down.

$$\begin{array}{cccc} A & B & C & D \end{array}$$
$$\begin{bmatrix} 0 & -2 & -5 & -5 \\ 0 & 3 & 3 & 0 \end{bmatrix}$$

⟵ **Write the vertices as a matrix.**

$$\begin{bmatrix} 5 & 5 & 5 & 5 \\ -3 & -3 & -3 & -3 \end{bmatrix}$$

⟵ **Write the translation matrix. Since the first row represents the x-coordinates, place 5 in each entry. Since the second row represents the y-coordinates, place -3 in each entry.**

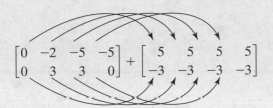

$$\begin{bmatrix} 0 & -2 & -5 & -5 \\ 0 & 3 & 3 & 0 \end{bmatrix} + \begin{bmatrix} 5 & 5 & 5 & 5 \\ -3 & -3 & -3 & -3 \end{bmatrix}$$

⟵ **Add the two matrices. Draw arrows connecting corresponding entries. Use a different colored pencil for each arrow.**

$$\begin{array}{cccc} A' & B' & C' & D' \end{array}$$
$$= \begin{bmatrix} 5 & 3 & 0 & 0 \\ -3 & 0 & 0 & -3 \end{bmatrix}$$

⟵ **Represent the translated points by A′, B′, C′, and D′ respectively.**

$A'(5, -3)$, $B'(3, 0)$, $C'(0, 0)$, $D'(0, -3)$

⟵ **Write the vertices as ordered pairs.**

⟵ **Graph the original figure and its image. Label each point.**

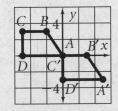

Exercises

A quadrilateral has vertices $A(0, 0)$, $B(-2, 3)$, $C(1, 4)$, and $D(3, 2)$. Use a matrix to translate the vertices according to the following. Graph the original figure and the image on graph paper.

1. a translation 1 unit right and 2 units down

2. a translation 3 units left and 1 unit down

3. a translation 4 units left and 3 units up

4. a translation 2 units right and 4 units up

Practice 4-4

· ·

For Exercises 1–11, use △ABC at the right. Find the coordinates of the image under each transformation. Express your answer as a matrix.

1. a dilation of 11

2. a translation 1 unit right and 4 units up

3. a dilation of 1.5

4. a translation 2 units right and 6 units down

5. a reflection in $y = x$

6. a rotation of 270°

7. a rotation of 90°

8. a translation 1 unit left and 2 units down

9. a translation 3 units left and 1 unit up

10. a dilation of $\frac{1}{2}$

11. a reflection in the x-axis

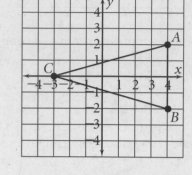

Graph each figure and its image after the given transformation.

12. $\begin{bmatrix} 2 & -3 & 6 & 4 \\ 0 & 1 & 1 & -4 \end{bmatrix}$; a dilation of 2

13. $\begin{bmatrix} 8 & 3 & -2 & -5 & 2 \\ 7 & 6 & 1 & 0 & -4 \end{bmatrix}$; a translation 2 units left and 1 unit up

14. $\begin{bmatrix} 2 & 4 & 5 & 3 \\ 1 & 1 & 3 & 5 \end{bmatrix}$; a translation 5 units left and 4 units down

15. $\begin{bmatrix} 2 & 1 & 6 & -4 \\ 0 & -3 & 5 & -2 \end{bmatrix}$; a rotation of 180°

16. $\begin{bmatrix} 6 & 5 & 1 & -3 & 6 \\ -1 & 6 & 2 & 0 & -4 \end{bmatrix}$; a reflection in the y-axis

The coordinates of the vertices of a polygon are given. Represent each transformation with matrices. Then express the coordinates of the vertices of the image as a matrix.

17. $I(21, -14), J(0, -7), K(-14, 0), L(0, 7)$; a dilation of $\frac{1}{7}$

18. $M(2, 0), N(0, -2), P(-2, 0)$; a translation 2 units down

19. $Q(2, 0), R(0, -2), S(-2, 0)$; a reflection in $y = -x$

Reteaching 4-5

2 × 2 Matrices, Determinants, and Inverses

OBJECTIVE: Finding and using the inverse of a 2 × 2 matrix

MATERIALS: None

- The inverse of a matrix A is the matrix A^{-1} such that the product $AA^{-1} = I$, the identity matrix. Suppose $A = \begin{bmatrix} a & b \\ c & d \end{bmatrix}$. If $ad - bc \neq 0$, then A has an inverse and $A^{-1} = \dfrac{1}{ad - bc}\begin{bmatrix} d & -b \\ -c & a \end{bmatrix}$.

Example

Write the inverse of the matrix $A - \begin{bmatrix} 2 & 4 \\ 1 & 3 \end{bmatrix}$.

$$ad - bc = (2)(3) - (4)(1)$$
$$2 \neq 0$$

← Calculate $ad - bc$. Since $ad - bc \neq 0$, the inverse does exist.

$$A^{-1} = \frac{1}{2}\begin{bmatrix} 3 & -4 \\ -1 & 2 \end{bmatrix}$$

← Substitute values into the matrix inverse formula.

$$= \begin{bmatrix} \frac{3}{2} & -2 \\ -\frac{1}{2} & 1 \end{bmatrix}$$

← Multiply each entry by $\frac{1}{2}$.

$$\begin{matrix} A & A^{-1} & I \end{matrix}$$

$$\begin{bmatrix} 2 & 4 \\ 1 & 3 \end{bmatrix}\begin{bmatrix} \frac{3}{2} & -2 \\ -\frac{1}{2} & 1 \end{bmatrix} = \begin{bmatrix} 1 & 0 \\ 0 & 1 \end{bmatrix}$$

← Check the results by verifying that $AA^{-1} = I$.

because

$$\begin{bmatrix} 2\left(\frac{3}{2}\right) + 4\left(-\frac{1}{2}\right) & 2(-2) + 4(1) \\ 1\left(\frac{3}{2}\right) + 3\left(-\frac{1}{2}\right) & 1(-2) + 3(1) \end{bmatrix} = \begin{bmatrix} 1 & 0 \\ 0 & 1 \end{bmatrix}$$

← Multiply each row of A by each column of A^{-1} to calculate the product of A and A^{-1}.

Exercises

Find the inverse of each 2 × 2 matrix. If it does not exist, write *no inverse.*

1. $\begin{bmatrix} 5 & -2 \\ -7 & 3 \end{bmatrix}$

2. $\begin{bmatrix} 9 & -2 \\ 5 & -1 \end{bmatrix}$

3. $\begin{bmatrix} 3 & 4 \\ 5 & 7 \end{bmatrix}$

4. $\begin{bmatrix} 6 & -3 \\ -2 & 1 \end{bmatrix}$

5. $\begin{bmatrix} -2 & 17 \\ 1 & 8 \end{bmatrix}$

6. $\begin{bmatrix} 7 & 4 \\ 3 & 2 \end{bmatrix}$

7. $\begin{bmatrix} 7 & -3 \\ -1 & 1 \end{bmatrix}$

8. $\begin{bmatrix} -9 & 3 \\ 6 & -2 \end{bmatrix}$

9. $\begin{bmatrix} 3 & 4 \\ 5 & 6 \end{bmatrix}$

Practice 4-5

2 × 2 Matrices, Determinants, and Inverses

Find the matrix E^{-1} for each.

1. $E = \begin{bmatrix} 2 & -2 \\ -1 & 2 \end{bmatrix}$

2. $E = \begin{bmatrix} 1 & -1 \\ 1 & 1 \end{bmatrix}$

3. $E = \begin{bmatrix} 2 & -1 \\ 1 & 0 \end{bmatrix}$

4. $E = \begin{bmatrix} 2 & 3 \\ 1 & 1 \end{bmatrix}$

5. $E = \begin{bmatrix} 1 & 4 \\ 1 & 3 \end{bmatrix}$

6. $E = \begin{bmatrix} 4 & 7 \\ 3 & 5 \end{bmatrix}$

Find the inverse of each matrix, if it exists. If it does not exist, write
no inverse **and explain why not.**

7. $\begin{bmatrix} 3 & 4 \\ -3 & 4 \end{bmatrix}$

8. $\begin{bmatrix} 3 & 4 \\ 3 & 4 \end{bmatrix}$

9. $\begin{bmatrix} 1 & 2 \\ 3 & 4 \end{bmatrix}$

10. $\begin{bmatrix} 30 & -4 \\ -25 & 3 \end{bmatrix}$

Solve each matrix equation.

11. $\begin{bmatrix} 1 & 2 \\ -1 & -2 \end{bmatrix} X = \begin{bmatrix} 2 \\ -2 \end{bmatrix}$

12. $\begin{bmatrix} 1 & 1 \\ 1 & -1 \end{bmatrix} X = \begin{bmatrix} 3 \\ -1 \end{bmatrix}$

13. $\begin{bmatrix} -2 & 3 \\ -4 & 5 \end{bmatrix} X = \begin{bmatrix} 6 \\ 8 \end{bmatrix}$

Evaluate the determinant of each matrix.

14. $\begin{bmatrix} -3 & 4 \\ 1 & -1 \end{bmatrix}$

15. $\begin{bmatrix} 3 & 9 \\ 3 & 2 \end{bmatrix}$

16. $\begin{bmatrix} 1 & -4 \\ 2 & 6 \end{bmatrix}$

17. $\begin{bmatrix} 4 & -3 \\ 1 & -8 \end{bmatrix}$

18. $\begin{bmatrix} 5 & 4 \\ 4 & 5 \end{bmatrix}$

19. $\begin{bmatrix} 1 & -12 \\ 3 & 0 \end{bmatrix}$

Determine whether the matrices are multiplicative inverses.

20. $\begin{bmatrix} 2 & 1 \\ 5 & 3 \end{bmatrix}, \begin{bmatrix} 3 & -1 \\ -5 & 2 \end{bmatrix}$

21. $\begin{bmatrix} 4 & 9 \\ 2 & 6 \end{bmatrix}, \begin{bmatrix} 1 & -\frac{3}{2} \\ -\frac{1}{3} & \frac{2}{3} \end{bmatrix}$

22. $\begin{bmatrix} 1 & 2 \\ 3 & 4 \end{bmatrix}, \begin{bmatrix} -2 & 1 \\ \frac{3}{2} & -\frac{1}{2} \end{bmatrix}$

Reteaching 4-6

3 × 3 Matrices, Determinants, and Inverses

OBJECTIVE: Finding the determinant of a 3 × 3 matrix

MATERIALS: Colored pencils

Like 2 × 2 matrices, a 3 × 3 matrix, $A = \begin{bmatrix} a_1 & b_1 & c_1 \\ a_2 & b_2 & c_2 \\ a_3 & b_3 & c_3 \end{bmatrix}$, has a determinant, det A.

$\det A = (a_1b_2c_3 + a_2b_3c_1 + a_3b_1c_2) - (a_1b_3c_2 + a_2b_1c_3 + a_3b_2c_1)$

Write matrix A, then copy matrix A to the right of the first matrix, aligning rows. In your first matrix, use three colored pencils and the first part of the formula to show what is being multiplied. In the second matrix, use other colors and the second part of the formula to show what is being multiplied. Do you see a pattern? This pattern will help you calculate the determinant of A.

Example

Find the determinant of A if $A = \begin{bmatrix} 3 & 2 & 1 \\ 4 & 3 & -2 \\ 5 & 0 & 0 \end{bmatrix}$.

$\det A = [3(3)(0) + 4(0)(1) + 5(2)(-2)]$ ⟵ **Use the definition.**
     $- [3(0)(-2) + 4(2)(0) + 5(3)(1)]$

    $= [0 + 0 + -20] - [0 + 0 + 15]$ ⟵ **Multiply.**

    $= -20 - 15 = -35$ ⟵ **Simplify.**

Exercises

Evaluate the determinant of each matrix.

1. $\begin{bmatrix} 1 & -1 & -1 \\ -2 & 0 & 1 \\ 1 & -1 & 2 \end{bmatrix}$ **2.** $\begin{bmatrix} 0 & 1 & 2 \\ 3 & 2 & 1 \\ 4 & 0 & 3 \end{bmatrix}$ **3.** $\begin{bmatrix} 1 & 0 & 3 \\ 4 & 2 & -1 \\ -1 & 0 & 4 \end{bmatrix}$

4. $\begin{bmatrix} 3 & 1 & 12 \\ -2 & 0 & -6 \\ 3 & 5 & -1 \end{bmatrix}$ **5.** $\begin{bmatrix} 1 & 2 & -2 \\ -1 & 3 & 1 \\ 1 & -1 & 2 \end{bmatrix}$ **6.** $\begin{bmatrix} 1 & 2 & 3 \\ -4 & 5 & -4 \\ 2 & 6 & 7 \end{bmatrix}$

Practice 4-6

3 × 3 Matrices, Determinants, and Inverses

Where necessary, use a graphing calculator. Find the inverse (A^{-1}) of each matrix, if it exists. If it does not exist, write *no inverse*.

1. $\begin{bmatrix} 1 & 2 & 0 \\ -2 & 0 & -3 \\ 3 & -1 & 5 \end{bmatrix}$
2. $\begin{bmatrix} 1 & 1 & 1 \\ 2 & 1 & 0 \\ 0 & 2 & 3 \end{bmatrix}$
3. $\begin{bmatrix} 2 & 4 & 3 \\ 0 & 5 & -1 \\ 1 & -1 & 2 \end{bmatrix}$
4. $\begin{bmatrix} 0 & 2 & 0 \\ 2 & 0 & 2 \\ 0 & 2 & 0 \end{bmatrix}$

5. $\begin{bmatrix} 4 & 5 & 6 \\ 0 & 1 & 2 \\ 8 & 9 & 5 \end{bmatrix}$
6. $\begin{bmatrix} 1 & -1 & 1 \\ 0 & 0 & 0 \\ 0 & 0 & 1 \end{bmatrix}$
7. $\begin{bmatrix} -1 & 0 & -1 \\ 0 & -2 & 0 \\ -2 & 0 & 3 \end{bmatrix}$
8. $\begin{bmatrix} -3 & -2 & -1 \\ 0 & 1 & 2 \\ 3 & 4 & -4 \end{bmatrix}$

Solve each equation for *X*.

9. $\begin{bmatrix} 1 & 0 & 0 \\ 0 & 1 & 0 \\ 0 & 0 & 1 \end{bmatrix} X = \begin{bmatrix} 4 \\ -5 \\ 3 \end{bmatrix}$
10. $\begin{bmatrix} 1 & 2 & 0 \\ -2 & 0 & -3 \\ 3 & -1 & 5 \end{bmatrix} X = \begin{bmatrix} -1 \\ 12 \\ -20 \end{bmatrix}$
11. $\begin{bmatrix} 0 & 0 & 1 \\ 0 & 0 & 1 \\ 1 & 1 & 1 \end{bmatrix} X = \begin{bmatrix} 3 \\ 4 \\ 3 \end{bmatrix}$

Evaluate the determinant of each matrix.

12. $\begin{bmatrix} -1 & 2 & -2 \\ 0 & 1 & 3 \\ 4 & 2 & -1 \end{bmatrix}$
13. $\begin{bmatrix} 2 & 1 & 2 \\ -1 & 0 & 5 \\ 0 & 4 & 1 \end{bmatrix}$
14. $\begin{bmatrix} 2 & 4 & 3 \\ -3 & 0 & -2 \\ -1 & 3 & 0 \end{bmatrix}$

15. $\begin{bmatrix} 2 & 6 & -1 \\ 1 & 0 & 0 \\ 1 & 3 & -2 \end{bmatrix}$
16. $\begin{bmatrix} -4 & 0 & 3 \\ 0 & -2 & 3 \\ -1 & 4 & -2 \end{bmatrix}$
17. $\begin{bmatrix} 7 & -1 & 3 \\ 1 & 2 & 6 \\ 4 & 1 & 3 \end{bmatrix}$

Determine whether the matrices are multiplicative inverses.

18. $A = \begin{bmatrix} -2 & 2 & 3 \\ 1 & -1 & 0 \\ 0 & 1 & 4 \end{bmatrix}, B = \begin{bmatrix} -\frac{4}{3} & -\frac{5}{3} & 1 \\ -\frac{4}{3} & -\frac{8}{3} & 1 \\ 1 & \frac{2}{3} & 0 \end{bmatrix}$

19. $A = \begin{bmatrix} 2 & -17 & 11 \\ -1 & 11 & -7 \\ 0 & 3 & -2 \end{bmatrix}, B = \begin{bmatrix} 1 & 1 & 2 \\ 2 & 4 & -3 \\ 3 & 6 & -5 \end{bmatrix}$

Reteaching 4-7

Inverse Matrices and Systems

OBJECTIVE: Solving systems using inverse matrices	**MATERIALS:** Graphing calculator

- A system of linear equations can be solved by using inverse matrices when the system has exactly one solution.

- The determinant of $\begin{bmatrix} a & b \\ c & d \end{bmatrix}$ is $ad - bc$.

- If the determinant is zero, the matrix has no inverse.

- If the determinant is zero, the matrix equation has no solution or an infinite number of solutions. To solve, use another method.

Example

Use an inverse matrix to solve the linear system $\begin{cases} 4x + 3y = -4 \\ 3x - y = -3 \end{cases}$.

$$\begin{matrix} A & X & B \end{matrix}$$

$$\begin{bmatrix} 4 & 3 \\ 3 & -1 \end{bmatrix} \begin{bmatrix} x \\ y \end{bmatrix} = \begin{bmatrix} -4 \\ -3 \end{bmatrix}$$ ← **Write the system as a matrix equation**

```
MATRIX[A]    2 ×2
[ 4     3          ]
[ 3     −1         ]

2 , 2 = −1
```
← **Store the coefficient matrix as matrix A.**

```
MATRIX[B]    2 ×1
[ −4               ]
[ −3               ]

2 , 1 = −3
```
← **Store the constant matrix as matrix B.**

```
[A]⁻¹[B]
              [ [−1]
                [0 ] ]

```
← **Multiply the matrices A^{-1} and B.**

Check the solution $(-1, 0)$ by substitution.

Exercises

Use a graphing calculator to solve each system. Check your solutions by substitution.

1. $\begin{cases} 2x - 7y = -3 \\ x + 5y = 7 \end{cases}$ **2.** $\begin{cases} x + 3y = 5 \\ x + 4y = 6 \end{cases}$ **3.** $\begin{cases} p - 3q = -1 \\ -5p + 16q = 5 \end{cases}$ **4.** $\begin{cases} 4m - 2n = -6 \\ -2m + n = 3 \end{cases}$

Practice 4-7

Inverse Matrices and Systems

Solve each system.

1. $\begin{cases} x + y + z = 0.621 \\ 3x - 3y + 2z = -0.007 \\ 4x + 5y - 10z = 1.804 \end{cases}$

2. $\begin{cases} 3x + 4y + 2z = 0.5 \\ 8x - 5y - 5z = 8.1 \\ 5x + 5y + 5z = 1 \end{cases}$

3. $\begin{cases} 5x - 4y + 3z = -30 \\ 18x - 2y - 19z = 103 \\ 2.9x + 0.06y + 17z = -81.8 \end{cases}$

4. $\begin{cases} x + 3y = 5 \\ x + 4y = 6 \end{cases}$

5. $\begin{cases} 4x + y + z = 0 \\ 5x + 2y + 3z = -15 \\ 6x - 5y - 5z = 52 \end{cases}$

6. $\begin{cases} 2x + 3y = 12 \\ x + 2y = 7 \end{cases}$

7. $\begin{cases} x + y + z = 31 \\ x - y + z = 1 \\ x - 2y + 2z = 7 \end{cases}$

8. $\begin{cases} x - 3y = -1 \\ -6x + 19y = 6 \end{cases}$

9. $\begin{cases} x + y + z = 8.8 \\ 2x - 5y + 9z = -4.8 \\ 3x + 2y - 7z = -7.6 \end{cases}$

10. $\begin{cases} -3x + 4y = 2 \\ x - y = -1 \end{cases}$

11. $\begin{cases} 0.5x + 1.5y + z = 7 \\ 3x + 3y + 5z = 3 \\ 2x + y + 2z = -1 \end{cases}$

12. $\begin{cases} x + y + z = -2 \\ 1.5x + 3y + 0.5z = 8 \\ 9x + 4y + 5z = 4 \end{cases}$

Write each system as a matrix equation. Identify the coefficient matrix, the variable matrix, and the constant matrix.

13. $\begin{cases} 6x + 9y = 36 \\ 4x + 13y = 2 \end{cases}$

14. $\begin{cases} 3x - 4y = -9 \\ 7y = 24 \end{cases}$

15. $\begin{cases} 4x - z = 9 \\ 12x + 2y = 17 \\ x - y + 12z = 3 \end{cases}$

Write a system of equations. Solve the system using an inverse matrix.

16. In 1992, there were 548,303 doctors under the age of 65 in the United States. Of those under age 45, 25.53415% were women. Of those between the ages of 45 and 64, 11.67209% were women. There were 110,017 women doctors under the age of 65. How many doctors were under age 45?

17. An apartment building has 50 units. All are one- or two-bedroom units. One-bedroom units rent for \$425/mo, and two-bedroom units rent for \$550/mo. When all units are occupied, the total monthly income is \$25,000. How many apartments of each type are there?

Solve each matrix equation. If the coefficient matrix has no inverse, write *no unique solution.*

18. $\begin{bmatrix} 0.25 & -0.75 \\ 3.5 & 2.25 \end{bmatrix} \begin{bmatrix} x \\ y \end{bmatrix} = \begin{bmatrix} 1.5 \\ -3.75 \end{bmatrix}$

19. $\begin{bmatrix} 3 & -9 \\ 1 & -6 \end{bmatrix} \begin{bmatrix} a \\ b \end{bmatrix} = \begin{bmatrix} 12 \\ 0 \end{bmatrix}$

20. $\begin{bmatrix} 3 & -6 \\ -1 & 2 \end{bmatrix} \begin{bmatrix} u \\ v \end{bmatrix} = \begin{bmatrix} 4 \\ 9 \end{bmatrix}$

21. $\begin{bmatrix} 12 & -3 \\ 16 & 4 \end{bmatrix} \begin{bmatrix} x \\ y \end{bmatrix} = \begin{bmatrix} 144 \\ -64 \end{bmatrix}$

Determine whether each system has a unique solution.

22. $\begin{cases} 4d + 2e = 4 \\ d + 3e = 6 \end{cases}$

23. $\begin{cases} 3x - 2y = 43 \\ 9x - 6y = 40 \end{cases}$

24. $\begin{cases} -y - z = 3 \\ x + 2y + 3z = 1 \\ 4x - 5y - 6z = -50 \end{cases}$

Reteaching 4-8

OBJECTIVE: Using the augmented matrix to solve systems of equations

MATERIALS: None

Remember the row operations:

- Switch any two rows.
- Multiply a row by a constant.
- Add one row to another.
- Combine one or more of these steps.

Example

Use an augmented matrix to solve the system $\begin{cases} 2x + 4y = 8 \\ 3x + 5y = 15 \end{cases}$.

After the row operations, you want the system to be in the form $\begin{bmatrix} 1 & 0 & | & m \\ 0 & 1 & | & n \end{bmatrix}$.
The solution to the system is (m, n).

Write the augmented matrix. $\longrightarrow \begin{bmatrix} 2 & 4 & | & 8 \\ 3 & 5 & | & 15 \end{bmatrix}$

To make element a_{11} equal to 1, multiply Row 1 by $\frac{1}{2}$. $\quad \frac{1}{2}(2 \ 4 \ 8) = (1 \ 2 \ 4) \quad \longrightarrow \begin{bmatrix} 1 & 2 & | & 4 \\ 3 & 5 & | & 15 \end{bmatrix}$
Then replace Row 1 with the result.

To make element a_{21} equal to 0, multiply Row 1
by -3. Then add the result to Row 2, and replace
Row 2 with this sum.

$$
\begin{array}{rrr}
-3(1 \ 2 \ 4) & = & (-3 \ -6 \ -12) \\
-3 & -6 & -12 \\
3 & 5 & 15 \\
\hline
0 & 1 & 3
\end{array}
\longrightarrow \begin{bmatrix} 1 & 2 & | & 4 \\ 0 & -1 & | & 3 \end{bmatrix}
$$

To make element a_{22} equal to 1, multiply Row 2
by -1. Then replace Row 2 with the result. $\quad -1(0 \ -1 \ 3) = (0 \ 1 \ -3) \quad \longrightarrow \begin{bmatrix} 1 & 2 & | & 4 \\ 0 & 1 & | & -3 \end{bmatrix}$

To make element a_{12} equal to 0, multiply Row 2
by -2. Then add the result to Row 1, and replace
Row 1 with this sum.

$$
\begin{array}{rrr}
-2(0 \ 1 \ -3) & = & (0 \ -2 \ 6) \\
0 & -2 & 6 \\
1 & 2 & 4 \\
\hline
1 & 0 & 10
\end{array}
\longrightarrow \begin{bmatrix} 1 & 0 & | & 10 \\ 0 & 1 & | & -3 \end{bmatrix}
$$

The solution to the system is $(10, -3)$. You can check the solution by

substituting $x = 10$ and $y = -3$ into each of the original equations.

Exercises

1. $\begin{cases} x - 5y = 4 \\ -2x + y = 1 \end{cases}$

2. $\begin{cases} x - 3y = 5 \\ 3x - y = -1 \end{cases}$

3. $\begin{cases} 2x - y = 6 \\ 3x - y = 2 \end{cases}$

Practice 4-8

Write a system of equations for each augmented matrix.

1. $\begin{bmatrix} 4 & -2 & | & 3 \\ 6 & 11 & | & 9 \end{bmatrix}$

2. $\begin{bmatrix} 12 & 6 & | & -4 \\ -1 & 0 & | & 2 \end{bmatrix}$

3. $\begin{bmatrix} -2 & 9 & -2 & | & 20 \\ 3 & -1 & 2 & | & 29 \\ 6 & 5 & 5 & | & -4 \end{bmatrix}$

Use Cramer's Rule to solve each system.

4. $\begin{cases} 2x + y = 1 \\ 3x - y = 9 \end{cases}$

5. $\begin{cases} 2x - y = 10 \\ x - 3y = 0 \end{cases}$

6. $\begin{cases} 3x + 5y = 1 \\ x + 6y = 9 \end{cases}$

7. $\begin{cases} x + y + z = 1.28 \\ x - 3y + 2z = 1.26 \\ 3x + 2y + 4z = 4.06 \end{cases}$

8. $\begin{cases} 2x + y - z = 0.75 \\ 3x + 3y + 2z = 4 \\ x - 5y + 3z = -2 \end{cases}$

9. $\begin{cases} x + y - z = 6 \\ 3x - 9y + z = -2 \\ 0.2x - 0.3y + 0.71z = -1.12 \end{cases}$

Write an augmented matrix for each system.

10. $\begin{cases} -3x + 4y = -8 \\ 2x - 8y = 16 \end{cases}$

11. $\begin{cases} u + 3v = -30 \\ 4u + v = 1 \end{cases}$

12. $\begin{cases} x - 4y + z = -9 \\ 3x + 2y - 3z = 9 \\ 4x + 2z = -4 \end{cases}$

Use an augmented matrix to solve each system.

13. $\begin{cases} x + y + z = 0 \\ 2x - 2y + 3z = 46 \\ 3x + 7y + 11z = 80 \end{cases}$

14. $\begin{cases} 3x + y + z = 18 \\ 4x + 2y + 3z = 12 \\ 7x + 8y + 5z = 9 \end{cases}$

15. $\begin{cases} 3x + 7y + 10z = 28 \\ 0.7x - 0.6y + 0.8z = 4.3 \\ 12x - 7y - 9z = 77 \end{cases}$

16. $\begin{cases} x - 2y - 3z = 2 \\ 2x + y - 5z = 30 \\ 7x - 11y - z = -48 \end{cases}$

17. $\begin{cases} x + y + z = 6.5 \\ 3x - 5y + 6z = -35 \\ 5x + 2y + 2z = 10 \end{cases}$

18. $\begin{cases} -x + y - z = -2 \\ 3x + 2y + 0.5z = -1.5 \\ 21x + 19y - 2z = -45 \end{cases}$

Use a graphing calculator to solve each system.

19. $\begin{cases} 4x - 2y + 3z = -2 \\ 2x + 2y + 5z = 16 \\ 8x - 5y - 2z = 4 \end{cases}$

20. $\begin{cases} x + y + z = -1 \\ 3x + 5y + 4z = 2 \\ 3x + 6y + 5z = 0 \end{cases}$

21. $\begin{cases} x + 3y - 2z = -3 \\ 2x + y - z = -6 \\ 3x - 2y + 4z = 8 \end{cases}$

Reteaching 5-1

Modeling Data with Quadratic Functions

OBJECTIVE: Recognizing and using a quadratic function

MATERIALS: Graphing calculator

A quadratic function can be written in standard form:

$$f(x) = ax^2 + bx + c, \text{ where } a \neq 0.$$

quadratic   linear   constant
term   term   term

Example

Rewrite the function in standard form. Indicate whether the function is quadratic. Graph the function to check your answer.

$f(x) = (1 + x)(9 + x)$ ⟵   **Multiply and simplify to put in standard form.**

$f(x) = 9 + x + 9x + x^2$ ⟵   **Use the FOIL Method to apply the Distributive Property.**

$f(x) = x^2 + 10x + 9$ ⟵   **Combine like terms and simplify.**

Since it has a quadratic term, this is a quadratic function.

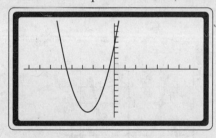   ⟵   **Use a graphing calculator to check your answer. This is a quadratic function, since its graph is a parabola.**

Exercises

Rewrite each function in standard form. Indicate whether the function is quadratic. Then graph to check.

1. $f(x) = (-5x - 4)(-5x - 4)$ **2.** $y = 3(x - 1) + 3$

3. $y = x^2 + 24 - 11x - x^2$ **4.** $g(x) = (x - 7)(x + 7)$

5. $f(x) = (3 - x)(x + 3)$ **6.** $g(x) = x^2$

7. $f(x) = 3x(x + 1) - x$ **8.** $f(x) = (x + 4)(x - 4)$

9. $f(x) = 4x^2 + 5x$ **10.** $y = 2(x + 2)^2 - 2x^2$

Practice 5-1

Find a quadratic model for each set of values.

1. $(-1, 1), (1, 1), (3, 9)$

2. $(-4, 8), (-1, 5), (1, 13)$

3. $(-1, 10), (2, 4), (3, -6)$

4.

x	−1	0	2
$f(x)$	1	−1	7

5.

x	−4	0	1
$f(x)$	1	9	16

6.

x	−1	2	3
$f(x)$	12	3	4

Identify the vertex and the axis of symmetry of each parabola.

7.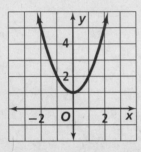

8.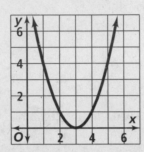

9.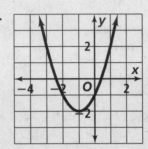

Determine whether each function is linear or quadratic. Identify the quadratic, linear, and constant terms.

10. $y = (x - 2)(x + 4)$

11. $y = 3x(x + 5)$

12. $y = 5x(x - 5) - 5x^2$

13. $f(x) = 7(x - 2) + 5(3x)$

14. $f(x) = 3x^2 - (4x - 8)$

15. $y = 3x(x - 1) - (3x + 7)$

16. $y = 3x^2 - 12$

17. $f(x) = (2x - 3)(x + 2)$

18. $y = 3x - 5$

For each parabola, identify points corresponding to P and Q.

19.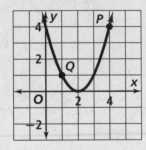

20.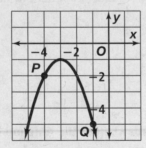

21.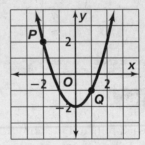

22. A toy rocket is shot upward from ground level. The table shows the height of the rocket at different times.

Time (seconds)	0	1	2	3	4
Height (feet)	0	256	480	672	832

a. Find a quadratic model for this data.

b. Use the model to estimate the height of the rocket after 1.5 seconds.

Reteaching 5-2

OBJECTIVE: Graphing a parabola using the vertex and axis of symmetry   **MATERIALS:** Graph paper

---

- The graph of a quadratic function, $y = ax^2 + bx + c$, where $a \neq 0$, is a parabola.
- The axis of symmetry is the line $x = -\dfrac{b}{2a}$.
- The x-coordinate of the vertex is $-\dfrac{b}{2a}$. The y-coordinate of the vertex is $y = f\left(-\dfrac{b}{2a}\right)$, or the y-value when $x = -\dfrac{b}{2a}$.
- The y-intercept is $(0, c)$.

Example

Graph $y = 2x^2 - 8x + 5$.

$x = -\dfrac{b}{2a} = \dfrac{-(-8)}{2(2)} = \dfrac{8}{4} = 2$ $\longleftarrow$ **Find the equation of the axis of symmetry.**

x-coordinate of vertex: 2 $\longleftarrow$ $-\dfrac{b}{2a}$

$f\left(-\dfrac{b}{2a}\right) = f(2) = 2(2)^2 - 8(2) + 5$ $\longleftarrow$ **Find the y-value when $x = 2$.**

$\qquad\qquad = 8 - 16 + 5$

$\qquad\qquad = -3$

y-coordinate of vertex: -3 $\longleftarrow$ **The vertex is at $(2, -3)$.**

y-intercept: $(0, 5)$ $\longleftarrow$ **The y-intercept is at $(0, c) = (0, 5)$.**

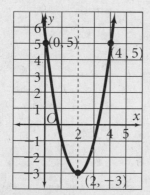

$\longleftarrow$ **Since a is positive, the graph opens upward, and the vertex is at the bottom of the graph. Plot the vertex and draw the axis of symmetry. Plot $(0, 5)$ and its corresponding point on the other side of the axis of symmetry.**

Exercises

Graph each parabola. Label the vertex and the axis of symmetry.

1. $y = x^2 - 4x + 7$

2. $y = x^2 + 8x + 11$

3. $y = -3x^2 + 6x - 9$

4. $y = -x^2 - 8x - 15$

5. $y = 2x^2 - 8x + 1$

6. $y = -2x^2 - 12x - 7$

Practice 5-2

Graph each function. If $a > 0$, find the minimum value. If $a < 0$, find the maximum value.

1. $y = -x^2 + 2x + 3$ **2.** $y = 2x^2 + 4x - 3$ **3.** $y = -3x^2 + 4x$

4. $y = x^2 - 4x + 1$ **5.** $y = -x^2 - x + 1$ **6.** $y = 5x^2 - 3$

7. $y = \frac{1}{2}x^2 - x - 4$ **8.** $y = 5x^2 - 10x - 4$ **9.** $y = 3x^2 - 12x - 4$

Graph each function.

10. $y = x^2 + 3$ **11.** $y = x^2 - 4$ **12.** $y = x^2 + 2x + 1$

13. $y = 2x^2 - 1$ **14.** $y = -3x^2 + 12x - 8$ **15.** $y = \frac{1}{3}x^2 + 2x - 1$

16. Suppose you are tossing an apple up to a friend on a third-story balcony. After t seconds, the height of the apple in feet is given by $h = -16t^2 + 38.4t + 0.96$. Your friend catches the apple just as it reaches its highest point. How long does the apple take to reach your friend, and at what height above the ground does your friend catch it?

17. The barber's profit p each week depends on his charge c per haircut. It is modeled by the equation $p = -200c^2 + 2400c - 4700$. Sketch the graph of the equation. What price should he charge for the largest profit?

18. A skating rink manager finds that revenue R based on an hourly fee F for skating is represented by the function $R = -480F^2 + 3120F$. What hourly fee will produce maximum revenues?

19. The path of a baseball after it has been hit is modeled by the function $h = -0.0032d^2 + d + 3$, where h is the height in feet of the baseball and d is the distance in feet the baseball is from home plate. What is the maximum height reached by the baseball? How far is the baseball from home plate when it reaches its maximum height?

20. A lighting fixture manufacturer has daily production costs of $C = 0.25n^2 - 10n + 800$, where C is the total daily cost in dollars and n is the number of light fixtures produced. How many fixtures should be produced to yield a minimum cost?

Graph each function. Label the vertex and the axis of symmetry.

21. $y = x^2 - 2x - 3$ **22.** $y = 2x - \frac{1}{4}x^2$ **23.** $y = x^2 + 6x + 7$

24. $y = x^2 + 2x - 6$ **25.** $y = x^2 - 8x$ **26.** $y = 2x^2 + 12x + 5$

27. $y = -3x^2 - 6x + 5$ **28.** $y = -2x^2 + 3$ **29.** $y = x^2 - 6$

Reteaching 5-3

OBJECTIVE: Writing equations in vertex and standard forms

MATERIALS: None

- Standard form of a quadratic function is $y = ax^2 + bx + c$.
  Vertex form of a quadratic function is $y = a(x - h)^2 + k$.

- For a parabola in vertex form, the coordinates of the vertex are (h, k).

Example

Write $y = 3x^2 - 24x + 50$ in vertex form.

$y = ax^2 + bx + c$

$y = 3x^2 - 24x + 50$ ⟵ **Verify that the equation is in standard form.**

$b = -24, a = 3$ ⟵ **Find b and a.**

$x\text{-coordinate} = -\left(\dfrac{-24}{2(3)}\right)$ ⟵ **For an equation in standard form, the x-coordinate of the vertex can be found by using $x = -\dfrac{b}{2a}$. Substitute.**

$= 4$ ⟵ **Simplify.**

$y\text{-coordinate} = 3(4)^2 - 24(4) + 50$ ⟵ **Substitute 4 into the standard form to find the y-coordinate.**

$= 2$ ⟵ **Simplify.**

$y = 3(x - 4)^2 + 2$ ⟵ **Substitute $(4, 2)$ for (h, k) into the vertex form.**

Once the conversion to vertex form is complete, check by multiplying.

$y = 3(x^2 - 8x + 16) + 2$

$y = 3x^2 - 24x + 50$

The result should be the standard form of the equation.

Exercises

Write each function in vertex form. Check.

1. $y = x^2 - 2x - 3$

2. $y = -x^2 + 4x + 6$

3. $y = x^2 + 3x - 10$

4. $y = x^2 - 9x$

5. $y = x^2 + x$

6. $y = x^2 + 5x + 4$

7. $y = 4x^2 + 8x - 3$

8. $y = \frac{3}{4}x^2 + 9x$

9. $y = -2x^2 + 2x + 1$

Write each function in standard form.

10. $y = (x - 3)^2 + 1$

11. $y = 2(x - 1)^2 - 3$

12. $y = -3(x + 4)^2 + 1$

Practice 5-3

Write the equation of the parabola in vertex form.

1.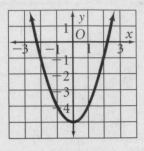

2.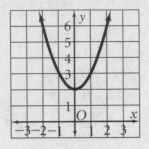

3.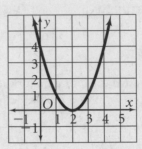

4.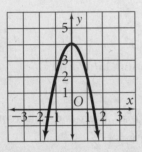

5.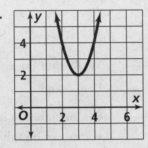

6.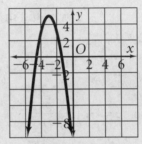

Graph each function.

7. $y = (x - 2)^2 - 3$

8. $y = (x - 6)^2 + 6$

9. $y = \frac{1}{2}(x - 1)^2 - 1$

10. $y = 8(x + 1)^2 - 2$

11. $y = -3(x - 1)^2 + 3$

12. $y = 3(x + 2)^2 + 4$

13. $y = \frac{1}{8}(x + 1)^2 - 1$

14. $y = \frac{1}{2}(x + 6)^2 - 2$

15. $y = 2(x + 3)^2 - 3$

16. $y = 4(x - 2)^2$

17. $y = -2(x + 1)^2 - 5$

18. $y = 4(x - 1)^2 - 2$

Write each function in vertex form.

19. $y = x^2 + 4x$

20. $y = 2x^2 + 8x + 3$

21. $y = -2x^2 - 8x$

22. $y = -x^2 + 4x + 4$

23. $y = x^2 - 4x - 4$

24. $y = x^2 + 5x$

25. $y = 2x^2 - 6$

26. $y = -3x^2 - x - 8$

27. $y = x^2 + 7x + 1$

28. $y = x^2 + 8x + 3$

29. $y = 2x^2 + 6x + 10$

30. $y = x^2 + 4x - 3$

Identify the vertex and the y-intercept of the graph of each function.

31. $y = 3(x - 2)^2 - 4$

32. $y = -\frac{1}{3}(x + 6)^2 + 5$

33. $y = 2(x - 1)^2 - 1$

34. $y = \frac{2}{3}(x + 4)^2 - 3$

35. $y = (x - 1)^2 + 2$

36. $y = -3(x - 2)^2 + 4$

37. $y = 4(x - 5)^2 + 1$

38. $y = -2(x + 5)^2 - 3$

39. $y = -5(x + 2)^2 + 5$

Reteaching 5-4

OBJECTIVE: Factoring quadratic expressions   **MATERIALS:** None

Example

Factor the expression $6x^2 - 5x - 4$.

$a = 6$, $b = -5$, and $c = -4$ ⟵ **Find a, b, and c; they are the coefficients of each term.**

$ac = -24$ and $b = -5$ ⟵ **We are looking for factors with product ac and sum b.**

Factors of −24	1, −24	−1, 24	2, −12	−2, 12	3, −8	−3, 8	4, −6	−4, 6
Sum of factors	−23	23	−10	10	−5	5	−2	2

The factors 3 and −8 are the combination whose sum is −5.

$\underbrace{6x^2 + 3x}\ \underbrace{-8x - 4}$ ⟵ **Rewrite the middle term using the factors you found.**

$3x(2x + 1) - 4(2x + 1)$ ⟵ **Find common factors by grouping the terms in pairs.**

$(3x - 4)(2x + 1)$ ⟵ **Rewrite using the Distributive Property.**

Check: $(3x - 4)(2x + 1)$ ⟵ **You can check your answer by multiplying it back together.**

$6x^2 + 3x - 8x - 4$

$6x^2 - 5x - 4$

Remember that not all quadratic expressions are factorable.

Exercises

Factor each expression.

1. $x^2 + 6x + 8$ **2.** $x^2 - 4x + 3$ **3.** $2x^2 - 6x + 4$

4. $2x^2 - 11x + 5$ **5.** $2x^2 - 7x - 4$ **6.** $4x^2 + 16x + 15$

7. $x^2 - 5x - 14$ **8.** $7x^2 - 19x - 6$ **9.** $x^2 - x - 72$

10. $2x^2 + 9x + 7$ **11.** $x^2 + 12x + 32$ **12.** $4x^2 - 28x + 49$

13. $x^2 - 3x - 10$ **14.** $2x^2 + 9x + 4$ **15.** $9x^2 - 6x + 1$

16. $x^2 - 10x + 9$ **17.** $x^2 + 4x - 12$ **18.** $x^2 + 7x + 10$

19. $x^2 - 8x + 12$ **20.** $2x^2 - 5x - 3$ **21.** $x^2 - 6x + 5$

22. $3x^2 + 2x - 8$ **23.** $2x^2 + 11x + 5$ **24.** $x^2 + 3x - 28$

Practice 5-4

Factoring Quadratic Expressions

Factor each expression completely.

1. $x^2 + 4x + 4$

2. $x^2 - 7x + 10$

3. $x^2 + 7x - 8$

4. $x^2 - 6x$

5. $2x^2 - 9x + 4$

6. $x^2 + 2x - 35$

7. $x^2 + 6x + 5$

8. $x^2 - 9$

9. $x^2 - 13x - 48$

10. $x^2 - 4$

11. $4x^2 + x$

12. $x^2 - 29x + 100$

13. $x^2 - x - 6$

14. $9x^2 - 1$

15. $3x^2 - 2x$

16. $x^2 - 64$

17. $x^2 - 25$

18. $x^2 - 81$

19. $x^2 - 36$

20. $x^2 - 100$

21. $x^2 - 1$

22. $4x^2 - 1$

23. $4x^2 - 36$

24. $9x^2 - 4$

25. $x^2 - 7x - 8$

26. $x^2 + 13x + 36$

27. $x^2 - 5x + 6$

28. $x^2 + 5x + 4$

29. $x^2 - 21x - 22$

30. $x^2 + 13x + 40$

31. $2x^2 - 5x - 3$

32. $x^2 + 10x - 11$

33. $x^2 - 14x + 24$

34. $5x^2 + 4x - 12$

35. $2x^2 - 5x - 7$

36. $2x^2 + 13x + 15$

37. $3x^2 - 7x - 6$

38. $3x^2 + 16x + 21$

39. $x^2 + 5x - 24$

40. $x^2 + 34x - 72$

41. $x^2 - 11x$

42. $3x^2 + 21x$

43. $x^2 + 8x + 12$

44. $x^2 - 10x + 24$

45. $x^2 + 7x - 30$

46. $x^2 - 2x - 168$

47. $x^2 - x - 72$

48. $4x^2 - 25$

49. $x^2 - 121$

50. $x^2 + 17x + 16$

51. $10x^2 - 17x + 3$

52. $4x^2 + 12x + 9$

53. $4x^2 - 4x - 15$

54. $9x^2 - 4$

55. $x^2 + 6x - 40$

56. $2x^2 - 8$

57. $x^2 + 18x + 77$

58. $2x^2 - 98$

59. $x^2 + 21x + 98$

60. $x^2 + 20x + 84$

61. $9x^2 + 30x + 16$

62. $8x^2 - 6x - 27$

63. $x^2 - 3x - 54$

64. $x^2 - 169$

65. $25x^2 - 9$

66. $7x^2 + 49$

67. $2x^2 - 10x - 28$

68. $x^2 + 8x + 12$

69. $x^2 - 2x - 35$

70. $x^2 + 2x - 63$

71. $20x^2 - 11x - 3$

72. $12x^2 + 4x - 5$

73. $4x^2 - 5x - 6$

74. $8x^2 + 22x - 21$

75. $3x^2 - 3x - 168$

Reteaching 5-5

Quadratic Equations

OBJECTIVE: Solving quadratic equations by graphing and factoring	**MATERIALS:** None

When graphing a quadratic equation, remember to use the formula $h = -\frac{b}{2a}$ to find the x-coordinate of the vertex of a parabola.

To complete the graph, plot the y-intercept $(0, c)$ and then make the parabola symmetrical.

Example

Solve the quadratic equation $x^2 + 6x + 8 = 0$ by graphing and factoring.

Graphing

Step 1
Graph the associated function $y = x^2 + 6x + 8$.

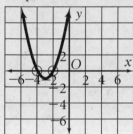

Step 2
Circle the place(s) where the graph crosses the x-axis.

Step 3
Find the values of x for the circled points.
$x = -4$ or $x = -2$

The values for x are the same for each method.

Factoring

Step 1
Factor the equation.
$(x + 4)(x + 2) = 0$

Step 2
Solve each factor for x.
$x + 4 = 0$ or $x + 2 = 0$
$x = -4$ or $x = -2$

Exercises

Solve each quadratic equation first by graphing and then by factoring.

1. $x^2 + 7x + 10 = 0$ **2.** $x^2 - 5x + 6 = 0$ **3.** $x^2 + 6x + 5 = 0$

4. $x^2 + 4x + 3 = 0$ **5.** $3x^2 + 10x + 3 = 0$ **6.** $0 = 2x^2 - 3x + 1$

Solve each quadratic equation by factoring.

7. $x^2 - 7x + 12 = 0$ **8.** $2x^2 + x - 15 = 0$ **9.** $x^2 + x - 2 = 0$

10. $3x^2 - 5x + 2 = 0$ **11.** $x^2 + 5x + 6 = 0$ **12.** $x^2 + x - 20 = 0$

Practice 5-5

Quadratic Equations

Solve each equation by factoring, by taking square roots, or by graphing.
When necessary, round your answer to the nearest hundredth.

1. $x^2 - 18x - 40 = 0$

2. $16x^2 = 56x$

3. $5x^2 = 15x$

4. $x^2 - 6x - 7 = 0$

5. $x^2 - 49 = 0$

6. $x^2 + 2x + 1 = 0$

7. $x^2 - 1 = 0$

8. $x^2 - 3x - 4 = 0$

9. $x^2 + 9x^2 + 20 = 0$

10. $6x^2 + 9 = -55x$

11. $(x + 5)^2 = 36$

12. $2x^2 - 3x = 0$

13. $2x^2 + x - 10 = 0$

14. $-4x^2 + 3x = -1$

15. $5x^2 - 6x + 1 = 0$

16. $3x^2 + 1 = -4x$

17. $-2x^2 + 2 = -3x$

18. $6x^2 + 1 = 5x$

19. $-2x^2 - x + 1 = 0$

20. $3x^2 + 5x = 2$

21. $x^2 - 6x = -8$

22. $x^2 + 6 = -7x$

23. $6x^2 + 18x = 0$

24. $2x^2 + 5 = 11x$

25. $3x^2 - 7x + 2 = 0$

26. $2x^2 - 3x = -1$

27. $2x^2 - x = 6$

28. $x^2 - 144 = 0$

29. $4x^2 + 2 = 6x$

30. $5x^2 + 2 = -7x$

31. $7x^2 + 6x - 1 = 0$

32. $2x^2 - 6x = -4$

33. $11x^2 - 12x + 1 = 0$

34. $7x^2 + 1 = -8x$

35. $x^2 + 9 = -10x$

36. $(x - 2)^2 = 18$

37. $x^2 - 8x + 7 = 0$

38. $x^2 - 16 = 0$

39. $x^2 + 6x = -8$

40. $x^2 + 3 = 4x$

41. $2x^2 + 6 = -7x$

42. $6x^2 + 2 = 7x$

43. $(x + 7)^2 = \frac{49}{16}$

44. $9x^2 - 8x = 1$

45. $10x^2 + 7x + 1 = 0$

46. $4x^2 + 2 = -9x$

47. $3x^2 + 4 = 8x$

48. $4x^2 + 5 + 9x = 0$

49. $9x^2 + 10x = -1$

50. $2x^2 + 9x + 4 = 0$

51. $2x^2 + 6x = -4$

52. $11x^2 - 1 = -10x$

53. $4x^2 = 1$

54. $6x^2 = 12x$

55. $25x^2 - 9 = 0$

56. $2x^2 + 11x = 6$

57. $8x^2 - 6x + 1 = 0$

58. $x^2 + 11 = -12x$

59. $6x^2 + 2 = 13x$

60. $x^2 = 121$

61. $4x^2 - 11x = 3$

62. $8x^2 + 6x + 1 = 0$

63. $x^2 + 9x + 8 = 0$

64. $x^2 + 8x = -12$

65. $x^2 + 6x = 40$

66. $2x^2 = 8$

67. $x^2 = x + 6$

68. $x^2 + 2x - 6 = 0$

69. $x^2 - 12 = 0$

70. $3x^2 + 4x = 6$

71. $7x^2 - 105 = 0$

72. $16x^2 = 81$

73. $x^2 + 5x + 4 = 0$

74. $x^2 + 36 = -13x$

75. $x^2 + 6 = 5x$

Reteaching 5-6

OBJECTIVE: Adding, subtracting, and multiplying complex numbers	**MATERIALS:** None

- A *complex number* consists of a real part and an imaginary part. It is written in the form $a + bi$, where a and b are real numbers.

- When adding or subtracting complex numbers, you combine the real parts and then combine the imaginary parts.

- When multiplying complex numbers, use the Distributive Property.

- $i^2 = (\sqrt{-1})(\sqrt{-1}) = -1$ and $i = \sqrt{-1}$

Examples

Simplify $(3 - i) + (2 + 3i)$.

$(3 - i) + (2 + 3i)$

$\quad = ③ - \boxed{i} + ② + \boxed{3i}$ ⟵ **Circle real parts. Put a square around imaginary parts.**

$\quad = (3 + 2) + (-1 + 3)i$ ⟵ **Combine.**

$\quad = 5 + 2i$

Simplify $(3 + 4i)(5 + 2i)$.

$(3 + 4i)(5 + 2i)$

$\quad = 3(5) + 3(2i) + 4i(5) + 4i(2i)$ ⟵ **Use the Distributive Property.**

$\quad = 15 + 6i + 20i + 8i^2$ ⟵ **Combine real parts and imaginary parts.**

$\quad = 15 + 26i + 8(-1)$ ⟵ **Substitute $i^2 = -1$.**

$\quad = 7 + 26i$

Exercises

Simplify each expression.

1. $2i + (-4 - 2i)$ **2.** $5i \cdot 12i$ **3.** $(2 + i)(2 - i)$

4. $(3 + i)(2 + i)$ **5.** $(4 + 3i)(1 + 2i)$ **6.** $3i(1 - 2i)$

7. $(6i)(-4i)$ **8.** $3i(4 - i)$ **9.** $3 - (-2 + 3i) + (-5 + i)$

10. $4i(6 - 2i)$ **11.** $2i + (3i)^2$ **12.** $(5 + 6i) + (-2 + 4i)$

13. $-14i(-4)$ **14.** $3i\sqrt{-6}$ **15.** $9(11 + 5i)$

Practice 5-6

Complex Numbers

Find the first three output values for each function. Use $z = 0$ for the first input value.

1. $f(z) = z^2 + 2i$

2. $f(z) = z^2 + 1 + i$

Find the additive inverse of each of the following.

3. $2 + 3i$

4. $-4 + i$

5. $2i$

6. $-1 - i$

7. $-6i$

8. $5 - 2i$

9. $-2 + 3i$

10. 4

Find each absolute value.

11. $|-2i|$

12. $|5 + 12i|$

13. $|-1 - i|$

14. $|2 + i|$

15. $|4 + 3i|$

16. $|5 - 2i|$

17. $|3 - 2i|$

18. $|-2 + i|$

19. $|3 - 3i|$

20. $|3i|$

21. $|2i|$

22. $|4 + i|$

23. $|6 - 3i|$

24. $|-3 + i|$

25. $|4|$

Simplify each expression.

26. $\sqrt{40}$

27. $\sqrt{-88}$

28. $-\sqrt{-36}$

29. $(1 + 5i) + (1 - 5i)$

30. $(3 + 2i) - (3 + 2i)$

31. $4 - \sqrt{-25}$

32. $(2 + 6i) - (7 + 9i)$

33. $(1 + 5i)(1 - 5i)$

34. $(1 + 5i)(6 - 3i)$

35. $(5 - 6i)(6 - 2i)$

36. $(3 + 4i)(3 + 4i)$

37. $(2 + 3i)(2 - 3i)$

38. $(2 + 2i)(2 - 2i)$

39. $(-3 - 2i)(1 - 3i)$

40. $(3 + 3i) - (4 - 3i)$

41. $\sqrt{-48}$

42. $\sqrt{-300}$

43. $\sqrt{-75}$

44. $\sqrt{-16} + 2$

45. $(4 - i)(4 - i)$

46. $(4 + 2i)(1 - 7i)$

47. $(1 + 3i)(1 - 7i)$

48. $(2 + 4i)(-3 - 2i)$

49. $(11 - 12i)(11 + 12i)$

50. $(2 + 3i) + (-4 + 5i)$

51. $(5 + 14i) - (10 - 2i)$

52. $(5 + 12i)(5 - 12i)$

53. $(3 + 4i)(1 - 2i)$

54. $(6 + 2i)(1 - 2i)$

55. $(5 - 13i)(5 - 13i)$

56. $\sqrt{-44}$

57. $-\sqrt{-63}$

58. $\sqrt{-8}$

59. $(2 + 3i)(4 + 5i)$

60. $(5 + 4i) - (-1 - 2i)$

61. $(1 + 2i)(-1 - 2i)$

62. $(-1 + 4i)(1 - 2i)$

63. $(6 + 2i) + (1 - 2i)$

64. $(3 + 2i)(3 + 2i)$

65. $(-2 + 3i) + (4 + 5i)$

66. $(5 + 4i)(1 + 2i)$

67. $(-1 - 5i)(-1 + 5i)$

Solve each equation.

68. $x^2 + 80 = 0$

69. $5x^2 + 500 = 0$

70. $2x^2 + 40 = 0$

71. $3x^2 + 36 = 0$

72. $3x^2 + 75 = 0$

73. $2x^2 + 144 = 0$

74. $4x^2 + 1600 = 0$

75. $4x^2 + 1 = 0$

76. $2x^2 + 10 = 0$

77. $4x^2 + 100 = 0$

78. $x^2 + 9 = 0$

79. $9x^2 + 90 = 0$

Reteaching 5-7

Completing the Square

• •

OBJECTIVE: Solving quadratic equations by completing the square

MATERIALS: None

• Perfect square trinomials are equations in the form $x^2 + 2kx + k^2$, which can be factored into $(x + k)^2$. Completing the square produces a perfect square trinomial.

• To complete the square, you must write the equation so that the coefficient of the x^2 term equals 1.

Example

Complete the square to solve the quadratic equation.

$$2x^2 + 20x - 22 = 0$$

$2x^2 + 20x - 22 = 0$	⟵ **Look to see whether the x^2 coefficient is 1.**
$x^2 + 10x - 11 = 0$	⟵ **Divide each side by 2 to eliminate the x^2 coefficient.**
$x^2 + ⑩x - 11 = 0$	⟵ **Circle the coefficient of the linear term.**
$x^2 + ⑩x = 11$	⟵ **Add 11 to each side to get the variables on one side of the equal sign.**
$x^2 + ⑩x + 25 = 11 + 25$	⟵ **Divide the circled number by 2, square it, and add the result to each side.**
$(x + 5)^2 = 36$	⟵ **Factor the perfect square trinomial.**
$x + 5 = \pm 6$	⟵ **Take the square root of each side.**
$x = -5 \pm 6$	⟵ **Solve for x.**
$x = 1 \text{ and } -11$	⟵ **Simplify.**

Exercises

Solve each equation by completing the square.

1. $x^2 + 4x = 21$ **2.** $x^2 - 8x = 33$ **3.** $x^2 + 10x = -5$

4. $3x^2 + 10x + 3 = 0$ **5.** $3x^2 + 4x = 3$ **6.** $x^2 - 5x - 5 = 0$

7. $x^2 + 7x = 0$ **8.** $2x^2 - 7x - 4 = 0$ **9.** $x^2 - x - 7 = 0$

10. $x^2 - 8x + 4 = 0$ **11.** $x^2 - 6x + 6 = 0$ **12.** $x^2 + 2x = 15$

13. $x^2 + 2x - 5 = 0$ **14.** $2x^2 + 8x - 10 = 0$ **15.** $4x^2 + 4x = 3$

Practice 5-7

Completing the Square

Complete the square.

1. $x^2 + 6x +$ ■

2. $x^2 - 7x +$ ■

3. $x^2 + 12x +$ ■

4. $x^2 + 3x +$ ■

5. $x^2 - 8x +$ ■

6. $x^2 + 16x +$ ■

7. $x^2 + 21x +$ ■

8. $x^2 - 2x +$ ■

Rewrite each equation in vertex form. Then find the vertex.

9. $y = x^2 + 4x - 6$

10. $y = x^2 - 6x + 6$

11. $y = 4x^2 + 8x - 4$

12. $y = 4x^2 + 4x + 1$

13. $y = 2x^2 + 4x - 5$

14. $y = -3x^2 - 4x - 1$

15. $y = -3x^2 + 3x - 1$

16. $y = x^2 + 2x + 1$

17. $y = -5x^2 + 10x + 1$

18. $y = -2x^2 + 4x + 3$

19. $y = x^2 + 5x + \frac{5}{4}$

20. $y = -2x^2 + 10x - 11$

21. $y = 6x^2 - 12x + 1$

22. $y = -2x^2 + 8x - 9$

23. $y = 3x^2 + 9x + 6$

Solve each quadratic equation by completing the square.

24. $x^2 + 12x + 4 = 0$

25. $x^2 - x - 5 = 0$

26. $3x^2 = -12x - 3$

27. $x^2 - x - 1 = 0$

28. $4x^2 - 8x + 1 = 0$

29. $5x^2 = 8x - 6$

30. $2x^2 - 4x - 3 = 0$

31. $x^2 + 11x = 0$

32. $x^2 = 5x + 14$

33. $2x^2 + x - 1 = 0$

34. $2x^2 + 6x - 7 = 0$

35. $2x^2 = -8x + 45$

36. $x^2 = -3x - 3$

37. $4x^2 = -2x + 1$

38. $3x^2 = -6x + 9$

39. $x^2 = 7x + 12$

40. $x^2 = 3x + 7$

41. $3x^2 = 6x - 9$

42. $x^2 = -3x + 2$

43. $x^2 = -7x - 1$

44. $4x^2 = -3x + 2$

45. $2x^2 = 4x - 5$

46. $2x^2 = 5x + 5$

47. $2x^2 = 6x + 5$

48. $x^2 = 3x$

49. $x^2 = 8x$

50. $4x^2 = -2x - 3$

51. $2x^2 = -2x + 5$

52. $2x^2 = -5x - 5$

53. $3x^2 = -5x + 1$

54. $2x^2 = 2x + 4$

55. $3x^2 = 7x + 8$

56. $2x^2 = -6x + 4$

57. $x^2 = -7x - 9$

58. $2x^2 = 5x$

59. $3x^2 = -42x$

60. $2x^2 = -4x + 5$

61. $4x^2 = -x + 5$

62. $3x^2 = -3x + 1$

63. $x^2 = 3x + 4$

64. $2x^2 = 2x + 8$

65. $3x^2 = x + 4$

Solve each equation.

66. $x^2 + 2x + 1 = 9$

67. $3x^2 - 18x + 27 = 125$

68. $x^2 - 4x + 4 = 5$

69. $x^2 + 3x + \frac{9}{4} = \frac{13}{4}$

70. $x^2 + 3x + \frac{9}{4} = -\frac{15}{4}$

71. $x^2 + 3x + \frac{9}{4} = \frac{41}{4}$

72. $x^2 + 7x + \frac{49}{4} = \frac{53}{4}$

73. $x^2 + 3x + \frac{9}{4} = \frac{29}{4}$

74. $x^2 - 6x + 9 = 7$

Algebra 2 Chapter 5

Reteaching 5-8

OBJECTIVE: Solving quadratic equations by using the Quadratic Formula

MATERIALS: None

Follow each step below to solve any quadratic equation by using the Quadratic Formula.

1. Write the equation in the standard form $ax^2 + bx + c = 0$.

2. Substitute a-, b-, and c-values into the Quadratic Formula.

$$x = \frac{-b \pm \sqrt{b^2 - 4ac}}{2a}$$

3. Simplify. Use imaginary numbers if necessary.

4. Check the solution(s) by substituting the values into the original equation.

Example

Use the Quadratic Formula to solve $x^2 + 2 = -2x$. Check your solution.

$$x^2 + 2 = -2x$$

$$x^2 + 2x + 2 = 0 \qquad \longleftarrow \quad \textbf{Write in standard form.}$$

$$\underline{1}x^2 + \textcircled{2}x + \boxed{2} = 0 \qquad \longleftarrow \quad \textbf{Underline } a\textbf{, circle } b\textbf{, and put a square around } c.$$

$$x = \frac{-2 \pm \sqrt{2^2 - 4(1)(2)}}{2(1)} \qquad \longleftarrow \quad \textbf{Substitute 1 for } a\textbf{, 2 for } b\textbf{, and 2 for } c \textbf{ into the Quadratic Formula.}$$

$$= \frac{-2 \pm \sqrt{-4}}{2} \qquad \longleftarrow \quad \textbf{Simplify to find the values of } x.$$

$$= \frac{-2 \pm 2i}{2}$$

$$= -1 \pm i$$

Check:

$$x^2 + 2 = -2x \qquad\qquad x^2 + 2 = -2x$$

$$(-1 + i)^2 + 2 \stackrel{?}{=} -2(-1 + i) \qquad (-1 - i)^2 + 2 \stackrel{?}{=} -2(-1 - i)$$

$$1 - 2i + i^2 + 2 \stackrel{?}{=} 2 - 2i \qquad\qquad 1 + 2i + i^2 + 2 \stackrel{?}{=} 2 + 2i$$

$$1 - 2i - 1 + 2 \stackrel{?}{=} 2 - 2i \qquad\qquad 1 + 2i - 1 + 2 \stackrel{?}{=} 2 + 2i$$

$$2 - 2i = 2 - 2i \checkmark \qquad\qquad 2 + 2i = 2 + 2i \checkmark$$

Exercises

Solve each equation using the Quadratic Formula.

1. $x^2 - 3x + 2 = 0$ **2.** $-x^2 + 5x = 9$ **3.** $10x - 6 = 5x^2$

4. $x + 2x^2 + 1 = -1 - x$ **5.** $2x^2 + x = 10$ **6.** $2x + 1 = 2x^2$

Practice 5-8

The Quadratic Formula

Evaluate the discriminant of each equation. Tell how many solutions each equation has and whether the solutions are real or imaginary.

1. $y = x^2 + 10x - 25$ **2.** $y = x^2 + 10x + 10$ **3.** $y = 9x^2 - 24x$

4. $y = 4x^2 - 4x + 1$ **5.** $y = 4x^2 - 5x + 1$ **6.** $y = 4x^2 - 3x + 1$

7. $y = x^2 + 3x + 4$ **8.** $y = x^2 + 7x - 3$ **9.** $y = -2x^2 + 3x - 5$

10. $y = x^2 - 5x + 4$ **11.** $y = x^2 + 12x + 36$ **12.** $y = x^2 + 2x + 3$

13. $y = 2x^2 - 13x - 7$ **14.** $y = -5x^2 + 6x - 4$ **15.** $y = -4x^2 - 4x - 1$

Solve each equation using the Quadratic Formula.

16. $x^2 + 6x + 9 = 0$ **17.** $x^2 - 15x + 56 = 0$ **18.** $3x^2 - 5x + 2 = 0$

19. $2x^2 + 3x + 5 = 0$ **20.** $10x^2 - 23x + 12 = 0$ **21.** $4x^2 + x - 5 = 0$

22. $x^2 + 8x + 15 = 0$ **23.** $3x^2 + 2x + 1 = 0$ **24.** $4x^2 + x + 5 = 0$

25. $x^2 - 4x - 12 = 0$ **26.** $x^2 = 3x + 2$ **27.** $2x^2 - 5x + 2 = 0$

28. $x^2 + 6x - 4 = 0$ **29.** $x^2 = 2x - 5$ **30.** $3x^2 + 7 = -6x$

31. $2x^2 + 6x + 3 = 0$ **32.** $x^2 = -18x - 80$ **33.** $x^2 + 9x - 13 = 0$

34. $x^2 - 8x + 25 = 0$ **35.** $4x^2 + 13x = 12$ **36.** $3x^2 - 5x = -12$

37. $3x^2 + 4x + 5 = 0$ **38.** $2x^2 = 3x - 7$ **39.** $5x^2 + 2x + 1 = 0$

40. $5x^2 + x + 3 = 0$ **41.** $5x^2 + x = 3$ **42.** $5x^2 - 2x + 7 = 0$

43. $x^2 - 2x + 3 = 0$ **44.** $-2x^2 + 3x = 24$ **45.** $4x^2 = 5x - 6$

46. $x^2 + 6x + 5 = 0$ **47.** $x^2 - 6x = -8$ **48.** $x^2 - 6x = -6$

Solve.

49. A model of the daily profits p of a gas station based on the price per gallon g is $p = -15,000g^2 + 34,500g - 16,800$. Use the discriminant to find whether the station can profit $4000 per day. Explain.

Solve each equation using the Quadratic Formula. Find the exact solutions. Then approximate any radical solutions. Round to the nearest hundredth.

50. $x^2 - 2x - 3 = 0$ **51.** $x^2 + 5x + 4 = 0$ **52.** $x^2 - 2x - 8 = 0$

53. $7x^2 - 12x + 3 = 0$ **54.** $5x^2 + 5x - 1 = 0$ **55.** $4x^2 + 5x + 1 = 0$

56. $6x^2 + 5x - 4 = 0$ **57.** $x^2 + x = 6$ **58.** $x^2 - 13x = 48$

59. $2x^2 + 5x = 0$ **60.** $x^2 + 3x - 3 = 0$ **61.** $x^2 - 4x + 1 = 0$

62. $9x^2 - 6x - 7 = 0$ **63.** $x^2 - 35 = 2x$ **64.** $x^2 + 7x + 10 = 0$

Reteaching 6-1

Polynomial Functions

OBJECTIVE: Comparing models of real data	**MATERIALS:** Graphing calculator

---

You can use your graphing calculator to model data and determine whether a linear, quadratic, or cubic model best fits the data. You can use the equation for that model to estimate values of data.

Example

The table shows winning times in the 400-meter run.

Men's Olympic Track and Field, 400-Meter Run

Year	1968	1972	1976	1980	1984	1988	1992	1996	2000
Seconds	43.86	44.66	44.26	44.60	44.27	43.87	43.50	43.49	43.84

Source: *The World Almanac and Book of Facts 2001*

a. Find and graph a linear model, a quadratic model, and a cubic model for the data.

Linear model	Quadratic model	Cubic model
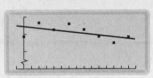	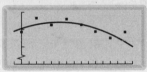	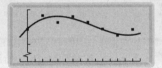
$y = -0.02433x + 44.42822$	$y = -0.00127x^2 + 0.01640x + 44.23812$	$y = 0.00032x^3 - 0.01665x^2 + 0.20197x + 43.89364$

b. The cubic model appears to be the best fit. Use it to estimate the winning time in 2004. Does your estimate seem reasonable?

Let $x =$ the years since 1968 and $y =$ the number of seconds. Substitute 36 for x and simplify.

$y = 0.00032(36)^3 - 0.01665(36)^2 + 0.20197(36) + 43.89364 = 44.51$

This estimate does not seem reasonable, since the times are generally decreasing. We would expect the time for the 2004 Olympic games to be less than the time for the 2000 Olympic games.

Exercises

Find a linear, quadratic, and cubic model for the data. Use the model that best fits the data to estimate the diving record in 2004.

Men's Olympic Springboard Diving Records

Year	1980	1984	1988	1992	1996	2000
Points	905.02	754.41	730.80	676.53	701.46	708.72

Source: *The World Almanac and Book of Facts 2001*

Name _____ Class _____ Date _____

Practice 6-1

Polynomial Functions

• •

Find a cubic model for each function. Then use your model to estimate the value of y when $x = 7$.

1.

x	0	2	4	6	8	10
y	25	21	20	23	19	17

2.

x	0	2	4	6	8	10
y	3.1	4.2	4.3	4.4	5.1	6.7

Write each polynomial in standard form. Then classify it by degree and by number of terms.

3. $4x + x + 2$

4. $-3 + 3x - 3x$

5. $6x^4 - 1$

6. $1 - 2s + 5s^4$

7. $5m^2 - 3m^2$

8. $x^2 + 3x - 4x^3$

9. $-1 + 2x^2$

10. $5m^2 - 3m^3$

11. $5x - 7x^2$

12. $2 + 3x^3 - 2$

13. $6 - 2x^3 - 4 + x^3$

14. $6x - 7x$

15. $a^3(a^2 + a + 1)$

16. $x(x + 5) - 5(x + 5)$

17. $p(p - 5) + 6$

18. $(3c^2)^2$

19. $-(3 - b)$

20. $6(2x - 1)$

21. $\frac{2}{3} + s^2$

22. $\frac{2x^4 + 4x - 5}{4}$

23. $\frac{3 - z^5}{3}$

24. The lengths of the sides of a triangle are $x + 4$ units, x units, and $x + 1$ units. Express the perimeter of the triangle as a polynomial in standard form.

25. Find a cubic function to model the data below. (Hint: Use the number of years past 1940 for x.) Then use the function to estimate the average monthly Social Security Benefit for a retired worker in 2005.

Average Monthly Social Security Benefits, 1940–1999

Year	1940	1950	1960	1970	1980	1990	1999
Amount (in dollars)	22.71	29.03	81.73	123.82	321.10	550.50	757.71

Source: *www.infoplease.com*

26. Find a cubic function to model the data below. (Hint: Use x to represent the gestation period.) Then use the function to estimate the longevity of an animal with a gestation period of 151 days.

Gestation and Longevity of Certain Animals

Animal	Rat	Squirrel	Pig	Cow	Elephant
Gestation (in days)	21	44	115	280	624
Longevity (in years)	3	9	10	12	40

Source: *www.infoplease.com*

Algebra 2 Chapter 6

Reteaching 6-2

OBJECTIVE: Writing a polynomial function from its zeros	**MATERIALS:** None

- A polynomial function in factored form can be rewritten in standard form if you know its zeros.

- Use the Zero-Product Property to find values that will make the polynomial equal zero.

Example

Write a polynomial function in standard form with zeros at $0, 4,$ and -2.

$(x + 0)(x - 4)(x + 2)$ ⟵ **Write the factors using the zeros.**

$f(x) = x(x - 4)(x + 2)$ ⟵ **Write the polynomial function in factored form.**

$= x(x^2 - 2x - 8)$ ⟵ **Multiply $(x - 4)(x + 2)$ to convert to standard form.**

$= x^3 - 2x^2 - 8x$ ⟵ **Multiply by x using the Distributive Property.**

The polynomial function written in standard form is
$f(x) = x^3 - 2x^2 - 8x$.

Exercises

Write a polynomial function with the given zeros.

1. $5, -1, 3$ **2.** $1, 7, -5$ **3.** $-1, 1, -6$ **4.** $2, -2, -3$

5. $2, 1, 3$ **6.** $2, 3, -3, -1$ **7.** $0, -8, 2$ **8.** $-10, 0, 2$

9. $-1, 1, -6$ **10.** $2, -2, -3$ **11.** $-2, 2, -\frac{3}{2}$ **12.** $-1, \frac{2}{3}$

13. $1, -3, -\frac{4}{3}$ **14.** $-2, -2, -3$ **15.** $4, -2$ (mult. 2)   **16.** $2, -1$ (mult. 2)

Find the zeros of each function.

17. $y = x(x + 8)(x - 2)$ **18.** $y = (x^2 - 4)(x^2 - 9)$ **19.** $y = (x - 3)(x + 3)$

20. $y = (3x + 2)(x - 5)$ **21.** $y = 6x(x - 8)$ **22.** $y = (x^2 - 1)(x^2 - 16)$

23. $y = x(x + 2)(x - 10)$ **24.** $y = (x^2 - 4)(x + 3)^2$ **25.** $y = (2x + 1)(x - 5)(x + 3)$

26. $y = 3x(x + 4)(2x - 3)$ **27.** $y = x^2(x^2 - 5)$ **28.** $y = 4x^2(x^2 - 36)$

Practice 6-2

Polynomials and Linear Factors

For each function, determine the zeros. State the multiplicity of any multiple zeros.

1. $y = (x - 5)^3$

2. $y = x(x - 8)^2$

3. $y = (x - 2)(x + 7)^3$

4. $f(x) = x^4 - 8x^3 + 16x^2$

5. $f(x) = 9x^3 - 81x$

6. $y = (2x + 5)(x - 3)^2$

Write each function in standard form.

7. $y = (x - 5)(x + 5)(2x - 1)$

8. $y = (2x + 1)(x - 3)(5 - x)$

9. A rectangular box is 24 in. long, 12 in. wide, and 18 in. high. If each dimension is increased by x in., write a polynomial function in standard form modeling the volume V of the box.

Write a polynomial function in standard form with the given zeros.

10. $-1, 3, 4$

11. $1, 1, 2$

12. $-3, 0, 0, 5$

13. -2 multiplicity 3

Write each expression as a polynomial in standard form.

14. $x(x - 1)^2$

15. $(x + 3)^2(x + 1)$

16. $(x + 4)(2x - 5)(x + 5)^2$

Write each function in factored form. Check by multiplication.

17. $y = 2x^3 + 10x^2 + 12x$

18. $y = x^4 - x^3 - 6x^2$

19. $y = -3x^3 + 18x^2 - 27x$

Find the zeros of each function. Then graph the function.

20. $y = (x + 1)(x - 1)(x - 3)$

21. $y = (x + 2)(x - 3)$

22. $y = x(x - 2)(x + 5)$

Find the relative maximum, relative minimum, and zeros of each function.

23. $f(x) = x^3 - 7x^2 + 10x$

24. $f(x) = x^3 - x^2 - 9x + 9$

Write each polynomial in factored form. Check by multiplication.

25. $x^3 - 6x^2 - 16x$

26. $x^3 + 7x^2 + 12x$

27. $x^3 - 8x^2 + 15x$

28. A rectangular box has a square base. The combined length of a side of the square base, and the height is 20 in. Let x be the length of a side of the base of the box.

  a. Write a polynomial function in factored form modeling the volume V of the box.

  b. What is the maximum possible volume of the box?

Reteaching 6-3

OBJECTIVE: Dividing polynomials   **MATERIALS:** None

Example

Divide $2x^2 + 6x - 7$ by $x + 1$.

$$\begin{array}{r} 2x \\ x+1 \overline{)2x^2 + 6x + 7} \end{array}$$

Step 1: To find the first term of the quotient, divide the highest-degree term of $2x^2 + 6x + 7$ by the highest-degree term of the divisor, $x + 1$. Circle these terms before dividing.

$$\begin{array}{r} 2x \\ x + 1 \overline{)2x^2 + 6x + 7} \\ 2x^2 + 2x \\ \hline \end{array}$$

Step 2: Multiply $x + 1$ by the new term in the quotient. Align like terms.

$$\begin{array}{r} 2x \\ x + 1 \overline{)2x^2 + 6x + 7} \\ 2x^2 + 2x \\ \hline 4x + 7 \end{array}$$

Step 3: Subtract. Bring down the next term.

$$\begin{array}{r} 2x + 4 \\ x + 1 \overline{)2x^2 + 6x + 7} \\ 2x^2 + 2x \\ \hline 4x + 7 \\ 4x + 4 \\ \hline 3 \end{array}$$

Step 4: Divide the highest-degree term of $4x + 7$ by the highest-degree term of $x + 1$. Circle these terms before dividing.

Step 5: Repeat Steps 2 and 3. The *remainder* is 3 because its degree is less than the degree of $x + 1$.

$2x^2 + 6x + 7$ divided by $x + 1$ is $2x + 4$, with a remainder of 3.

Exercises

Divide using long division.

1. $(3x^2 - 8x + 7) \div (x - 1)$

2. $x + 6 \overline{)x^3 + 5x^2 - 3x - 4}$

3. $x - 5 \overline{)x^2 + 3x - 8}$

4. $(x^2 + 6x + 14) \div (x + 3)$

5. $(x^3 - 7x^2 + 11x + 3) \div (x - 3)$

6. $x - 2 \overline{)2x^3 - 3x^2 - x - 2}$

7. $(2x^2 - 4x + 7) \div (x - 3)$

8. $x + 7 \overline{)x^3 + 2x^2 - 20x + 4}$

9. $x - 1 \overline{)x^2 - 5x + 2}$

10. $(2x^3 + 3x^2 + x + 6) \div (x + 3)$

Practice 6-3

Dividing Polynomials

Determine whether each binomial is a factor of $x^3 + 3x^2 - 10x - 24$.

1. $x + 4$ **2.** $x - 3$ **3.** $x + 6$ **4.** $x + 2$

Divide using synthetic division.

5. $(x^3 - 8x^2 + 17x - 10) \div (x - 5)$ **6.** $(x^3 + 5x^2 - x - 9) \div (x + 2)$

7. $(-2x^3 + 15x^2 - 22x - 15) \div (x - 3)$ **8.** $(x^3 + 7x^2 + 15x + 9) \div (x + 1)$

9. $(x^3 + 2x^2 + 5x + 12) \div (x + 3)$ **10.** $(x^3 - 5x^2 - 7x + 25) \div (x - 5)$

11. $(x^4 - x^3 + x^2 - x + 1) \div (x - 1)$ **12.** $\left(x^4 + \frac{5}{3}x^3 - \frac{2}{3}x^2 + 6x - 2 \right) \div \left(x - \frac{1}{3} \right)$

13. $(x^4 - 5x^3 + 5x^2 + 7x - 12) \div (x - 4)$ **14.** $(2x^4 + 23x^3 + 60x^2 - 125x - 500) \div (x + 4)$

Use synthetic division and the Remainder Theorem to find $P(a)$.

15. $P(x) = 3x^3 - 4x^2 - 5x + 1; a = 2$ **16.** $P(x) = x^3 + 7x^2 + 12x - 3; a = -5$

17. $P(x) = x^3 + 6x^2 + 10x + 3; a = -3$ **18.** $P(x) = 2x^4 - 9x^3 + 7x^2 - 5x + 11; a = 4$

Divide using long division. Check your answers.

19. $(x^2 - 13x - 48) \div (x + 3)$ **20.** $(2x^2 + x - 7) \div (x - 5)$

21. $(x^3 + 5x^2 - 3x - 1) \div (x - 1)$ **22.** $(3x^3 - x^2 - 7x + 6) \div (x + 2)$

Use synthetic division and the given factor to completely factor each polynomial function.

23. $y = x^3 + 3x^2 - 13x - 15; (x + 5)$ **24.** $y = x^3 - 3x^2 - 10x + 24; (x - 2)$

Divide.

25. $(6x^3 + 2x^2 - 11x + 12) \div (3x + 4)$ **26.** $(x^4 + 2x^3 + x - 3) \div (x - 1)$

27. $(2x^4 + 3x^3 - 4x^2 + x + 1) \div (2x - 1)$ **28.** $(x^5 - 1) \div (x - 1)$

29. $(x^4 - 3x^2 - 10) \div (x - 2)$ **30.** $(3x^3 - 2x^2 + 2x + 1) \div \left(x + \frac{1}{3} \right)$

31. A box is to be mailed. The volume in cubic inches of the box can be expressed as the product of its three dimensions: $V(x) = x^3 - 16x^2 + 79x - 120$. The length is $x - 8$. Find linear expressions for the other dimensions. Assume that the width is greater than the height.

Reteaching 6-4

OBJECTIVE: Solving polynomial equations by factoring

MATERIALS: None

Example

Solve $2x^3 + 16 = 0$ by factoring. Find all complex roots.

$2x^3 + 16 = 0$

$2(x^3 + 8) = 0$ ⟵   **Since 2 is a common factor to each term, factor out 2.**

$2(x + 2)(x^2 - 2x + 4) = 0$ ⟵   **Factor the remaining cubic expression.**

$2 = 0$ or $(x + 2) = 0$ or $(x^2 - 2x + 4) = 0$ ⟵   **Use the Zero-Product Property.**

$x = -2$ or $x = \dfrac{2 \pm \sqrt{4 - 4(1)(4)}}{2(1)}$ ⟵   **Solve each equation for x. Use the Quadratic Formula when necessary.**

$x = -2$ or $x = \dfrac{2 \pm 2i\sqrt{3}}{2}$

$x = -2$ or $x = 1 \pm i\sqrt{3}$ ⟵   **Simplify.**

The solutions are -2 and $1 \pm i\sqrt{3}$.

Exercises

Solve each equation by factoring. Find all complex roots.

1. $x^3 - 8 = 0$ **2.** $4x^3 + 4 = 0$

3. $x^4 - x^2 - 72 = 0$ **4.** $x^4 + 9x^2 = -20$

5. $x^4 - 27x = 0$ **6.** $8x^3 = -1$

7. $7x^4 = -28x^2 - 21$ **8.** $x^3 = 64$

9. $8x^3 + 27 = 0$ **10.** $x^4 - 7x^2 = -12$

11. $2x^4 + 16x^2 = 40$ **12.** $2x^4 - 16x = 0$

13. $9x^4 - 25 = 0$ **14.** $2x^4 - x^2 = 3$

15. $x^4 + 5x^2 = -4$ **16.** $x^4 - 7x^2 - 8 = 0$

17. $2x^3 + 16 = 0$ **18.** $x^4 - 5x^2 - 24 = 0$

Practice 6-4

Solving Polynomial Equations

Factor the expression on the left side of each equation. Then solve the equation.

1. $8x^3 - 27 = 0$

2. $x^3 + 64 = 0$

3. $2x^3 + 54 = 0$

4. $2x^3 - 250 = 0$

5. $4x^3 - 32 = 0$

6. $27x^3 + 1 = 0$

7. $64x^3 - 1 = 0$

8. $x^3 - 27 = 0$

9. $x^4 - 5x^2 + 4 = 0$

10. $x^4 - 12x^2 + 11 = 0$

11. $x^4 - 10x^2 + 16 = 0$

12. $x^4 - 8x^2 + 16 = 0$

13. $x^4 - 9x^2 + 14 = 0$

14. $x^4 + 13x^2 + 36 = 0$

15. $x^4 - 10x^2 + 9 = 0$

16. $x^4 + 3x^2 - 4 = 0$

17. Over 3 yr, Lucia saved $550, $600, and $650 from baby-sitting jobs. The polynomial $550x^3 + 600x^2 + 650x$ represents her savings, with interest, after 3 yr. The annual interest rate equals $x - 1$. Find the interest needed so that she will have $2000 after 3 yr.

Solve each equation by graphing. Where necessary, round to the nearest hundredth.

18. $2x^4 = 9x^2 - 4$

19. $x^2 - 16x = -1$

20. $6x^3 + 10x^2 + 5x = 0$

21. $36x^3 + 6x^2 = 9x$

22. $15x^4 = 11x^3 + 14x^2$

23. $x^4 = 81x^2$

24. The product of three consecutives integers $n - 1$, n, and $n + 1$ is -336. Write and solve an equation to find the numbers.

Factor each expression.

25. $x^3 - 125$

26. $x^4 - 8x^2 + 15$

27. $x^4 + x^2 - 2$

28. $x^3 + 1$

29. $x^4 - 2x^2 - 24$

30. $x^4 + 10x^2 + 9$

31. $x^3 + 27$

32. $x^4 + 7x^2 - 18$

Solve each equation.

33. $x^4 - x = 0$

34. $3x^4 + 18 = 21x^2$

35. $2x^4 - 26x^2 - 28 = 0$

36. $5x^4 + 50x^2 + 80 = 0$

37. $x^4 - 81 = 0$

38. $x^4 = 25$

39. $x^5 = x^3 + 12x$

40. $x^4 + 12x^2 = 8x^3$

Reteaching 6-5

Theorems about Roots of Polynomial Equations

OBJECTIVE: Writing a polynomial equation from its roots

MATERIALS: None

Example

Find a third-degree polynomial equation with rational coefficients that has roots -4 and $2 - 3i$.

Roots: $-4, 2 - 3i, 2 + 3i$ ← **Since $2 - 3i$ is a root, its complex conjugate $2 + 3i$ is also a root.**

$(x + 4)\,[x - (2 - 3i)][x - (2 + 3i)]$ ← **Write the factored form of the polynomial.**

$(x + 4)[x^2 - x(2 + 3i) - x(2 - 3i) + (2 - 3i)(2 + 3i)]$ ← **Multiple the factors.**

$(x + 4)[x^2 - 2x - 3ix - 2x + 3ix + 4 + 6i - 6i - 9i^2]$

$(x + 4)[x^2 - 4x + 4 - 9i^2]$ ← **Simplify.**

$(x + 4)(x^2 - 4x + 13)$ ← **Multiply.**

$x^3 + 4x^2 - 4x^2 - 16x + 13x + 52$

$x^3 - 3x + 52$ ← **Simplify.**

A third-degree polynomial equation with rational coefficients and roots -4 and $2 - 3i$ is $x^3 - 3x + 52 = 0$.

Exercises

Find a third-degree polynomial equation with rational coefficients that has the given roots.

1. $1, 2 - i$ **2.** $5 + 2i, -2$

3. $3, 6 + i$ **4.** $-4, \sqrt{2}$

5. $2 - \sqrt{3}, -1$ **6.** $0, 3 - \sqrt{3}$

7. $3i, 7$ **8.** $2 + \sqrt{5}, 3$

9. $-3, i$ **10.** $1 - i, 8$

11. $1, 5i$ **12.** $2, 4 + i$

13. $3, -4i$ **14.** $0, 2 - i$

15. $-7, 1 - \sqrt{2}$ **16.** $-4, -\sqrt{7}$

Practice 6-5

Theorems about Roots of Polynomial Equations

**A polynomial equation with rational coefficients has the given roots.
Find two additional roots.**

1. $2 + 3i$ and $\sqrt{7}$

2. $3 - \sqrt{2}$ and $1 + \sqrt{3}$

3. $-4i$ and $6 - i$

4. $5 - \sqrt{6}$ and $-2 + \sqrt{10}$

**Find a fourth-degree polynomial equation with integer coefficients that has
the given numbers as roots.**

5. $2i$ and $4 - i$

6. $\sqrt{2}$ and $2 - \sqrt{3}$

7. $3i$ and $\sqrt{6}$

8. $2 + i$ and $1 - \sqrt{5}$

Find the roots of each polynomial equation.

9. $x^3 - 5x^2 + 2x + 8 = 0$

10. $x^3 + x^2 - 17x + 15 = 0$

11. $2x^3 + 13x^2 + 17x - 12 = 0$

12. $x^3 - x^2 - 34x - 56 = 0$

13. $x^3 - 18x + 27 = 0$

14. $x^4 - 5x^2 + 4 = 0$

15. $x^3 - 6x^2 + 13x - 10 = 0$

16. $x^3 - 5x^2 + 4x + 10 = 0$

17. $x^3 - 5x^2 + 17x - 13 = 0$

18. $x^3 + x + 10 = 0$

19. $x^3 - 5x^2 - x + 5 = 0$

20. $x^3 - 12x + 16 = 0$

21. $x^3 - 2x^2 - 5x + 6 = 0$

22. $x^3 - 8x^2 - 200 = 0$

23. $x^3 + x^2 - 5x + 3 = 0$

24. $4x^3 - 12x^2 - x + 3 = 0$

25. $x^3 + x^2 - 7x + 2 = 0$

26. $12x^3 + 31x^2 - 17x - 6 = 0$

**Use the Rational Root Theorem to list all possible rational roots for each
polynomial equation. Then find any actual rational roots.**

27. $x^3 + 5x^2 - 2x - 15 = 0$

28. $36x^3 + 144x^2 - x - 4 = 0$

29. $2x^3 + 5x^2 + 4x + 1 = 0$

30. $12x^4 + 14x^3 - 5x^2 - 14x - 4 = 0$

31. $5x^3 - 11x^2 + 7x - 1 = 0$

32. $x^3 + 81x^2 - 49x - 49 = 0$

**Find a third-degree polynomial equation with rational coefficients that has
the given numbers as roots.**

33. $3, 2 - i$

34. $5, 2i$

35. $-1, 3 + i$

36. $-7, i$

37. $-4, 4i$

38. $6, 3 - 2i$

Reteaching 6-6

The Fundamental Theorem of Algebra

OBJECTIVE: Finding all zeros of a polynomial function

MATERIALS: None

Example

Find all zeros of the function $f(x) = x^3 + 4x^2 - x - 10$.

The possible rational roots are $\pm 1, \pm 2, \pm 5, \pm 10$.

$$
\begin{array}{r|rrrr}
1 & 1 & 4 & -1 & -10 \\
  &   & 1 & 5 & 4 \\
\hline
  & 1 & 5 & 4 & -6
\end{array}
\qquad
\begin{array}{r|rrrr}
-1 & 1 & 4 & -1 & -10 \\
   &   & -1 & -3 & 4 \\
\hline
   & 1 & 3 & -4 & -6
\end{array}
$$

$$
\begin{array}{r|rrrr}
2 & 1 & 4 & -1 & -10 \\
  &   & 2 & 12 & 22 \\
\hline
  & 1 & 6 & 11 & 12
\end{array}
\qquad
\begin{array}{r|rrrr}
-2 & 1 & 4 & -1 & -10 \\
   &   & -2 & -4 & 10 \\
\hline
   & 1 & 2 & -5 & 0
\end{array}
$$

← Use synthetic division to test each possible rational root until you get a remainder of zero.

So -2 is one of the roots.

$x^3 + 4x^2 - x - 10 = (x + 2)(x^2 + 2x - 5)$ ← Use the coefficients from synthetic division to obtain the quadratic factor.

$x = \dfrac{-b \pm \sqrt{b^2 - 4ac}}{2a}$ ← Since $x^2 + 2x - 5$ cannot be factored, use the Quadratic Formula to solve $x^2 + 2x - 5 = 0$.

$x = \dfrac{-2 \pm \sqrt{4 - 4(1)(-5)}}{2(1)}$

$x = \dfrac{-2 \pm \sqrt{24}}{2}$

$x = \dfrac{-2 \pm 2\sqrt{6}}{2}$

$x = -1 \pm \sqrt{6}$

The polynomial function $f(x) = x^3 + 4x^2 - x - 10$ has one rational zero, -2, and two irrational zeros, $-1 + \sqrt{6}$ and $-1 - \sqrt{6}$.

Exercises

Find all the zeros of each function.

1. $f(x) = x^3 - 2x^2 + 4x - 3$

2. $f(x) = x^3 - 3x^2 - 15x + 125$

3. $f(x) = 3x^3 - 2x^2 - 15x + 10$

4. $f(x) = x^4 - 4x^3 + 8x^2 - 16x + 16$

5. $f(x) = x^4 - 3x^2 + 2$

6. $f(x) = x^3 - 2x^2 - 17x - 6$

Practice 6-6

The Fundamental Theorem of Algebra

Find all the zeros of each function.

1. $y = 5x^3 - 5x$

2. $f(x) = x^3 - 16x$

3. $g(x) = 12x^3 - 2x^2 - 2x$

4. $y = 6x^3 + x^2 - x$

5. $f(x) = 5x^3 + 6x^2 + x$

6. $y = -4x^3 + 100x$

For each equation, state the number of complex roots, the possible number of real roots, and the possible rational roots.

7. $2x^2 + 5x + 3 = 0$

8. $3x^2 + 11x - 10 = 0$

9. $2x^4 - 18x^2 + 5 = 0$

10. $4x^3 - 12x + 9 = 0$

11. $6x^5 - 28x + 15 = 0$

12. $x^3 - x^2 - 2x + 7 = 0$

13. $x^3 - 6x^2 - 7x - 12 = 0$

14. $2x^4 + x^2 - x + 6 = 0$

15. $4x^5 - 5x^4 + x^3 - 2x^2 + 2x - 6 = 0$

16. $7x^6 + 3x^4 - 9x^2 + 18 = 0$

17. $5 + x + x^2 + x^3 + x^4 + x^5 = 0$

18. $6 - x + 2x^3 - x^3 + x^4 - 8x^5 = 0$

Find all the zeros of each function.

19. $f(x) = x^3 - 9x^2 + 27x - 27$

20. $y = 2x^3 - 8x^2 + 18x - 72$

21. $y = x^3 - 10x - 12$

22. $y = x^3 - 4x^2 + 8$

23. $f(x) = 2x^3 + x - 3$

24. $y = x^3 - 2x^2 - 11x + 12$

25. $g(x) = x^3 + 4x^2 + 7x + 28$

26. $f(x) = x^3 + 3x^2 + 6x + 4$

27. $g(x) = x^4 - 5x^2 - 36$

28. $y = x^4 - 7x^2 + 12$

29. $y = 9x^4 + 5x^2 - 4$

30. $y = 4x^4 - 11x^2 - 3$

Name _____ Class _____ Date _____

Reteaching 6-7

Permutations and Combinations

• •

OBJECTIVE: Find permutations and combinations   **MATERIALS:** Calculator

---

- A *permutation* of a set of items is an ordered arrangement of the items.

- If n and r are positive integers with $r \leq n$, then $_nP_r$ denotes the number of permutations of n distinct items taken r at a time.

$$_nP_r = \frac{n!}{(n-r)!}$$

- A *combination* is a selection of items in which order does not matter.

- The number of combinations of n objects of a set chosen r objects at a time is given by the following formula:

$$_nC_r = \frac{n!}{r!(n-r)!}; \text{ for } 0 \leq r \leq n$$

Example

If order is not important, in how many ways can five letters be chosen from the alphabet?

n = alphabet = 26   ⟵ **Decide what number represents n and what number represents r.**
r = chosen letters = 5

$_{26}C_5 = \dfrac{26!}{5!(21!)}$ ⟵ **Use the formula to write the equation.**

$= \dfrac{7,893,600}{120}$ ⟵ **Evaluate the factorials. Use the ! option of a calculator.**

$= 65,780$ ⟵ **Simplify.**

There are 65,780 ways in which five letters can be chosen from the alphabet.

Exercises

1. How many permutations of six letters are there from A, E, B, L, N, O, S, T, and Y?

2. A chemist is making a solution of five chemicals in water. How many possible permutations are there in which to add the chemicals one at a time?

3. You have 12 CDs in your collection. You have time to listen to two CDs. How many combinations of CDs do you have to choose from?

4. Your biology teacher chooses six students from a class of 26 to do a special project. Find the total number of combinations.

5. In how many ways can a family of six line up for a photograph?

6. In how many ways can a president, vice president, secretary, and treasurer be elected from a club with 15 members?

7. A health food store offers ten toppings for yogurt. How many different three-topping yogurt sundaes can be formed with the ten toppings? (Assume that no topping is used twice.)

• •

Practice 6-7

Indicate whether each situation involves a combination or a permutation.

1. Five apples chosen at random from a case of apples.

2. Ten applicants line up for a job interview.

3. Three students elected president, secretary, and treasurer of the student body.

4. Four students chosen at random from the student body.

Evaluate each expression.

5. $_{12}C_{11}$ **6.** $_{12}C_{10}$ **7.** $_{12}C_5$ **8.** $_{12}C_1$

9. $_{12}C_{12}$ **10.** $_5C_4 + {_5}C_3$ **11.** $\dfrac{_5C_3}{_5C_2}$ **12.** $4(_7C_2)$

How many combinations of five can you make from each set?

13. Xul, Ben, Sue, Tom, and Ria

14. $\{0, 1, 2, 3, 4, 5, 6, 7, 8, 9\}$

15. 14 novels on a reading list

16. 50 states

Evaluate each expression.

17. $8!$ **18.** $\dfrac{11!}{9!}$ **19.** $6!4!$ **20.** $3(5!)$

21. $_{12}P_{11}$ **22.** $_{12}P_{10}$ **23.** $_{12}P_5$ **24.** $_{12}P_1$

25. In how many ways can four distinct positions for a relay race be assigned from a team of nine runners?

26. A committee must choose 3 finalists from 15 scholarship candidates. How many ways can the committee choose the three finalists?

27. A traveler can choose from three airlines, five hotels, and four rental car companies. How many arrangements of these services are possible?

28. In how many ways can four students be seated at a table with six chairs?

Assume a and b arc positive integers. Decide whether each statement is true or false. If it is true, explain why. If it is false, give a counterexample.

29. $a!b! = b!a!$ **30.** $(a^2)! = (a!)^2$ **31.** $a \cdot b! = (ab)!$

32. $(a + 0)! = a!$ **33.** $(a + b)! = a! + b!$ **34.** $(a!)! = (a!)^2$

Reteaching 6-8

OBJECTIVE: Using the Binomial Theorem	**MATERIALS:** None

- The *Binomial Theorem* states that for any binomial $(a + b)$ and any positive integer n,

$$(a + b)^n = {}_nC_0a^n + {}_nC_1a^{n-1}b + {}_nC_2a^{n-2}b^2 + \ldots + {}_nC_{n-1}ab^{n-1} + {}_nC_nb^n.$$

- The theorem provides an effective method for expanding any power of a binomial.

Example

Use the Binomial Theorem to expand $(3x + 2)^3$.

Step 1
Determine $a, b,$ and n.
$a = 3x, b = 2, n = 3$

Step 2
Use the formula to write the equation.
$$(3x + 2)^3 = {}_3C_0(3x)^3 + {}_3C_1(3x)^2(2) + {}_3C_2(3x)(2)^2 + {}_3C_3(2)^3$$

Step 3
Simplify.
$$= 1(27x^3) + 3(9x^2)(2) + 3(3x)(4) + 1(8)$$
$$= 27x^3 + 54x^2 + 36x + 8$$

Exercises

Fill in the correct coefficients, variables, and exponents for the expanded form of each binomial.

1. $(x + y)^4 = x^{\square} + \square x^3y + 6x^{\square}y^2 + \square xy^{\square} + \square^4$

2. $(z - y)^3 = z^{\square} - \square z^2y + \square zy^{\square} - \square^3$

3. $(x + z)^5 = x^{\square} + \square x^4z + 10x^{\square}z^2 + \square x^2z^{\square} + \square xz^4 + \square^5$

Use the Binomial Theorem to expand each binomial.

4. $(x + y)^5$ 5. $(x - y)^5$ 6. $(2x + y)^3$

7. $(x + 3y)^4$ 8. $(x - 2y)^5$ 9. $(2x - y)^5$

10. $(x - 3y)^4$ 11. $(4x - y)^3$ 12. $(x - 1)^5$

13. $(1 - x)^3$ 14. $(x^2 + 1)^3$ 15. $(y^2 + a)^4$

Practice 6-8

The Binomial Theorem

Use the Binomial Theorem to expand each binomial.

1. $(x + 2)^4$

2. $(a + 2)^7$

3. $(x + y)^7$

4. $(d - 2)^9$

5. $(2x - 3)^8$

6. $(x - 1)^9$

7. $(2x^2 - 2y^2)^6$

8. $(x^5 + 2y)^7$

9. What is the probability that you will roll exactly five sixes in ten tosses of a number cube?

10. One airline recently had a rate of 52 complaints per 100,000 departures, or a 0.00052 probability of a complaint on each flight.

   a. What is the probability that the airline will not have a complaint in 20 flights?

   b. What is the probability that the airline will not have a complaint in 100 flights?

   c. What is the probability that the airline will have a complaint in 100 flights?

11. 6% of the circuit boards assembled at a certain production plant are defective. If five circuit boards are chosen at random, what is the probability that exactly two are defective?

12. The probability that a baby will be a boy is $\frac{1}{2}$. What is the probability that a family with five children has all boys?

13. Your friend's batting average is 0.225. What is the probability of her getting three or more hits in the next five times at bat?

14. If a classmate randomly guesses on ten multiple choice questions, what is the probability that six or more answers will be right? The probability of each answer being correct is 0.2.

Use Pascal's Triangle to expand each binomial.

15. $(n - 3)^3$

16. $(2n + 2)^4$

17. $(n - 6)^5$

18. $(n - 1)^6$

19. $(2a + 2)^3$

20. $(x^2 - y^2)^4$

21. $(2x + 3y)^5$

22. $(2x^2 + y^2)^6$

23. $(x^2 - y^2)^3$

24. $(2b + c)^4$

25. $(3m - 2n)^5$

26. $(x^3 - y^4)^6$

Expand each binomial.

27. $(x + 1)^7$

28. $(x + 4)^8$

29. $(x - 3y)^6$

30. $(x + 2)^5$

31. $(x^2 - y^2)^5$

32. $(3 + y)^5$

33. $(x^2 + 3)^6$

34. $(x - 5)^7$

35. $(x - 4y)^4$

Reteaching 7-1

OBJECTIVE: Simplifying radical expressions	**MATERIALS:** None

- For any real numbers a and b, and any positive integer n, if $a^n = b$, then a is an nth root of b.

- For any negative real number a, $\sqrt[n]{a^n} = |a|$ when n is even.

Examples

Simplify $\sqrt[3]{1000x^3y^9}$.

$$\sqrt[3]{1000x^3y^9} = \sqrt[3]{10^3x^3(y^3)^3} \quad \longleftarrow \textbf{Write each factor as a cube.}$$

$$= \sqrt[3]{(10xy^3)^3} \quad \longleftarrow \textbf{Write as the cube of a product.}$$

$$= 10xy^3 \quad \longleftarrow \textbf{Simplify.}$$

Simplify $\sqrt[4]{\dfrac{256g^8}{h^4k^{16}}}$.

$$\sqrt[4]{\frac{256g^8}{h^4k^{16}}} = \sqrt[4]{\frac{4^4(g^2)^4}{h^4(k^4)^4}}$$

$$= \sqrt[4]{\left(\frac{4g^2}{hk^4}\right)^4} = \frac{4g^2}{|h|k^4}$$

The absolute value symbols are needed to ensure the root is positive when h is negative. Note that $4g^2$ and k^4 are never negative.

Exercises

Simplify. Use absolute value symbols when needed.

1. $\sqrt{36x^2}$ 　　　　　　**2.** $\sqrt[3]{216y^3}$ 　　　　　　**3.** $\sqrt{\dfrac{1}{100x^2}}$

4. $\dfrac{\sqrt{x^{20}}}{\sqrt{y^8}}$ 　　　　　　**5.** $\sqrt[3]{\dfrac{(x+3)^3}{(x-4)^6}}$ 　　　　　　**6.** $\sqrt[5]{x^{10}y^{15}z^5}$

7. $\sqrt[3]{\dfrac{27z^3}{(z+12)^6}}$ 　　　　　　**8.** $\sqrt[4]{2401x^{12}}$ 　　　　　　**9.** $\sqrt[3]{\dfrac{1331}{x^3}}$

10. $\sqrt[4]{\dfrac{(y-4)^8}{(z+9)^4}}$ 　　　　　　**11.** $\sqrt[3]{\dfrac{a^6b^6}{c^3}}$ 　　　　　　**12.** $\sqrt[3]{-x^3y^6}$

Practice 7-1

Roots and Radical Expressions

Find each real-number root.

1. $\sqrt{144}$ **2.** $-\sqrt{25}$ **3.** $\sqrt{-0.01}$ **4.** $\sqrt[3]{0.001}$

5. $\sqrt[4]{0.0081}$ **6.** $\sqrt[3]{27}$ **7.** $\sqrt[3]{-27}$ **8.** $\sqrt{0.09}$

Find all the real cube roots of each number.

9. 216   **10.** -343 **11.** -0.064 **12.** $\dfrac{1000}{27}$

Find all the real square roots of each number.

13. 400   **14.** -196 **15.** 10,000   **16.** 0.0625

Find all the real fourth roots of each number.

17. -81 **18.** 256   **19.** 0.0001   **20.** 625

Simplify each radical expression. Use absolute value symbols when needed.

21. $\sqrt{81x^4}$ **22.** $\sqrt{121y^{10}}$ **23.** $\sqrt[3]{8g^6}$ **24.** $\sqrt[3]{125x^9}$

25. $\sqrt[5]{243x^5y^{15}}$ **26.** $\sqrt[3]{(x-9)^3}$ **27.** $\sqrt{25(x+2)^4}$ **28.** $\sqrt[3]{\dfrac{64x^9}{343}}$

Find the two real-number solutions of each equation.

29. $x^2 = 4$ **30.** $x^4 = 81$ **31.** $x^2 = 0.16$ **32.** $x^2 = \dfrac{16}{49}$

33. A cube has volume $V = s^3$, where s is the length of a side. Find the side length for a cube with volume 8000 cm^3.

34. The velocity of a falling object can be found using the formula $v^2 = 64h$, where v is the velocity (in feet per second) and h is the distance the object has already fallen.

     a. What is the velocity of the object after a 10-foot fall?

     b. How much does the velocity increase if the object falls 20 feet rather than 10 feet?

Reteaching 7-2

Multiplying and Dividing Radical Expressions

OBJECTIVE: Rationalizing the denominator and simplifying

MATERIALS: None

- If $\sqrt[n]{a}$ and $\sqrt[n]{b}$ are real numbers and $b \neq 0$, then $\dfrac{\sqrt[n]{a}}{\sqrt[n]{b}} = \sqrt[n]{\dfrac{a}{b}}$.
- Rationalizing the denominator means that you are rewriting the expression so that no radicals appear in the denominator and there are no fractions inside the radical.

Example

Rationalize the denominator and simplify. Assume that all variables are positive.

$$\frac{\sqrt{9y}}{\sqrt{2x}} = \sqrt{\frac{9y}{2x}} \qquad \longleftarrow \textbf{Rewrite as a square root of a fraction.}$$

$$= \sqrt{\frac{9y \cdot 2x}{2x \cdot 2x}} \qquad \longleftarrow \textbf{Make the denominator a perfect square.}$$

$$= \sqrt{\frac{18xy}{4x^2}} \qquad \longleftarrow \textbf{Simplify.}$$

$$= \frac{\sqrt{18xy}}{\sqrt{2^2 \cdot x^2}}$$

$$= \frac{\sqrt{18xy}}{2x}$$

$$= \frac{\sqrt{3^2 \cdot 2 \cdot x \cdot y}}{2x} \qquad \longleftarrow \textbf{Simplify the numerator.}$$

$$= \frac{3\sqrt{2xy}}{2x}$$

Exercises

Rationalize the denominator of each expression. Assume that all variables are positive.

1. $\dfrac{\sqrt{5}}{\sqrt{x}}$

2. $\dfrac{\sqrt[3]{6ab^2}}{\sqrt[3]{2a^4b}}$

3. $\dfrac{\sqrt[4]{9y}}{\sqrt[4]{x}}$

4. $\dfrac{\sqrt{10xy^3}}{\sqrt{12y^2}}$

5. $\dfrac{4\sqrt[3]{k^9}}{16\sqrt[3]{k^5}}$

6. $\sqrt{\dfrac{3x^5}{5y}}$

7. $\dfrac{\sqrt[4]{10}}{\sqrt[4]{z^2}}$

8. $\sqrt[3]{\dfrac{19a^2b}{abc^4}}$

Practice 7-2

Multiplying and Dividing Radical Expressions

Multiply and simplify. Assume that all variables are positive.

1. $\sqrt{4} \cdot \sqrt{6}$

2. $\sqrt{9x^2} \cdot \sqrt{9y^5}$

3. $\sqrt[3]{50x^2z^5} \cdot \sqrt[3]{15y^3z}$

4. $4\sqrt{2x} \cdot 3\sqrt{8x}$

5. $\sqrt{xy} \cdot \sqrt{4xy}$

6. $9\sqrt{2} \cdot 3\sqrt{y}$

Rationalize the denominator of each expression. Assume that all variables are positive.

7. $\sqrt{\dfrac{9x}{2}}$

8. $\dfrac{\sqrt{xy}}{\sqrt{3x}}$

9. $\sqrt[3]{\dfrac{x^2}{3y}}$

10. $\dfrac{\sqrt[4]{2x}}{\sqrt[4]{3x^2}}$

11. $\sqrt{\dfrac{x}{8y}}$

12. $\sqrt[3]{\dfrac{3a}{4b^2c}}$

Multiply. Simplify if possible. Assume that all variables are positive.

13. $\sqrt{4} \cdot \sqrt{25}$

14. $\sqrt{81} \cdot \sqrt{36}$

15. $\sqrt{3} \cdot \sqrt{27}$

16. $\sqrt[3]{-3} \cdot \sqrt[3]{9}$

17. $\sqrt{3x} \cdot \sqrt{6x^3}$

18. $\sqrt[3]{2xy^2} \cdot \sqrt[3]{4x^2y^7}$

Simplify. Assume that all variables are positive.

19. $\sqrt{36x^3}$

20. $\sqrt[3]{125y^2z^4}$

21. $\sqrt{18k^6}$

22. $\sqrt[3]{-16a^{12}}$

23. $\sqrt{x^2y^{10}z}$

24. $\sqrt[4]{256s^7t^{12}}$

25. $\sqrt[3]{216x^4y^3}$

26. $\sqrt{75r^3}$

27. $\sqrt[4]{625u^5v^8}$

Divide and simplify. Assume that all variables are positive.

28. $\dfrac{\sqrt{6x}}{\sqrt{3x}}$

29. $\dfrac{\sqrt[3]{4x^2}}{\sqrt[3]{x}}$

30. $\sqrt[4]{\dfrac{243k^3}{3k^7}}$

31. $\dfrac{\sqrt{(2x)^2}}{\sqrt{(5y)^4}}$

32. $\dfrac{\sqrt[3]{18y^2}}{\sqrt[3]{12y}}$

33. $\sqrt{\dfrac{162a}{6a^3}}$

34. The volume of a sphere of radius r is $V = \dfrac{4}{3}\pi r^3$.

   a. Use the formula to find r in terms of V. Rationalize the denominator.

   b. Use your answer to part (a) to find the radius of a sphere with volume 100 cubic inches. Round to the nearest hundredth.

Reteaching 7-3

OBJECTIVE: Multiplying and dividing binomial radical expressions

MATERIALS: None

- Conjugates, such as $\sqrt{a} + \sqrt{b}$ and $\sqrt{a} - \sqrt{b}$, differ only in the sign of the second term. If a and b are rational numbers, then the product of conjugates produces a rational number:

$$\left(\sqrt{a} + \sqrt{b}\right)\left(\sqrt{a} - \sqrt{b}\right) = \left(\sqrt{a}\right)^2 - \left(\sqrt{b}\right)^2 = a - b.$$

- You can use the conjugate of a radical denominator to rationalize the denominator.

Examples

Multiply $\left(2\sqrt{7} - \sqrt{5}\right)\left(2\sqrt{7} + \sqrt{5}\right)$.

$$\left(2\sqrt{7} - \sqrt{5}\right)\left(2\sqrt{7} + \sqrt{5}\right) \qquad \longleftarrow \textbf{These are conjugates.}$$

$$= \left(2\sqrt{7}\right)^2 - \left(\sqrt{5}\right)^2 \qquad \longleftarrow \textbf{Use the difference of squares formula.}$$

$$= 28 - 5 = 23 \qquad \longleftarrow \textbf{Simplify.}$$

Rationalize the denominator of $\dfrac{4\sqrt{2}}{1 + \sqrt{3}}$.

$$\frac{4\sqrt{2}}{1 + \sqrt{3}}$$

$$= \frac{4\sqrt{2}}{1 + \sqrt{3}} \cdot \frac{1 - \sqrt{3}}{1 - \sqrt{3}} \qquad \longleftarrow \textbf{Use the conjugate of } \mathbf{1 + \sqrt{3}} \text{ to rationalize the denominator.}$$

$$= \frac{4\sqrt{2} - 4\sqrt{6}}{1 - 3} \qquad \longleftarrow \textbf{Multiply.}$$

$$= \frac{4\sqrt{2} - 4\sqrt{6}}{-2} = -\frac{\left(4\sqrt{2} - 4\sqrt{6}\right)}{2} \qquad \longleftarrow \textbf{Simplify.}$$

$$= \frac{-4\sqrt{2} + 4\sqrt{6}}{2} = -2\sqrt{2} + 2\sqrt{2}$$

Exercises

Simplify. Rationalize all denominators.

1. $\left(3 + \sqrt{6}\right)\left(3 - \sqrt{6}\right)$

2. $\dfrac{2\sqrt{3} + 1}{5 - \sqrt{3}}$

3. $\left(4\sqrt{6} - 1\right)\left(\sqrt{6} + 4\right)$

4. $\dfrac{2 - \sqrt{7}}{2 + \sqrt{7}}$

5. $\left(2\sqrt{8} - 6\right)\left(\sqrt{8} - 4\right)$

6. $\dfrac{\sqrt{5}}{2 + \sqrt{3}}$

Practice 7-3

Binomial Radical Expressions

Multiply each pair of conjugates.

1. $\left(3\sqrt{2} - 9\right)\left(3\sqrt{2} + 9\right)$

2. $\left(1 - \sqrt{7}\right)\left(1 + \sqrt{7}\right)$

3. $\left(5\sqrt{3} + \sqrt{2}\right)\left(5\sqrt{3} - \sqrt{2}\right)$

Add or subtract if possible.

4. $9\sqrt{3} + 2\sqrt{3}$

5. $5\sqrt{2} + 2\sqrt{3}$

6. $3\sqrt{7} - 7\sqrt[3]{x}$

7. $14\sqrt[3]{xy} - 3\sqrt[3]{xy}$

Rationalize each denominator. Simplify the answer.

8. $\dfrac{2}{2\sqrt{3} - 4}$

9. $\dfrac{5}{2 + \sqrt{3}}$

10. $\dfrac{1 + \sqrt{5}}{1 - \sqrt{5}}$

11. $\dfrac{2 + \sqrt{12}}{5 - \sqrt{12}}$

Simplify.

12. $3\sqrt{32} + 2\sqrt{50}$

13. $\sqrt{200} - \sqrt{72}$

14. $\sqrt[3]{81} - 3\sqrt[3]{3}$

15. $2\sqrt[4]{48} + 3\sqrt[4]{243}$

Multiply.

16. $\left(1 - \sqrt{5}\right)\left(2 + \sqrt{5}\right)$

17. $\left(1 + 4\sqrt{10}\right)\left(2 - \sqrt{10}\right)$

18. $\left(1 - 3\sqrt{7}\right)\left(4 - 3\sqrt{7}\right)$

19. $\left(4 - 2\sqrt{3}\right)^2$

20. $\left(\sqrt{2} + \sqrt{7}\right)^2$

21. $\left(2\sqrt{3} + 3\sqrt{2}\right)^2$

Simplify. Rationalize all denominators. Assume that all variables are positive.

22. $\sqrt{28} + 4\sqrt{63} - 2\sqrt{7}$

23. $6\sqrt{40} - 2\sqrt{90} + 3\sqrt{160}$

24. $3\sqrt{12} + 7\sqrt{75} - \sqrt{54}$

25. $4\sqrt[3]{81} + 2\sqrt[3]{72} - 3\sqrt[3]{24}$

26. $3\sqrt{225x} + 5\sqrt{144x}$

27. $6\sqrt{45y^2} + 4\sqrt{20y^2}$

28. $\left(3\sqrt{y} - \sqrt{5}\right)\left(2\sqrt{y} + 5\sqrt{5}\right)$

29. $\left(\sqrt{x} - \sqrt{3}\right)\left(\sqrt{x} + \sqrt{3}\right)$

30. $\dfrac{3 - \sqrt{10}}{\sqrt{5} - \sqrt{2}}$

31. $\dfrac{2 + \sqrt{14}}{\sqrt{7} + \sqrt{2}}$

32. $\dfrac{2 + \sqrt[3]{x}}{\sqrt[3]{x}}$

33. A park in the shape of a triangle has a sidewalk dividing it into two parts.

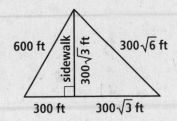

600 ft   sidewalk $300\sqrt{3}$ ft $300\sqrt{6}$ ft

300 ft $300\sqrt{3}$ ft

a. If a man walks around the perimeter of the park, how far will he walk?

b. What is the area of the park?

Reteaching 7-4

OBJECTIVE: Simplifying expressions with rational exponents   **MATERIALS:** None

---

- You can simplify a number with a rational exponent using the properties of exponents or by converting the expression to a radical expression.

- To write an expression with rational exponents in simplest form, write every exponent as a positive number using the following rules for $a \neq 0$. $a^{-n} = \frac{1}{a^n}$ and $\frac{1}{a^{-m}} = a^m$

Example

Write $(8x^9y^{-3})^{-\frac{2}{3}}$ in simplest form.

$$(8x^9y^{-3})^{-\frac{2}{3}} = (2^3x^9y^{-3})^{-\frac{2}{3}}$$ ⟵ **Factor any numerical coefficients.**

$$= (2^3)^{-\frac{2}{3}}(x^9)^{-\frac{2}{3}}(y^{-3})^{-\frac{2}{3}}$$ ⟵ **Use the property $(ab)^m = a^m b^m$.**

$$= 2^{-2}x^{-6}y^2$$ ⟵ **Multiply exponents, using the property $(a^m)^n = a^{mn}$.**

$$= \frac{y^2}{2^2x^6}$$ ⟵ **Write every exponent as a positive number.**

$$= \frac{y^2}{4x^6}$$ ⟵ **Simplify.**

Exercises

Write each expression in simplest form. Assume that all variables are positive.

1. $y^{\frac{2}{3}}y^{\frac{3}{5}}$
2. $(16x^2y^8)^{-\frac{1}{2}}$
3. $(z^{-3})^{\frac{1}{9}}$

4. $(2x^{\frac{1}{4}})^4$
5. $\left(\frac{49x^{-6}}{9x^2}\right)^{\frac{1}{2}}$
6. $(25x^{-6}y^2)^{\frac{1}{2}}$

7. $\frac{x^{\frac{2}{3}}y^2}{x^{\frac{5}{3}}y^2}$
8. $(8a^{-3}b^9)^{\frac{2}{3}}$
9. $\left(\frac{16z^4}{25x^8}\right)^{-\frac{1}{2}}$

10. $a^{\frac{3}{4}} \cdot a^{\frac{3}{4}}$
11. $\left(\frac{x^2}{y^{-1}}\right)^{\frac{1}{5}}$
12. $(27m^9n^{-3})^{-\frac{2}{3}}$

13. $(2x^{\frac{1}{6}})(3x^{\frac{2}{6}})$
14. $\left(\frac{32r^2}{2s^4}\right)^{\frac{1}{4}}$
15. $(9z^{10})^{\frac{3}{2}}$

Practice 7-4

Rational Exponents

Simplify each expression. Assume that all variables are positive.

1. $27^{\frac{1}{3}}$

2. $\left(81^{\frac{1}{4}}\right)^4$

3. $\left(32^{\frac{1}{5}}\right)^5$

4. $(256^4)^{\frac{1}{4}}$

5. 7^0

6. $8^{\frac{2}{3}}$

7. $(-1)^{\frac{1}{5}}$

8. $(-27)^{\frac{2}{3}}$

9. $16^{\frac{1}{4}}$

10. $x^{\frac{1}{2}} \cdot x^{\frac{1}{3}}$

11. $2y^{\frac{1}{2}} \cdot y$

12. $(8^2)^{\frac{1}{3}}$

13. 3.6^0

14. $\left(\frac{1}{16}\right)^{\frac{1}{4}}$

15. $\left(\frac{27}{8}\right)^{\frac{2}{3}}$

16. $\sqrt[8]{0}$

17. $\left(3x^{\frac{1}{2}}\right)\left(4x^{\frac{2}{3}}\right)$

18. $\frac{12y^{\frac{1}{3}}}{4y^{\frac{1}{2}}}$

19. $\left(3a^{\frac{1}{2}}b^{\frac{1}{3}}\right)^2$

20. $\left(y^{\frac{2}{3}}\right)^{-9}$

21. $\left(a^{\frac{2}{3}}b^{-\frac{1}{2}}\right)^{-6}$

22. $y^{\frac{2}{5}} \cdot y^{\frac{3}{8}}$

23. $\left(\frac{x^{\frac{4}{7}}}{x^{\frac{2}{3}}}\right)$

24. $\left(2a^{\frac{1}{4}}\right)^3$

25. $81^{-\frac{1}{2}}$

26. $\left(2x^{\frac{2}{5}}\right)\left(6x^{\frac{1}{4}}\right)$

27. $\left(9x^4y^{-2}\right)^{\frac{1}{2}}$

28. The interest rate r required to increase your investment p to the amount a in t years is found by $r = \left(\frac{a}{p}\right)^{\frac{1}{t}} - 1$. What interest rate would be required to increase your investment of \$2700 to \$3600 over three years? Round your answer to the nearest tenth of a percent.

Write each expression in radical form.

29. $x^{\frac{4}{3}}$

30. $(2y)^{\frac{1}{3}}$

31. $a^{1.5}$

32. $b^{\frac{1}{5}}$

33. $z^{\frac{2}{3}}$

34. $(ab)^{\frac{1}{4}}$

35. $m^{2.4}$

36. $t^{-\frac{2}{7}}$

37. $a^{-1.6}$

Write each expression in exponential form.

38. $\sqrt{x^3}$

39. $\sqrt[3]{m}$

40. $\sqrt{5y}$

41. $\sqrt[3]{2y^2}$

42. $\left(\sqrt[4]{b}\right)^3$

43. $\sqrt{-6}$

44. $\sqrt{(6a)^4}$

45. $\sqrt[5]{n^4}$

46. $\sqrt[4]{(5ab)^3}$

Reteaching 7-5

Solving Radical Equations

OBJECTIVE: Solving radical equations   **MATERIALS:** None

- Equations containing radicals can be solved by isolating the radical on one side of the equation and then raising both sides to the same power that would undo the radical.

- An extraneous solution satisfies later equations in your work but does not make the original equation true.

Example

Solve $\sqrt{17 - x} - 3 = x$. Check your solution(s).

$$\sqrt{17 - x} - 3 = x$$

$$\sqrt{17 - x} = x + 3 \qquad \longleftarrow \textbf{Add 3 to each side to get the radical alone on one side of the equal sign.}$$

$$\left(\sqrt{17 - x}\right)^2 = (x + 3)^2 \qquad \longleftarrow \textbf{Square each side.}$$

$$17 - x = x^2 + 6x + 9$$

$$0 = x^2 + 7x - 8 \qquad \longleftarrow \textbf{Rewrite in standard form.}$$

$$0 = (x - 1)(x + 8) \qquad \longleftarrow \textbf{Factor.}$$

$$x - 1 = 0 \ \text{ or } \ x + 8 = 0 \qquad \longleftarrow \textbf{Set each factor equal to 0 using the Zero Product Property.}$$

$$x = 1 \ \text{ or } \qquad x = -8$$

Check:

$$\sqrt{17 - x} - 3 \overset{?}{=} x \qquad\qquad \sqrt{17 - x} - 3 \overset{?}{=} x$$

$$\sqrt{17 - 1} - 3 \overset{?}{=} 1 \qquad\qquad \sqrt{17 - (-8)} - 3 \overset{?}{=} -8$$

$$\sqrt{16} - 3 \overset{?}{=} 1 \qquad\qquad\qquad \sqrt{25} - 3 \overset{?}{=} -8$$

$$1 = 1 ✔ \qquad\qquad\qquad\qquad 2 \neq -8$$

The only solution is 1.

Exercises

Solve. Check for extraneous solutions.

1. $x^{\frac{1}{2}} = 13$

2. $3\sqrt{2x} = 12$

3. $\sqrt{5x + 1} = \sqrt{4x + 3}$

4. $\sqrt{x^2} + 3 = x + 1$

5. $\sqrt{3x} = \sqrt{x + 6}$

6. $x = \sqrt{x + 7} + 5$

7. $x - 3\sqrt{x - 4} = 0$

8. $\sqrt{x + 2} = x - 4$

9. $\sqrt[3]{5y + 2} - 3 = 0$

Practice 7-5

Solving Radical Equations

· ·

Solve. Check for extraneous solutions.

1. $(x - 2)^{\frac{1}{3}} = 5$

2. $3x^{\frac{4}{3}} + 5 = 53$

3. $4x^{\frac{3}{2}} - 5 = 103$

4. $\sqrt{x + 1} = x - 1$

5. $\sqrt{2x + 1} = -3$

6. $x^{\frac{1}{2}} - 5 = 0$

7. $\sqrt{x + 7} = x - 5$

8. $(2x + 1)^{\frac{1}{3}} = -3$

9. $2x^{\frac{1}{3}} - 2 = 0$

10. $\sqrt{2x - 5} = 7$

11. $\sqrt{2x - 4} = x - 2$

12. $\sqrt{x} + 6 = x$

13. $\sqrt{x + 2} = 10 - x$

14. $\sqrt{4x + 2} = \sqrt{3x + 4}$

15. $(7x - 3)^{\frac{1}{2}} = 5$

16. $(x - 2)^{\frac{2}{3}} - 4 = 5$

17. $2\sqrt{x - 1} = \sqrt{26 + x}$

18. $2x^{\frac{3}{4}} = 16$

19. $\sqrt{7x - 6} - \sqrt{5x + 2} = 0$

20. $\sqrt{3x - 3} - 6 = 0$

21. $5\sqrt{x} + 2 = 12$

22. $2x^{\frac{4}{3}} - 2 = 160$

23. $4x^{\frac{1}{2}} - 5 = 27$

24. $\sqrt{x + 1} = x + 1$

25. $\sqrt{2x + 1} = -5$

26. $x^{\frac{1}{6}} - 2 = 0$

27. $\sqrt{x + 2} = x - 18$

28. $(2x + 1)^{\frac{1}{3}} = 1$

29. $x^{\frac{1}{4}} + 3 = 0$

30. $\sqrt[3]{2x - 4} = -2$

31. $x^{\frac{1}{4}} - 1 = 0$

32. $(x - 2)^{\frac{1}{3}} = -5$

33. $x^{\frac{1}{3}} - 2 = 0$

34. $\sqrt{3x} = 6$

35. $(2x + 7)^{\frac{1}{2}} - x = 2$

36. $\sqrt{4x} - 8 = 0$

37. $\sqrt{3x + 1} - 5 = 0$

38. $3(2x + 4)^{\frac{4}{3}} = 48$

39. $2\sqrt{x} = \sqrt{x + 6}$

40. $(2x + 1)^{\frac{1}{2}} = (5 - 2x)^{\frac{1}{2}}$

41. $(x + 14)^{\frac{1}{4}} = (2x)^{\frac{1}{2}}$

42. $\sqrt[3]{x - 2} = 4$

Reteaching 7-6

Function Operations

OBJECTIVE: Combining functions	**MATERIALS:** Highlighter pens of three different colors

- One way to combine two functions is by forming a composite.
- A composite is written $(g \circ f)$ or $g(f(x))$. The two different functions are g and f.
- Evaluate the inner function $f(x)$ first.
- Use this value, the first output, as the input for the second function, $g(x)$.

Example

Evaluate the expression $g(f(2))$ given the inner function, $f(x) = 3x - 5$ and the outer function, $g(x) = x^2 + 2$.

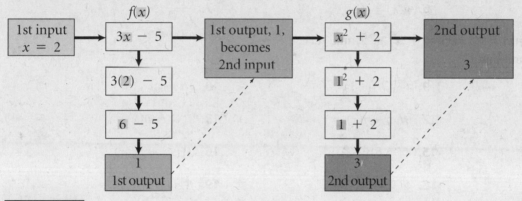

Exercises

Evaluate the expression $g(f(5))$ using the same functions for g and f as in the Example. Fill in blanks 1–8 on the chart.

Use one color highlighter to highlight the first input. Use a second color to highlight the first output and the second input. Use a third color to highlight the second output, which is the answer.

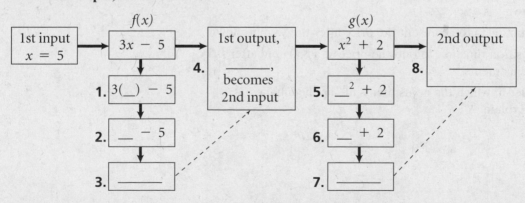

Given $f(x) = x^2 + 4x$ and $g(x) = 2x + 3$, evaluate each expression.

9. $f(g(2))$ **10.** $g(f(2.5))$ **11.** $g(f(-5))$ **12.** $f(g(-5))$

Practice 7-6

Function Operations

1. A boutique prices merchandise by adding 80% to its cost. It later decreases by 25% the price of items that don't sell quickly.

   a. Write a function $f(x)$ to represent the price after the 80% markup.

   b. Write a function $g(x)$ to represent the price after the 25% markdown.

   c. Use a composition function to find the price of an item after both price adjustments that originally costs the boutique $150.

   d. Does the order in which the adjustments are applied make a difference? Explain.

Let $f(x) = 4x - 1$ and $g(x) = 2x^2 + 3$. Perform each function operation and then find the domain.

2. $f(x) + g(x)$

3. $f(x) - g(x)$

4. $f(x) \cdot g(x)$

5. $\dfrac{f(x)}{g(x)}$

6. $g(x) - f(x)$

7. $\dfrac{g(x)}{f(x)}$

Let $f(x) = -3x + 2, g(x) = \frac{x}{5}, h(x) = -2x^2 + 9,$ and $j(x) = 5 - x.$ Find each value or expression.

8. $(f \circ j)(3)$

9. $(j \circ h)(-1)$

10. $(h \circ g)(-5)$

11. $(g \circ f)(a)$

12. $f(x) + j(x)$

13. $f(x) - h(x)$

14. $(g \circ f)(-5)$

15. $(f \circ g)(-2)$

16. $3f(x) + 5g(x)$

17. $g(f(2))$

18. $g(f(x))$

19. $f(g(1))$

Let $g(x) = x^2 - 5$ and $h(x) = 3x + 2$. Perform each function operation.

20. $(h \circ g)(x)$

21. $g(x) \cdot h(x)$

22. $-2g(x) + h(x)$

23. A department store has marked down its merchandise by 25%. It later decreases by $5 the price of items that have not sold.

   a. Write a function $f(x)$ to represent the price after the 25% markdown.

   b. Write a function $g(x)$ to represent the price after the $5 markdown.

   c. Use a composition function to find the price of a $50 item after both price adjustments.

   d. Does the order in which the adjustments are applied make a difference? Explain.

Reteaching 7-7

OBJECTIVE: Finding the inverse of a function   **MATERIALS:** None

- Inverse operations "undo" each other. Addition and subtraction are inverse operations. So are multiplication and division. The inverse of cubing a number is taking its cube root.

- If two functions are inverses, they consist of inverse operations performed in the opposite order.

Example

Find the inverse of $f(x) = x + 1$.

$f(x) = x + 1$

$y = x + 1$ ← **Rewrite the equation using *y*, if necessary.**

$x = y + 1$ ← **Interchange *x* and *y*.**

$x - 1 = y$ ← **Solve for *y*.**

$y = x - 1$ ← **The resulting function is the inverse of the original function.**

So, $f^{-1}(x) = x - 1$.

Exercises

Find the inverse of each function.

1. $y = 4x - 5$ **2.** $y = 3x^3 + 2$ **3.** $y = (x + 1)^3$

4. $y = 0.5x + 2$ **5.** $f(x) = x + 3$ **6.** $f(x) = 2(x - 2)$

7. $f(x) = \frac{x}{5}$ **8.** $f(x) = 4x + 2$ **9.** $y = x$

10. $y = x - 3$ **11.** $y = \frac{x - 1}{2}$ **12.** $y = x^3 - 8$

13. $f(x) = \sqrt{x + 2}$ **14.** $f(x) = \frac{2}{3}x - 1$ **15.** $f(x) = \frac{x + 3}{5}$

16. $f(x) = 2(x - 5)^2$ **17.** $y = \sqrt{x} + 4$ **18.** $y = 8x + 1$

Practice 7-7

Graph each relation and its inverse.

1. $y = \dfrac{x + 3}{3}$

2. $y = \dfrac{1}{2}x + 5$

3. $y = 2x + 5$

4. $y = 4x^2$

5. $y = \dfrac{1}{2}x^2$

6. $y = \dfrac{2}{3}x^2$

Find the inverse of each function. Is the inverse a function?

7. $y = x^2 + 2$

8. $y = x + 2$

9. $y = 3(x + 1)$

10. $y = -x^2 - 3$

11. $y = 2x - 1$

12. $y = 1 - 3x^2$

13. $y = 5x^2$

14. $y = (x + 3)^2$

15. $y = 6x^2 - 4$

16. $y = 3x^2 - 2$

17. $y = (x + 4)^2 - 4$

18. $y = -x^2 + 4$

For each function f, find f^{-1} and the domain and range of f and f^{-1}. Determine whether f^{-1} is a function.

19. $f(x) = \dfrac{1}{6}x$

20. $f(x) = -\dfrac{1}{5}x + 2$

21. $f(x) = x^2 - 2$

22. $f(x) = x^2 + 4$

23. $f(x) = \sqrt{x - 1}$

24. $f(x) = \sqrt{3x}$

Find the inverse of each relation. Graph the given relation and its inverse.

25.

x	−2	−1	0	1
y	−3	−2	−1	0

26.

x	0	1	2	3
y	−3	−1	0	−2

Let $f(x) = 2x + 5$. Find each value.

27. $(f^{-1} \circ f)(-1)$

28. $(f \circ f^{-1})(3)$

29. $(f \circ f^{-1})\left(-\dfrac{1}{2}\right)$

30. The equation $f(x) = 198,900x + 635,600$ can be used to model the number of utility trucks under 6000 pounds that are sold each year in the U.S. with $x = 0$ representing the year 1992. Find the inverse of the function. Use the inverse to estimate in which year the number of utility trucks under 6000 pounds sold in the U.S. will be 4,000,000.
Source: *www.infoplease.com*

Reteaching 7-8

Graphing Radical Functions

OBJECTIVE: Graphing radical functions   **MATERIALS:** None

The graph of $y = a\sqrt{x - h} + k$ is a translation h units horizontally and k units vertically of $y = a\sqrt{x}$. The value of a determines a vertical stretch or compression of $y = \sqrt{x}$.

Example

Graph $y = 2\sqrt{x - 5} + 3$.

$$y = 2\sqrt{x - 5} + 3$$

$$\uparrow \qquad \uparrow \qquad \uparrow$$

$$a = 2 \quad h = 5 \quad k = 3$$

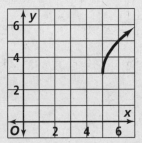

Translate the graph of $y = 2\sqrt{x}$ right five units and up three units. The graph of $y = 2\sqrt{x}$ looks like the graph of $y - \sqrt{x}$ with a vertical stretch by a factor of 2.

Exercises

Graph each function.

1. $y = \sqrt{x - 4} + 1$ **2.** $y = \sqrt{x} - 4$

3. $y = \sqrt{x + 1}$ **4.** $y = -\sqrt{x + 2} - 3$

5. $y = 2\sqrt{x - 1}$ **6.** $y = -2\sqrt{x + 3} + 4$

7. $y = -\sqrt{x} + 1$ **8.** $y = \sqrt{x + 3} - 4$

9. $y = 3\sqrt{x} + 2$ **10.** $y = -\sqrt{x - 2}$

11. $y = \sqrt{x - 1} - 2$ **12.** $y = -\sqrt{x + 4} - 1$

Practice 7-8

Graphing Radical Functions

Graph each function.

1. $y = -\sqrt{x + 2}$

2. $y = \sqrt{x - 3}$

3. $y = \sqrt{x} + 1$

4. $y = -\sqrt{x} - 1$

5. $y = \sqrt{x - 4} + 2$

6. $y = \sqrt{x + 1} - 3$

7. $y = \sqrt{x + 2} - 6$

8. $y = -\sqrt{x - 2} + 3$

9. $y = -\sqrt{x - 3} + 3$

10. $y = \sqrt{x + 3} - 2$

11. $y = \sqrt{x - 1} - 5$

12. $y = -\sqrt{x - 2} + 5$

13. $y = -\sqrt{x + 1} - 4$

14. $y = -\sqrt{x - 1} + 2$

15. $y = \sqrt{x - 1} + 3$

16. $y = \sqrt{x - 2} + 1$

17. $y = \sqrt{x + 2} - 2$

18. $y = \sqrt{x - 1} + 2$

19. $y = \sqrt{x + 1} + 4$

20. $y = \sqrt{x - 3} + 3$

21. $y = \sqrt{x + 1} - 2$

22. $y = \sqrt{x - 1} - 1$

23. $y = \sqrt{x + 3} - 3$

24. $y = \sqrt{x + 4} - 1$

25. $y = \sqrt{x - 2} - 4$

26. $y = \sqrt{x + 2} + 1$

27. $y = \sqrt{x - 2} + 3$

28. If you know the area A of a circle, you can use the equation $r = \sqrt{\dfrac{A}{\pi}}$ to find the radius r.

    a. Graph the equation.

    b. What is the radius of a circle with an area of 350 ft^2?

Rewrite each function to make it easy to graph using a translation. Describe the graph.

29. $y = \sqrt{81x + 162}$

30. $y = -\sqrt{4x + 20}$

31. $y = \sqrt[3]{125x - 250}$

32. $y = -\sqrt{64x + 192}$

33. $y = -\sqrt[3]{8x - 56} + 4$

34. $y = \sqrt{25x + 75} - 1$

Graph each function.

35. $y = \sqrt[3]{x - 1}$

36. $y = \sqrt[3]{x + 2} - 3$

37. $y = \sqrt[3]{x + 1} - 2$

38. $y = -\sqrt[3]{x} + 2$

39. $y = 2\sqrt[3]{x - 3}$

40. $y = \sqrt[3]{x + 3} - 1$

Reteaching 8-1

OBJECTIVE: Modeling exponential growth and decay	**MATERIALS:** None

- The general form of an exponential function is $y = ab^x$. This can model either growth or decay. When the value of b is greater than 1, the function models growth. When the value of b is between zero and 1, the function models decay.

- When you see words like *increase* or *appreciation*, think growth. When you see words like *decrease* and *depreciation*, think decay.

Example

Carl's weight at 12 yr is 82 lb. Assume that his weight increases at a rate of 16% each year. Write an exponential function to model the increase. Calculate his weight after 5 yr.

Step 1: Find a and b.

$a = 82$ ⟵ **a is the original amount.**

$b = 1 + 0.16$ ⟵ **b is the growth or decay factor. If you are modeling growth, b equals 1 plus the percent. If you are modeling decay, b equals 1 minus the percent. Carl's weight**

$= 1.16$ **increases, so add.**

Step 2: Write the exponential function.

$y = ab^x$ ⟵ **Use the formula.**

$y = 82(1.16)^x$ ⟵ **Substitute.**

Step 3: Calculate.

$y = 82(1.16)^5$ ⟵ **Substitute 5 for x.**

$y = 172.228$ ⟵ **Use a calculator.**

If the model is correct, Carl will weigh about 172 lb in 5 yr.

Exercises

Write an exponential function to model each situation. Find each amount after the specified time.

1. A tree 3 ft tall grows 8% each year. How tall will the tree be at the end of 14 yr? Round the answer to the nearest hundredth.

2. The price of a new home is $126,000. The value of the home appreciates 2% each year. How much will the home be worth in 10 yr?

3. A motorcycle purchased for $9,000 today will be worth 6% less each year. For what can you expect to sell the motorcycle at the end of 5 yr?

Practice 8-1

Exploring Exponential Models

Without graphing, determine whether each equation represents exponential growth or exponential decay.

1. $y = 72(1.6)^x$ **2.** $y = 24(0.8)^x$ **3.** $y = 3\left(\dfrac{6}{5}\right)^x$ **4.** $y = 7\left(\dfrac{2}{3}\right)^x$

Sketch the graph of each function. Identify the horizontal asymptote.

5. $y = (0.3)^x$ **6.** $y = 3^x$ **7.** $y = 2\left(\dfrac{1}{5}\right)^x$ **8.** $y = \dfrac{1}{2}(3)^x$

9. A new car that sells for \$18,000 depreciates 25% each year. Write a function that models the value of the car. Find the value of the car after 4 yr.

10. A new truck that sells for \$29,000 depreciates 12% each year. Write a function that models the value of the truck. Find the value of the truck after 7 yr.

11. The bear population increases at a rate of 2% per year. There are 1573 bear this year. Write a function that models the bear population. How many bears will there be in 10 yr?

12. An investment of \$75,000 increases at a rate of 12.5% per year. Find the value of the investment after 30 yr.

13. The population of an endangered bird is decreasing at a rate of 0.75% per year. There are currently about 200,000 of these birds. Write a function that models the bird population. How many birds will there be in 100 yr?

Write an exponential function $y = ab^x$ for a graph that includes the given points.

14. $(0, 2), (1, 1.3)$ **15.** $(-1, 12.5), (4, 4.096)$ **16.** $(1, 0.84), (2, 1.008)$

For each annual rate of change, find the corresponding growth or decay factor.

17. $+45\%$ **18.** -10% **19.** -40% **20.** $+200\%$

For each function, find the annual percent increase or decrease that the function models.

21. $y = 1700(0.75)^x$ **22.** $y = 30.698\left(\dfrac{5}{8}\right)^x$ **23.** $y = 984.5(1.73)^x$

24. The value of a piece of equipment has a decay factor of 0.80 per year. After 5 yr, the equipment is worth \$98,304. What was the original value of the equipment?

Reteaching 8-2

OBJECTIVE: Graphing exponential functions	**MATERIALS:** Graphing calculator, graph paper

Example

Sketch the graph of $y = 2\left(\frac{1}{3}\right)^{x+1} - 4$ as a translation of $y = 2\left(\frac{1}{3}\right)^{x}$.

Step 1: Determine the base of the function $y = 2\left(\frac{1}{3}\right)^{x}$. Since $b < 1$, the graph will represent exponential decay.

Step 2: Make a table. Find more values if necessary to get a good picture of the graph.

Step 3: Use the values for x and y from the table to graph the function.

x	$y = 2\left(\frac{1}{3}\right)^{x}$	y
-2	$2\left(\frac{1}{3}\right)^{-2} = 2(9)$	18
-1	$2\left(\frac{1}{3}\right)^{-1} = 2(3)$	6
0	$2\left(\frac{1}{3}\right)^{0} = 2(1)$	2
1	$2\left(\frac{1}{3}\right)^{1} = 2\left(\frac{1}{3}\right)$	$\frac{2}{3}$
2	$2\left(\frac{1}{3}\right)^{2} = 2\left(\frac{1}{9}\right)$	$\frac{2}{9}$

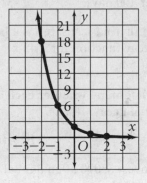

Step 4: For $y = 2\left(\frac{1}{3}\right)^{x+1} - 4$, $h = -1$ and $k = -4$. Shift the graph of the parent function above 1 unit left and 4 units down. The horizontal asymptote shifts down as well, from $y = 0$ to $y = -4$.

Step 5: Use a graphing calculator to check your graph.

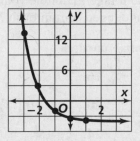

Exercises

Graph each exponential function.

1. $y = \left(\frac{1}{5}\right)^{x}$

2. $y = 3^{x} + 1$

3. $y = 5^{x}$

4. $y = -\left(\frac{1}{2}\right)^{x}$

5. $y = -\left(\frac{1}{2}\right)^{x} + 4$

6. $y = \left(\frac{1}{4}\right)^{x}$

7. $y = \left(\frac{1}{4}\right)^{x-1}$

8. $y = 4^{x} + 1$

9. $y = -(2)^{x}$

Practice 8-2

Properties of Exponential Functions

Evaluate each expression to four decimal places.

1. e^2 **2.** $e^{-2.5}$ **3.** $e^{\frac{1}{3}}$ **4.** $e^{\sqrt{2}}$

Find the amount in a continuously compounded account for the given conditions.

5. principal: $5000
   annual interest rate: 6.9%
   time: 30 yr

6. principal: $20,000
   annual interest rate: 3.75%
   time: 2 yr

7. Hg-197 is used in kidney scans. It has a half-life of 64.128 h. Write the exponential decay function for a 12-mg sample. Find the amount remaining after 72 h.

8. Sr-85 is used in bone scans. It has a half-life of 64.9 days. Write the exponential decay function for an 8-mg sample. Find the amount remaining after 100 days.

9. I-123 is used in thyroid scans. It has a half-life of 13.2 h. Write the exponential decay function for a 45-mg sample. Find the amount remaining after 5 h.

Without graphing, determine whether each equation represents exponential growth or exponential decay.

10. $y = \frac{5}{4}(0.11)^x$ **11.** $A(t) = 1000(1.075)^t$ **12.** $s(t) = 2.4(0.5)^t$

13. Suppose you invest $5000 at an annual interest of 6.9%, compounded monthly.

   a. How much will you have in the account after 10 years?

   b. Determine how much more you would have if the interest were compounded continuously.

14. How long would it take to double your principal at an annual interest rate of 7% compounded continuously?

Graph each exponential function.

15. $y = 2^x$ **16.** $y = 2^{x+1}$ **17.** $y = -(2)^{x+1}$ **18.** $y = 5(0.12)^x$

19. $y = 5^x$ **20.** $y = -0.1(5)^x$ **21.** $y = 5^{-x}$ **22.** $y = -0.1(5)^{-x}$

23. $y = \left(\frac{1}{3}\right)^x$ **24.** $y = 5\left(\frac{1}{3}\right)^x$ **25.** $y = -5\left(\frac{1}{3}\right)^x$ **26.** $y = 2(2)^{x+2}$

Reteaching 8-3

OBJECTIVE: Evaluating logarithmic expressions   **MATERIALS:** None

- A logarithmic function is the inverse or opposite of an exponential function.

- To evaluate logarithmic expressions, use the fact that $x = \log_b y$ means the same as $y = b^x$. Keep in mind that $x = \log y$ means $x = \log_{10} y$.

Example

Evaluate $\log_4 32$.

$x = \log_4 32$	⟵ **Write the equation in logarithmic form $x = \log_b y$.**
$32 = 4^x$	⟵ **Rewrite in exponential form $y = b^x$.**
$2^5 = (2^2)^x$	⟵ **Rewrite each side of the equation with like bases in order to solve the equation.**
$2^5 = 2^{2x}$	⟵ **Simplify.**
$5 = 2x$	⟵ **Set the exponents equal to each other.**
$x = \frac{5}{2}$	⟵ **Solve for x.**
$\log_4 32 = \frac{5}{2}$	

Exercises

Evaluate the logarithm.

1. $\log_2 64$ **2.** $\log_4 64$ **3.** $\log_3 3^4$

4. $\log 10$ **5.** $\log 0.1$ **6.** $\log 1$

7. $\log_8 2$ **8.** $\log_{32} 2$ **9.** $\log_9 3$

Write each equation in exponential form.

10. $x = \log_3 8$ **11.** $2 = \log_5 25$ **12.** $\log 0.1 = -1$

13. $\log 7 = 0.845$ **14.** $\log 1000 = 3$ **15.** $-2 = \log 0.01$

16. $\log_3 81 = 4$ **17.** $\log_{49} 7 = \frac{1}{2}$ **18.** $\log_8 \frac{1}{4} = -\frac{2}{3}$

19. $\log_2 128 = 7$ **20.** $\log_5 \frac{1}{625} = -4$ **21.** $\log_6 36 = 2$

Practice 8-3

Logarithmic Functions as Inverses

Write each equation in exponential form.

1. $\log_4 256 = 4$

2. $\log_7 1 = 0$

3. $\log_2 32 = 5$

4. $\log 10 = 1$

5. $\log_5 5 = 1$

6. $\log_8 \frac{1}{64} = -2$

7. $\log_9 59{,}049 = 5$

8. $\log_{17} 289 = 2$

9. $\log_{56} 1 = 0$

10. $\log_{12} \frac{1}{144} = -2$

11. $\log_2 \frac{1}{1024} = -10$

12. $\log_3 6561 = 8$

Write each equation in logarithmic form.

13. $9^2 = 81$

14. $25^2 = 625$

15. $8^3 = 512$

16. $13^2 = 169$

17. $2^9 = 512$

18. $4^5 = 1024$

19. $5^4 = 625$

20. $10^{-3} = 0.001$

21. $4^{-3} = \frac{1}{64}$

22. $5^{-2} = \frac{1}{25}$

23. $8^{-1} = \frac{1}{8}$

24. $11^0 = 1$

25. $6^1 = 6$

26. $6^{-3} = \frac{1}{216}$

27. $17^0 = 1$

28. $17^1 = 17$

29. A single-celled bacterium divides every hour. The number N of bacteria after t hours is given by the formula $\log_2 N = t$. After how many hours will there be 32 bacteria?

Evaluate each logarithm.

30. $\log_2 16$

31. $\log_2 8$

32. $\log_2 4$

33. $\log_2 2$

34. $\log_2 1$

35. $\log_2 \frac{1}{2}$

36. $\log_2 \frac{1}{4}$

37. $\log_2 \frac{1}{8}$

38. $\log_{16} 16$

39. $\log_5 125$

40. $\log_{11} 121$

41. $\log 0.1$

42. $\log 1$

43. $\log_3 1$

44. $\log_6 216$

45. $\log_{12} 12$

46. $\log_{30} 30$

47. $\log 100{,}000$

48. $\log_3 \frac{1}{9}$

49. $\log_3 \frac{1}{27}$

50. $\log \frac{1}{100}$

51. $\log_4 32$

52. $\log_7 \frac{1}{49}$

53. $\log_{81} 9$

For each pH given, find the concentration of hydrogen ions $[H^+]$. Use the formula $pH = -\log[H^+]$.

54. 7.2

55. 7.3

56. 8.2

57. 6.2

58. 5.6

59. 4.6

60. 7.0

61. 2.9

Graph each logarithmic function.

62. $y = \log x$

63. $y = \log_3 x$

64. $y = \log_6 x$

65. $y = \log_{\frac{1}{2}} x$

66. $y = \log_3(x + 1)$

67. $y = \log_2 x - 3$

68. $y = \log_6(x + 2)$

69. $y = \log_5(x - 4) + 1$

70. $y = \log_2(x - 3) + 1$

Algebra 2 Chapter 8

Reteaching 8-4

OBJECTIVE: Rewriting logarithmic expressions   **MATERIALS:** None

- Logarithmic expressions can be rewritten using the **properties of logarithms.**

  Product Property

  $\log_b MN = \log_b M + \log_b N$

  The log of a product is the sum of the logs of the factors.

  Quotient Property

  $\log_b \frac{M}{N} = \log_b M - \log_b N$

  The log of a quotient is the difference of the logs of the numerator and denominator.

  Power Property

  $\log_b M^x = x \log_b M$

  The log of an expression raised to an exponent is the exponent times the log of the expression.

Examples

Expand $\log_2 3x^4$.

$\log_2 3x^4 = \log_2 3 + \log_2 x^4 = \log_2 3 + 4 \log_2 x$

Write $\log_5 6 - \log_5 4$ as a single logarithm.

$\log_5 6 - \log_5 4 = \log_5 \frac{6}{4} = \log_5 \frac{3}{2}$

Exercises

Use properties of logarithms to expand the following expressions.

1. $\log \frac{2}{3}$

2. $\log 6y$

3. $\log \frac{1}{5}$

4. $\log_3 x^3$

5. $\log_3 6xy$

6. $\log_6 36x^2$

7. $\log_5 xy$

8. $\log_3 \frac{x}{4}$

9. $\log_7 x^4$

10. $\log_3 x^2 y$

11. $\log_8 y^7$

12. $\log_5 x^4 y^3$

Use properties of logarithms to write each logarithmic expression as a single logarithm.

13. $\log_3 13 + \log_3 3$

14. $2 \log x + \log 5$

15. $\log_4 2 - \log_4 6$

16. $3 \log_3 3 - \log_3 3$

17. $\log_5 8 + \log_5 x$

18. $\log 2 - 2 \log x$

19. $\log_2 x + \log_2 y$

20. $3 \log_7 x - 5 \log_7 y$

21. $4 \log x + 3 \log x$

22. $\log_5 x + 3 \log_5 y$

23. $3 \log_2 x - \log_2 y$

24. $\log_2 16 - \log_2 8$

Practice 8-4

Properties of Logarithms

For Exercises 1–2, use the formula $L = 10 \log \dfrac{I}{I_0}$.

1. A sound has an intensity of $5.92 \times 10^{25} \text{W/m}^2$. What is the loudness of the sound in decibels? Use $I_0 = 10^{-12} \text{W/m}^2$.

2. Suppose you decrease the intensity of a sound by 45%. By how many decibels would the loudness be decreased?

Assume that $\log 3 \approx 0.4771$, $\log 4 \approx 0.6021$, and $\log 5 \approx 0.6990$. Use the properties of logarithms to evaluate each expression. Do not use a calculator.

3. $\log 12$

4. $\log 16$

5. $\log \dfrac{3}{5}$

6. $\log 0.8$

7. $\log 75$

8. $\log \dfrac{16}{5}$

9. $\log_6 1 - \log 1$

10. $\log 60$

Write each logarithmic expression as a single logarithm.

11. $\log_5 4 + \log_5 3$

12. $\log_6 25 - \log_6 5$

13. $\log_2 4 + \log_2 2 - \log_2 8$

14. $5 \log_7 x - 2 \log_7 x$

15. $\log_4 60 - \log_4 4 + \log_4 x$

16. $\log 7 - \log 3 + \log 6$

17. $2 \log x - 3 \log y$

18. $\frac{1}{2} \log r + \frac{1}{3} \log s - \frac{1}{4} \log t$

19. $\log_3 4x + 2 \log_3 5y$

20. $5 \log 2 - 2 \log 2$

21. $\frac{1}{3} \log 3x + \frac{2}{3} \log 3x$

22. $2 \log 4 + \log 2 + \log 2$

23. $(\log 3 - \log 4) - \log 2$

24. $5 \log x + 3 \log x^2$

25. $\log_6 3 - \log_6 6$

26. $\log 2 + \log 4 - \log 7$

27. $\log_3 2x - 5 \log_3 y$

28. $\frac{1}{3}(\log_2 x - \log_2 y)$

29. $\frac{1}{2} \log x + \frac{1}{3} \log y - 2 \log z$

30. $3(4 \log t^2)$

31. $\log_5 y - 4(\log_5 r + 2 \log_5 t)$

Expand each logarithm.

32. $\log xyz$

33. $\log_2 \dfrac{x}{yz}$

34. $\log 6x^3 y$

35. $\log 7(3x - 2)^2$

36. $\log \sqrt{\dfrac{2rst}{5w}}$

37. $\log \dfrac{5x}{4y}$

38. $\log_5 5x^{-5}$

39. $\log \dfrac{2x^2 y}{3k^3}$

40. $\log_4 (3xyz)^2$

State the property or properties used to rewrite each expression.

41. $\log 6 - \log 3 = \log 2$

42. $6 \log 2 = \log 64$

43. $\log 3x = \log 3 + \log x$

44. $\frac{1}{3} \log_2 x = \log_2 \sqrt[3]{x}$

45. $\frac{2}{3} \log 7 = \log \sqrt[3]{49}$

46. $\log_4 20 - 3 \log_4 x = \log_4 \dfrac{20}{x^3}$

Reteaching 8-5

Exponential and Logarithmic Equations

OBJECTIVE: Using logarithms to solve exponential equations

MATERIALS: None

• When solving exponential equations, use inverse operations to isolate the variable. Remember that the inverse of raising to an exponent is taking the logarithm.

Example

Solve $7 - 5^{2x-1} = 4$.

$$7 - 5^{2x-1} = 4$$

$$-5^{2x-1} = -3 \qquad \longleftarrow \quad \textbf{First isolate the term that has the variable in the exponent. Begin by subtracting 7 from each side.}$$

$$5^{2x-1} = 3 \qquad \longleftarrow \quad \textbf{Multiply each side by } -1.$$

$$\log_5 5^{2x-1} = \log_5 3 \qquad \longleftarrow \quad \textbf{Since the variable is in the exponent, use logarithms. Take } \log_5 \textbf{ of each side since 5 is the base of the exponent.}$$

$$(2x - 1)\log_5 5 = \log_5 3 \qquad \longleftarrow \quad \textbf{Use the Power Property of Logarithms.}$$

$$2x - 1 = \log_5 3 \qquad \longleftarrow \quad \textbf{Simplify. (Recall that } \log_b b = 1.)$$

$$2x - 1 = \frac{\log 3}{\log 5} \qquad \longleftarrow \quad \textbf{Apply the Change of Base Formula.}$$

$$2x = \frac{\log 3}{\log 5} + 1 \qquad \longleftarrow \quad \textbf{Add 1 to each side.}$$

$$x = \frac{1}{2}\left(\frac{\log 3}{\log 5} + 1\right) \qquad \longleftarrow \quad \textbf{Divide each side by 2.}$$

$$x \approx 0.84 \qquad \longleftarrow \quad \textbf{Use a calculator to find a decimal approximation.}$$

Exercises

Solve each equation. Round the answer to the nearest hundredth.

1. $2^x = 5$ **2.** $10^{2x} = 8$ **3.** $5^{x+1} = 25$

4. $2^{x+3} = 9$ **5** $3^{2x-3} = 7$ **6.** $4^x - 5 = 3$

7. $5 + 2^{x+6} = 9$ **8.** $4^{3x} + 2 = 3$ **9.** $1 - 3^{2x} = -5$

10. $2^{3x} - 2 = 13$ **11.** $5^{2x+7} - 1 = 8$ **12.** $7 - 2^{x+7} = 5$

Practice 8-5

Exponential and Logarithmic Equations

Use the Change of Base Formula to evaluate each expression. Round answers to the nearest hundredth.

1. $\log_2 12$ **2.** $\log_3 40$ **3.** $\log_4 8$ **4.** $\log_5 3$ **5.** $\log_2 1$

6. $\log_5 10$ **7.** $\log_2 8$ **8.** $\log_3 6$ **9.** $\log_9 3$ **10.** $\log_8 3$

Solve each equation. Check your answer. Round answers to the nearest hundredth.

11. $2^x = 243$ **12.** $7^n = 12$ **13.** $5^{2x} = 20$ **14.** $8^{n+1} = 3$

15. $4^{n-2} = 3$ **16.** $4^{3n} = 5$ **17.** $15^{2n-3} = 245$ **18.** $4^x - 5 = 12$

Solve each equation. Check your answer. Round answers to the nearest hundredth.

19. $\log 3x = 2$ **20.** $4 \log x = 4$ **21.** $\log (3x - 2) = 3$

22. $2 \log x - \log 5 = -2$ **23.** $\log 8 - \log 2x = -1$ **24.** $\log (x + 21) + \log x = 2$

25. $8 \log x = 16$ **26.** $\log x = 2$ **27.** $\log 4x = 2$

28. $\log (x - 25) = 2$ **29.** $2 \log x = 2$ **30.** $\log 3x - \log 5 = 1$

Use the Change of Base Formula to solve each equation. Round answers to the nearest hundredth.

31. $10^x = 182$ **32.** $8^n = 12$ **33.** $10^{2x} = 9$ **34.** $5^{n+1} = 3$

35. $10^{n-2} = 0.3$ **36.** $3^{3n} = 50$ **37.** $10^{2n-5} = 500$ **38.** $11^x - 50 = 12$

The function $y = 1000(1.005)^x$ models the value of $1000 deposit at 6% per year (0.005 per month) x months after the money is deposited.

39. Use a graph (on your graphing calculator) to predict how many months it will be until the account is worth $1100.

40. Predict how many years it will be until the account is worth $5000.

Solve each equation. Round answers to the nearest hundredth.

41. $2 \log 3x - \log 9 = 1$ **42.** $\log x - \log 4 = -1$ **43.** $\log x - \log 4 = -2$

44. $\log x - \log 4 = 3$ **45.** $2 \log x - \log 4 = 2$ **46.** $\log (2x + 5) = 3$

47. $2 \log (2x + 5) = 4$ **48.** $\log 4x = -1$ **49.** $2 \log x \quad \log 3 - 1$

Solve by graphing. Round answers to the nearest hundredth.

50. $10^n = 3$ **51.** $10^{3y} = 5$ **52.** $10^{k-2} = 20$

53. $5^x = 4$ **54.** $2^{4x} = 8$ **55.** $3^{x+5} = 15$

Reteaching 8-6

OBJECTIVE: Solving equations using natural logarithms

MATERIALS: Graphing calculator

- To solve equations that involve natural logarithms, use the following inverse properties:

$$\ln e^x = x \qquad\qquad e^{\ln x} = x$$

Example

Solve $4e^{2x} = 5$.

$$4e^{2x} = 5$$

$$e^{2x} = \frac{5}{4} \qquad \longleftarrow \quad \textbf{Divide each side by 4.}$$

$$\ln e^{2x} = \ln 1.25 \qquad \longleftarrow \quad \textbf{Take the natural logarithm of each side since the base of the exponent is } \boldsymbol{e}.$$

$$2x = \ln 1.25 \qquad \longleftarrow \quad \textbf{Apply the inverse property } \ln e^x = x.$$

$$x = \frac{\ln 1.25}{2} \qquad \longleftarrow \quad \textbf{Divide each side by 2.}$$

$$x \approx 0.112 \qquad \longleftarrow \quad \textbf{Use a calculator to approximate.}$$

The solution is $x \approx 0.112$.

Exercises

Solve each equation. Check your answers. Round answers to the nearest thousandth.

1. $2e^x = 4$ **2.** $e^{4x} = 25$ **3.** $e^x = 72$

4. $e^{3x} = 124$ **5.** $12e^{3x-2} = 8$ **6.** $\ln(x - 3) = 2$

7. $\ln 2x = 4$ **8.** $1 + \ln x^2 = 2$ **9.** $\ln(2x - 5) = 3$

Use the formula $A = Pe^{rt}$ to solve.

10. If \$5000 is invested in a savings account that pays 7.85% interest compounded continuously, how much money will be in the account after 12 yr?

11. If \$10,000 is invested in a savings account that pays 8.65% interest compounded continuously, in how many years will the balance be \$250,000? Round to the nearest tenth.

Practice 8-6

Natural Logarithms

The formula $P = 50e^{-\frac{t}{25}}$ gives the power output P, in watts, available to run a certain satellite for t days. Find how long a satellite with the given power output will operate. Round answers to the nearest hundredth.

1. 10 W
2. 12 W
3. 14 W

The formula for the maximum velocity v of a rocket is $v = c \ln R$, where c is the velocity of the exhaust in km/s and R is the mass ratio of the rocket. A rocket must reach 7.8 km/s to attain a stable orbit. Round answers to the nearest hundredth.

4. Find the maximum velocity of a rocket with a mass ratio of about 18 and an exhaust velocity of 2.2 km/s. Can this rocket achieve a stable orbit?

5. What mass ratio would be needed to achieve a stable orbit for a rocket with an exhaust velocity of 2.5 km/s?

6. A rocket with an exhaust velocity of 2.4 km/s can reach a maximum velocity of 7.8 km/s. What is the mass ratio of the rocket?

Use natural logarithms to solve each equation. Round answers to the nearest hundredth.

7. $e^x = 15$
8. $4e^x = 10$
9. $e^{x+2} = 50$
10. $4e^{3x-1} = 5$

11. $e^{x-4} = 2$
12. $5e^{6x+3} = 0.1$
13. $e^x = 1$
14. $e^{\frac{x}{5}} = 32$

15. $3e^{3x-5} = 49$
16. $7e^{5x+8} = 0.23$
17. $6 - e^{12x} = 5.2$
18. $e^{\frac{x}{2}} = 25$

19. $e^{2x} = 25$
20. $e^{\ln 5x} = 20$
21. $e^{\ln x} = 21$
22. $e^{x+6} + 5 = 1$

Solve each equation. Check your answer. Round answers to the nearest hundredth.

23. $4 \ln x = -2$
24. $2 \ln (3x - 4) = 7$
25. $5 \ln (4x - 6) = -6$

26. $-7 + \ln 2x = 4$
27. $3 - 4 \ln (8x + 1) = 12$
28. $\ln x + \ln 3x = 14$

29. $2 \ln x + \ln x^2 = 3$
30. $\ln x + \ln 4 = 2$
31. $\ln x - \ln 5 = -1$

32. $\ln e^x = 3$
33. $3 \ln e^{2x} = 12$
34. $\ln e^{x+5} = 17$

35. $\ln 3x + \ln 2x = 3$
36. $5 \ln (3x - 2) = 15$
37. $7 \ln (2x + 5) = 8$

38. $\ln (3x + 4) = 5$
39. $\ln \frac{2x}{41} = 2$
40. $\ln (2x - 1)^2 = 4$

Write each expression as a single natural logarithm.

41. $\ln 16 - \ln 8$
42. $3 \ln 3 + \ln 9$
43. $a \ln 4 - \ln b$

44. $\ln z - 3 \ln x$
45. $\frac{1}{2} \ln 9 + \ln 3x$
46. $4 \ln x + 3 \ln y$

Reteaching 9-1

OBJECTIVE: Identifying and solving inverse variations	MATERIALS: None

- In a direct variation, $y = kx$, as the value of one variable increases, so does the other. For inverse variation, $y = \frac{k}{x}$, as the value of one variable increases, the value of the other decreases.

Example

The time t that is necessary to complete a task varies inversely as the number of people p working. If it takes 4 h for 12 people to paint the exterior of a house, how long would it take for 3 people to do the same job?

$t = \frac{k}{p}$ ⟵ **Write an inverse variation. Since time is dependent on people, t is the dependent variable and p is the independent variable.**

$4 = \frac{k}{12}$ ⟵ **Substitute 4 for t and 12 for p.**

$48 = k$ ⟵ **Multiply each side by 12 to solve for k, the constant of variation.**

$t = \frac{48}{p}$ ⟵ **Substitute 48 for k. This is the equation of the inverse variation.**

$t = \frac{48}{3} = 16$ ⟵ **Substitute 3 for p. Simplify to solve the equation.**

It would take 3 people 16 h to paint the exterior of the house.

Exercises

1. The time t needed to complete a task varies inversely as the number of people p. It takes 5 h for seven men to install a new roof. How long would it take ten men to complete the job?

2. The time t needed to drive a certain distance varies inversely as the speed r. It takes 7.5 h at 40 mi/h to drive a certain distance. How long would it take to drive the same distance at 60 mi/h?

3. The cost of each item bought is inversely proportional to the number of items when spending a fixed amount. When 42 items are bought, each costs $1.46. Find the number of items when each costs $2.16 each.

4. The length ℓ of a rectangle of a certain area varies inversely as the width w. The length of a rectangle is 9 cm when its width is 6 cm. Determine its length if its width is 8 cm.

Practice 9-1

Inverse Variation

Each ordered pair is from an inverse variation. Find the constant of variation.

1. $\left(3, \dfrac{1}{3}\right)$ **2.** $(0.2, 6)$ **3.** $(10, 5)$ **4.** $\left(\dfrac{5}{7}, \dfrac{2}{5}\right)$ **5.** $(3.5, 1.2)$

Suppose that x and y vary inversely. Write a function that models each inverse variation.

6. $x = 7$ when $y = 2$ **7.** $x = 4$ when $y = 9$ **8.** $x = -3$ when $y = 8$

9. $x = 5$ when $y = -6$ **10.** $x = 1$ when $y = 0.8$ **11.** $x = -4$ when $y = -2$

12. $x = \dfrac{3}{5}$ when $y = 5$ **13.** $x = 3$ when $y = 2.1$ **14.** $x = -\dfrac{1}{3}$ when $y = \dfrac{9}{10}$

Describe the combined variation that is modeled by each formula.

15. $I = \dfrac{120}{R}$ **16.** $A = \dfrac{1}{2}bh$ **17.** $h = \dfrac{3V}{B}$ **18.** $V = \dfrac{4}{3}\pi r^3$

Each pair of values is from an inverse variation. Find the missing value.

19. $(2, 4)$ and $(6, y)$ **20.** $\left(\dfrac{1}{3}, 6\right)$ and $\left(x, -\dfrac{1}{2}\right)$ **21.** $(1.2, 4.5)$ and $(2.7, y)$

Suppose that x and y vary inversely. Write a function that models each inverse variation, and find y when $x = 8$.

22. $x = 4$ when $y = 2$ **23.** $x = -3$ when $y = \dfrac{1}{3}$ **24.** $x = 6$ when $y = 1.2$

Write the function that models each relationship. Find z when $x = 6$ and $y = 4$.

25. z varies jointly with x and y. When $x = 7$ and $y = 2$, $z = 28$.

26. z varies directly with x and inversely with the cube of y. When $x = 8$ and $y = 2$, $z = 3$.

Is the relationship between the values in each table a direct variation, an inverse variation, or neither? Write equations to model the direct and inverse variations.

27.

x	2	4	5	20
y	10	5	4	1

28.

x	1	3	7	10
y	2	8	20	29

29.

x	1	2	5	7
y	6	12	30	42

30.

x	0.2	0.5	2	3
y	25	62.5	250	375

31.

x	0.1	0.5	1.5	2
y	31	7	3	2.5

32.

x	3	1.5	0.5	0.3
y	5	10	30	50

Reteaching 9-2

Graphing Inverse Variations

OBJECTIVE: Identifying asymptotes and graphing inverse variations

MATERIALS: None

- An inverse variation equation has the form $y = \frac{k}{x}$. Its graph has vertical and horizontal asymptotes on the x- and y-axes.

- When an equation is of the form $y = \frac{k}{x - b} + c$, it is a translation of the inverse variation graph $y = \frac{k}{x}$. This means that the graph is moved b units to the left or right and c units up or down. The asymptotes are found at $x = b$ and $y = c$.

Example

Sketch the graph of $y = -\frac{6}{x - 3} + 2$, and include any asymptotes.

$y = -\frac{6}{x - 3} + 2$ ←   **Check to see that the equation is in $y = \frac{k}{x - b} + c$ form.**

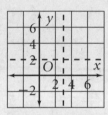 ←   **Because $b = 3$ and $c = 2$, the vertical asymptote will occur at $x = 3$ and the horizontal asymptote at $y = 2$.**

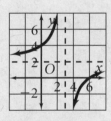 ←   **Because k is negative, the branches occur in the upper–left and lower–right regions. When k is positive, the branches occur in the upper–right and lower–left regions.**

Exercises

Sketch the asymptotes and the graph of each function.

1. $y = \frac{8}{x}$ **2.** $y = -\frac{4}{x}$ **3.** $xy = 2$

4. $y = \frac{2}{x + 4}$ **5.** $y = -\frac{4}{x - 8}$ **6.** $y = -\frac{2}{x} + 3$

7. $y = \frac{1}{x} - 4$ **8.** $y = -\frac{2}{x + 3} - 3$ **9.** $y = \frac{2}{x - 3} + 4$

10. $y = \frac{3}{x - 2} - 4$ **11.** $y = \frac{2}{3x} + \frac{3}{2}$ **12.** $y = -\frac{2}{x + 2} + 3$

Practice 9-2

Write an equation for a translation of $y = -\frac{3}{x}$ that has the given asymptotes.

1. $x = 2; y = 1$ **2.** $x = -1; y = 3$ **3.** $x = 4; y = -2$ **4.** $x = 0; y = 6$

5. $x = 3; y = 0$ **6.** $x = 1; y = 2$ **7.** $x = -3; y = -1$ **8.** $x = -2; y = 1$

Sketch the asymptotes and the graph of each equation.

9. $y = \frac{3}{x-1} + 2$ **10.** $y = \frac{2}{x+1}$ **11.** $y = \frac{11}{x+3} - 3$ **12.** $y = -\frac{4}{x-2} - 2$

13. $y = \frac{1}{x} + 3$ **14.** $y = \frac{1}{x+1} - 2$ **15.** $y = \frac{1}{x-2} + 1$ **16.** $y = \frac{1}{x-1} - 1$

17. $y = \frac{2}{x}$ **18.** $y = -\frac{3}{x-3} + 1$ **19.** $y = \frac{1}{x+1} + 2$ **20.** $y = \frac{3}{4x} + \frac{1}{2}$

21. $y = \frac{3}{x+3} - 1$ **22.** $y = \frac{2}{x-5}$ **23.** $y = -\frac{6}{x-3} - 2$ **24.** $y = \frac{5}{x}$

25. $y = \frac{1}{x-1} + 1$ **26.** $y = \frac{1}{x}$ **27.** $y = -\frac{3}{x-4} - 2$ **28.** $y = -\frac{1}{x-2} - \frac{1}{2}$

The length of a panpipe p (in feet) is inversely proportional to its pitch ℓ (in hertz). The inverse variation is modeled by the equation $p = \frac{495}{\ell}$.

29. Find the length required to produce a pitch of 220 Hz.

30. What pitch would be produced by a pipe with a length of 1.2 ft?

31. Find the pitch of a 0.6-ft pipe.

32. Find the pitch of a 3-ft pipe.

The junior class is buying keepsakes for the junior-senior prom. The price of each keepsake p is inversely proportional to the number of keepsakes s bought. The equation $p = \frac{1800}{s}$ models this inverse variation.

33. If they buy 240 keepsakes, how much can the class spend for each?

34. If they spend $5.55 for each keepsake, how many can the class buy?

35. If 400 keepsakes are bought, how much can be spent for each?

36. If the class buys 50 keepsakes, how much can be spent for each?

Compare the graphs of the inverse variations.

37. $y = \frac{1}{x}$ and $y = \frac{5}{x}$ **38.** $y = \frac{3}{x}$ and $y = -\frac{3}{x}$

39. $y = \frac{2}{x}$ and $y = \frac{20}{x}$ **40.** $y = -\frac{1}{x}$ and $y = -\frac{10}{x}$

41. $y = \frac{6}{x}$ and $y - \frac{6}{x}$ **42.** $y = \frac{0.2}{x}$ and $y = \frac{0.02}{x}$

Reteaching 9-3

OBJECTIVE: Finding and classifying points of discontinuity

MATERIALS: None

Rational functions may have two different types of points of discontinuity.

- A hole is present at $x = a$ when a is a zero of both the numerator and the denominator.

- A vertical asymptote is present at $x = a$ when a is a zero of the denominator only.

- Find points of discontinuity before attempting to graph the function.

Example

Find and classify any points of discontinuity for $y = \dfrac{x^2 + x - 6}{3x^2 - 12}$.

$$y = \frac{x^2 + x - 6}{3x^2 - 12}$$

$$y = \frac{(x - 2)(x + 3)}{3(x - 2)(x + 2)} \qquad \longleftarrow \quad \text{Factor the numerator and denominator completely.}$$

$$y = \frac{(x - 2)(x + 3)}{3(x - 2)(x + 2)} \qquad \longleftarrow \quad \text{Circle common factors in the numerator and denominator to indicate holes.}$$

$$x - 2 = 0 \qquad \longleftarrow \quad \text{Use the Zero-Product Property to find the point of discontinuity.}$$

$$x = 2$$

$$x + 2 = 0 \qquad \longleftarrow \quad \text{Use the Zero-Product Property with any remaining}$$
$$x = -2 \qquad \qquad \text{factors in the denominator to find the asymptotes.}$$

There is a hole at $x = 2$ and a vertical asymptote at $x = -2$.

Exercises

Find and classify any points of discontinuity.

1. $y = \dfrac{x}{x^2 - 9}$

2. $y = \dfrac{3x^2 - 1}{x^3}$

3. $y = \dfrac{6x^2 + 3}{x - 1}$

4. $y = \dfrac{5x^3 - 4}{x^2 + 4x - 5}$

5. $y = \dfrac{7x}{x^3 + 1}$

6. $y = \dfrac{12x^4 + 10x - 3}{3x^4}$

7. $y = \dfrac{12x + 24}{x^2 + 2x}$

8. $y = \dfrac{x^2 - 1}{x^2 + 3x + 2}$

9. $y = \dfrac{x^2 - 1}{x^2 - 2x - 3}$

Practice 9-3

Find any points of discontinuity for each rational function.

1. $y = \dfrac{x + 3}{(x - 4)(x + 3)}$

2. $y = \dfrac{x - 2}{x^2 - 4}$

3. $y = \dfrac{(x - 3)(x + 1)}{(x - 2)}$

4. $y = \dfrac{3x(x + 2)}{x(x + 2)}$

5. $y = \dfrac{2}{(x + 1)}$

6. $y = \dfrac{4x}{x^3 - 9x}$

Find the horizontal asymptote of the graph of each rational function.

7. $y = \dfrac{2}{x - 6}$

8. $y = \dfrac{x + 2}{x - 4}$

9. $y = \dfrac{(x + 3)}{2(x + 4)}$

10. $y = \dfrac{2x^2 + 3}{x^2 - 6}$

11. $y = \dfrac{3x - 12}{x^2 - 2}$

12. $y = \dfrac{3x^3 - 4x + 2}{2x^3 + 3}$

Sketch the graph of each rational function.

13. $y = \dfrac{3}{x - 2}$

14. $y = \dfrac{3}{(x - 2)(x + 2)}$

15. $y = \dfrac{x}{x(x - 6)}$

16. $y = \dfrac{2x}{x - 6}$

17. $y = \dfrac{x^2 - 1}{x^2 - 4}$

18. $y = \dfrac{2x^2 + 10x + 12}{x^2 - 9}$

19. $y = \dfrac{x}{x^2 + 4}$

20. $y = \dfrac{x + 2}{x - 1}$

21. $y = \dfrac{x + 3}{x + 1}$

Describe the vertical asymptotes and holes for the graph of each rational function.

22. $y = \dfrac{x - 2}{(x + 2)(x - 2)}$

23. $y = -\dfrac{x}{x(x - 1)}$

24. $y = \dfrac{5 - x}{x^2 - 1}$

25. $y = \dfrac{x^2 - 2}{x + 2}$

26. $y = \dfrac{x^2 - 4}{x^2 + 4}$

27. $y = \dfrac{x + 3}{x^2 - 9}$

28. $y = \dfrac{x^2 - 25}{x - 4}$

29. $y = \dfrac{(x - 2)(2x + 3)}{(5x + 4)(x - 3)}$

30. $y = \dfrac{15x^2 - 7x - 2}{x^2 - 4}$

31. Suppose you start a home business typing technical research papers for college students. You must spend \$3500 to replace your computer system. Then you estimate the cost of typing each page will be \$.02.

   a. Write a rational function modeling your average cost per page. Graph the function.

   b. How many pages must you type to bring your average cost per page to less than \$1.50 per page, the amount you plan to charge?

   c. How many pages must you type to have the average cost per page equal \$1.00?

   d. How many pages must you type to have the average cost per page equal \$.50?

   e. What are the vertical and horizontal asymptotes of the graph of the function?

Name _____ Class _____ Date _____

Reteaching 9-4

Rational Expressions

OBJECTIVE: Multiplying and dividing rational expressions	**MATERIALS:** None

Example

Divide $\dfrac{x^2-2x-35}{2x^3-3x^2}$ by $\dfrac{7x-49}{4x^3-9x}$.

$$\dfrac{x^2-2x-35}{2x^3-3x^2} \div \dfrac{7x-49}{4x^3-9x}$$

$$= \dfrac{x^2-2x-35}{2x^3-3x^2} \cdot \dfrac{4x^3-9x}{7x-49} \qquad \longleftarrow \quad \textbf{Multiply by the reciprocal of the second expression.}$$

$$= \dfrac{(x-7)(x+5)}{x \cdot x(2x-3)} \cdot \dfrac{x(2x-3)(2x+3)}{7(x-7)} \qquad \longleftarrow \quad \textbf{Factor expressions completely.}$$

$$= \dfrac{\cancel{(x-7)}(x+5)}{\cancel{x} \cdot x\cancel{(2x-3)}} \cdot \dfrac{\cancel{x}\cancel{(2x-3)}(2x+3)}{7\cancel{(x-7)}} \qquad \longleftarrow \quad \textbf{Divide out common factors.}$$

$$= \dfrac{2x^2+13x+15}{7x} \qquad \longleftarrow \quad \textbf{Multiply remaining factors.}$$

Exercises

Multiply or divide. Write the result in simplest form.

1. $\dfrac{x^2-y^2}{(x-y)^2} \cdot \dfrac{1}{x+y}$

2. $\dfrac{a^2-a-6}{a^2-7a+12} \cdot \dfrac{a^2-2a-8}{a^2-3a-10}$

3. $\dfrac{3x+12}{2x-8} \div \dfrac{x^2+8x+16}{x^2-8x+16}$

4. $\dfrac{2x}{3x-12} \div \dfrac{x^2-2x}{x^2-6x+8}$

5. $\dfrac{4x^2-4x}{x^2+2x-3} \cdot \dfrac{x^2+x-6}{4x}$

6. $\dfrac{x^2+3x}{x^2+6x+8} \cdot \dfrac{-(x^2+x-2)}{4x^3+12x^2}$

7. $\dfrac{2x^2-16x}{x^2-9x+8} \div \dfrac{2x}{5x-5}$

8. $\dfrac{x-3}{x^2-5x-14} \div \dfrac{x^2-x-6}{x-7}$

9. $\dfrac{2x-10}{3x-21} \div \dfrac{x-5}{4x-28}$

10. $\dfrac{x^2-9x+14}{x^3+2x^2} \div \dfrac{x-2}{x+2}$

11. $\dfrac{x^2+2x-8}{x^2} \cdot \dfrac{x^2-3x}{x^2+x-12}$

12. $\dfrac{x^2+3x}{x^2-3x+2} \cdot \dfrac{x^2+x-2}{3x^2+9x}$

13. $\dfrac{4x-16}{4x} \div \dfrac{x^2-2x-8}{3x+6}$

14. $\dfrac{3x-12}{2x^2-8x} \div \dfrac{x^2+x-6}{x^3-4x}$

15. $\dfrac{x^4-9x^2}{x^3+3x^2} \cdot \dfrac{3x}{x^2-3x}$

16. $\dfrac{1}{x^4-x^3-2x^2} \cdot \dfrac{x^2-x-2}{x^2}$

Practice 9-4

Rational Expressions

Simplify each rational expression. State any restrictions on the variable.

1. $\dfrac{20 + 40x}{20x}$

2. $\dfrac{4x + 6}{2x + 3}$

3. $\dfrac{3y^2 - 3}{y^2 - 1}$

4. $\dfrac{4x + 20}{3x + 15}$

5. $\dfrac{x^2 + x}{x^2 + 2x}$

6. $\dfrac{3x + 6}{5x + 10}$

7. $\dfrac{2y}{y^2 + 6y}$

8. $\dfrac{x^2 - 5x}{x^2 - 25}$

9. $\dfrac{x^2 + 3x - 18}{x^2 - 36}$

10. $\dfrac{x^2 + 13x + 40}{x^2 - 2x - 35}$

11. $\dfrac{3x^2 - 12}{x^2 - x - 6}$

12. $\dfrac{4x^2 - 36}{x^2 + 10x + 21}$

13. $\dfrac{2x^2 + 11x + 5}{3x^2 + 17x + 10}$

14. $\dfrac{6x^2 + 5x - 6}{3x^2 - 5x + 2}$

15. $\dfrac{7x - 28}{x^2 - 16}$

16. $\dfrac{x^2 - 9}{2x + 6}$

Multiply or divide. Write the answer in simplest form. State any restrictions on the variables.

17. $\dfrac{5a}{5a + 5} \cdot \dfrac{10a + 10}{a}$

18. $\dfrac{9 - x^2}{5x^3 + 17x^2 + 6x} \cdot \dfrac{5x^2 + 2x}{x - 3}$

19. $\dfrac{(x - 1)(2x - 4)}{x + 4} \cdot \dfrac{(x + 1)(x + 4)}{2x - 4}$

20. $\dfrac{(x + 3)(x + 4)}{(x + 1)(x + 3)} \cdot \dfrac{(x + 3)(x + 1)}{x + 4}$

21. $\dfrac{5y - 20}{3y + 15} \cdot \dfrac{7y + 35}{10y + 40}$

22. $\dfrac{3x^3}{x^2 - 25} \cdot \dfrac{x^2 + 6x + 5}{x^2}$

23. $\dfrac{3y + 3}{6y + 12} \div \dfrac{18}{5y + 5}$

24. $\dfrac{6x + 6}{7} \div \dfrac{4x + 4}{x - 2}$

25. $\dfrac{y^2 - 2y}{y^2 + 7y - 18} \cdot \dfrac{y^2 - 81}{y^2 - 11y + 18}$

26. $\dfrac{(y + 6)^2}{y^2 - 36} \cdot \dfrac{3y - 18}{2y + 12}$

27. $\dfrac{y^2 - 49}{(y - 7)^2} \div \dfrac{5y + 35}{y^2 - 7y}$

28. $\dfrac{x^2 - 3x - 10}{2x^2 - 11x + 5} \div \dfrac{x^2 - 5x + 6}{2x^2 - 7x + 3}$

29. $\dfrac{x^2 - 5x + 4}{x^2 - 1} \cdot \dfrac{x^2 + 5x + 4}{x^2 - 9}$

30. $\dfrac{x^2 - 5x}{x^2 + 3x} \cdot \dfrac{x + 3}{x - 5}$

31. $\dfrac{x^2 - 4}{x^2 + 6x + 9} \cdot \dfrac{x^2 - 9}{x^2 + 4x + 4}$

32. $\dfrac{x^2 - 6x}{x^2 - 36} \cdot \dfrac{x + 6}{x^2}$

33. $\dfrac{x^2 + 10x + 16}{x^2 - 6x - 16} \div \dfrac{x + 8}{x^2 - 64}$

34. $\dfrac{5y}{2x^2} \div \dfrac{5y^2}{8x^2}$

35. $\dfrac{6x^2 - 32x + 10}{3x^2 - 15x} \div \dfrac{3x^2 + 11x - 4}{2x^2 - 32}$

36. $\dfrac{7x^4}{24y^5} \div \dfrac{21x}{12y^4}$

37. $\dfrac{2x + 4}{10x} \cdot \dfrac{15x^2}{x + 2}$

38. $\dfrac{x^2 + 6x}{3x^2 + 6x - 24} \cdot \dfrac{x^2 + 2x - 8}{x + 6}$

39. $\dfrac{x^2 - 5x + 4}{x^2 + 3x - 28} \cdot \dfrac{x^2 + 2x - 3}{x^2 + 10x + 21}$

40. $\dfrac{x^2 + 2x + 1}{x^2 - 1} \cdot \dfrac{x^2 + 3x + 2}{x^2 + 4x + 4}$

Reteaching 9-5

Adding and Subtracting Rational Expressions

OBJECTIVE: Adding and subtracting rational expressions

MATERIALS: None

- To find the sum or difference of two rational expressions with like denominators, simply add or subtract their numerators. Then write the answer over the common denominator.

- To find the sum or difference of two rational expressions with unlike denominators, first find the least common denominator. Then multiply each fraction by the factors needed to get the least common denominator. Remember, the factor(s) multiplied should always be in fraction form and equivalent to 1—for example, $\frac{x+1}{x+1}$.

Example

Subtract: $\frac{2x}{3x+5} - \frac{14}{x+7}$. Simplify, if possible.

$$\frac{2x}{3x+5} - \frac{14}{x+7}$$

$$\frac{2x}{(3x+5)} - \frac{14}{(x+7)} \qquad \longleftarrow \quad \textbf{Circle the factors multiplied to get the least common denominator.}$$

$$= \frac{2x(x+7)}{(3x+5)(x+7)} - \frac{14(3x+5)}{(3x+5)(x+7)} \qquad \longleftarrow \quad \textbf{Multiply as necessary to rewrite with the least common denominator.}$$

$$= \frac{(2x^2+14x)}{(3x+5)(x+7)} - \frac{(42x+70)}{(3x+5)(x+7)} \qquad \longleftarrow \quad \textbf{Use the Distributive Property in the numerator.}$$

$$= \frac{2x^2+14x-42x-70}{(3x+5)(x+7)} \qquad \longleftarrow \quad \textbf{Subtract the numerators of the fractions.}$$

$$= \frac{2x^2-28x-70}{(3x+5)(x+7)} \qquad \longleftarrow \quad \textbf{Combine like terms.}$$

The difference is $\frac{2x^2-28x-70}{(3x+5)(x+7)}$.

Exercises

Add or subtract. Simplify, if possible.

1. $\frac{3}{2a+3} + \frac{2a}{2a+3}$

2. $\frac{y}{y-1} + \frac{2}{1-y}$

3. $\frac{3}{x+2} + \frac{2}{x^2-4}$

4. $\frac{y}{y^2-y-20} + \frac{2}{y+4}$

5. $\frac{x}{x^2+5x+6} - \frac{2}{x^2+3x+2}$

6. $\frac{4x+1}{x^2-4} - \frac{3}{x-2}$

7. $-\frac{2}{7x} - \frac{5}{4x}$

8. $\frac{12x^2-x+9}{3x+33} - \frac{16}{x+11}$

9. $\frac{4}{x^2+3x} + \frac{5}{x^3-2x^2}$

Practice 9-5

Adding and Subtracting Rational Expressions

Find the least common multiple of each pair of polynomials.

1. $3x(x + 2)$ and $6x(2x - 3)$

2. $2x^2 - 8x + 8$ and $3x^2 + 27x - 30$

3. $4x^2 + 12x + 9$ and $4x^2 - 9$

4. $2x^2 - 18$ and $5x^3 + 30x^2 + 45x$

Simplify.

5. $\dfrac{x^2}{5} + \dfrac{x^2}{5}$

6. $\dfrac{x^2 - 2}{12} + \dfrac{x}{6}$

7. $\dfrac{12}{xy^3} - \dfrac{9}{xy^3}$

8. $-\dfrac{2}{n + 4} - \dfrac{n^2}{n^2 - 16}$

9. $\dfrac{x}{9} - \dfrac{2x}{9}$

10. $\dfrac{2y + 1}{3y} + \dfrac{5y + 4}{3y}$

11. $\dfrac{6y - 4}{y^2 - 5} + \dfrac{3y + 1}{y^2 - 5}$

12. $\dfrac{6}{5x^2y} + \dfrac{5}{10xy^2}$

13. $\dfrac{3}{8x^3y^3} - \dfrac{1}{4xy}$

14. $\dfrac{4}{x^2 - 25} + \dfrac{6}{x^2 + 6x + 5}$

15. $\dfrac{3}{7x^2y} + \dfrac{4}{21xy^2}$

16. $\dfrac{xy - y}{x - 2} - \dfrac{y}{x + 2}$

17. $\dfrac{x + 2}{x^2 + 4x + 4} + \dfrac{2}{x + 2}$

18. $\dfrac{3}{x^2 - x - 6} + \dfrac{2}{x^2 + 6x + 5}$

19. $\dfrac{1}{6x^2 - 11x + 3} + \dfrac{1}{8x^2 - 18}$

20. $\dfrac{4}{x^2 - 3x} + \dfrac{6}{3x - 9}$

21. $\dfrac{3}{x^2 + 3x - 10} + \dfrac{1}{x^2 + 6x + 5}$

22. $\dfrac{3}{x - 9} + 4x$

23. $3 - \dfrac{1}{x^2 + 5}$

24. $5 + \dfrac{1}{x^2 - 5x + 6}$

25. $1 + \dfrac{2x + 7}{3x - 1}$

26. $\dfrac{2a}{a + 2} + \dfrac{3a}{a - 2}$

27. $\dfrac{4c}{c - 3} + \dfrac{4c}{c + 3}$

28. $\dfrac{f + 1}{fgh} + \dfrac{f - 1}{fgh}$

29. $\dfrac{2 - t}{t - 5} + \dfrac{2 + t}{t + 5}$

30. $\dfrac{4r}{r - 2} + \dfrac{4r}{r + 2}$

31. $\dfrac{x - y}{x + y} + \dfrac{y}{x}$

32. $\dfrac{\frac{2}{x}}{\frac{3}{y}}$

33. $\dfrac{1 + \frac{2}{x}}{4 - \frac{6}{x}}$

34. $\dfrac{\frac{1}{x - 2}}{2 + \frac{1}{x}}$

35. $\dfrac{y}{4y + 8} - \dfrac{1}{y^2 + 2y}$

36. $\dfrac{1 + \frac{2}{3}}{\frac{4}{9}}$

37. $\dfrac{6x^2}{3x - 2} + \dfrac{5x - 6}{3x - 2}$

38. $\dfrac{\frac{3}{x + 1}}{\frac{5}{x - 1}}$

39. $\dfrac{\frac{2}{x} + 6}{\frac{1}{y}}$

40. $\dfrac{2y}{y^2 - 4y - 12} + \dfrac{y}{y^2 - 10y + 24}$

41. The total resistance for a parallel circuit is given by

$$\frac{1}{R} = \frac{1}{R_1} + \frac{1}{R_2} + \frac{1}{R_3}.$$

a. If $R = 1$ ohm, $R_2 = 6$ ohms, and $R_3 = 8$ ohms, find R_1.

b. If $R_1 = 3$ ohms, $R_2 = 4$ ohms, and $R_3 = 6$ ohms, find R.

Reteaching 9-6
Solving Rational Equations

| OBJECTIVE: Solving rational equations | MATERIALS: None |

- When one side of a rational equation has a sum or difference, multiply each side by the LCD. This eliminates the fractions.

Example

Solve the equation.

$$\frac{6}{x} + \frac{x}{2} = 4$$

$$2x\left(\frac{6}{x}\right) + 2x\left(\frac{x}{2}\right) = 2x(4) \quad \longleftarrow \text{ Multiply the LCD, } 2x, \text{ by each term.}$$

$$2x\left(\frac{6}{x}\right) + 2x\left(\frac{x}{2}\right) = 2x(4) \quad \longleftarrow \text{ Cancel where possible.}$$

$$12 + x^2 = 8x \quad \longleftarrow \text{ Simplify.}$$

$$x^2 - 8x + 12 = 0 \quad \longleftarrow \text{ Write the equation in standard form.}$$

$$(x - 2)(x - 6) = 0 \quad \longleftarrow \text{ Factor.}$$

$$x - 2 = 0 \quad x - 6 = 0 \quad \longleftarrow \text{ Use the Zero-Product Property to solve for } x.$$

$$x = 2 \quad x = 6$$

Exercises

Solve each equation. Check each solution.

1. $\frac{10}{x + 3} + \frac{10}{3} = 6$

2. $-\frac{1}{x - 3} = \frac{x - 4}{x^2 - 27}$

3. $\frac{6}{x - 1} + \frac{2x}{x - 2} = 2$

4. $\frac{7}{3x - 12} - \frac{1}{x - 4} = \frac{2}{3}$

5. $\frac{2x}{5} = \frac{x^2 - 5x}{5x}$

6. $\frac{8(x - 1)}{x^2 - 4} = \frac{4}{x - 2}$

7. $x + \frac{4}{x} = \frac{25}{6}$

8. $\frac{2}{x} + \frac{6}{x - 1} = \frac{6}{x^2 - x}$

9. $\frac{2}{x} + \frac{1}{x} = 3$

10. $\frac{4}{x - 1} = \frac{5}{x - 1} + 2$

11. $\frac{1}{x} = \frac{5}{2x} + 3$

12. $\frac{x + 6}{5} = \frac{2x - 4}{5} - 3$

13. Quinn can refinish hardwood floors four times as fast as Jack. They have to refinish 100 ft² of flooring. Working together, Quinn and Jack can finish the job in 3 hours. How long would it take each of them working alone?

Practice 9-6

Solving Rational Equations

Solve each equation. Check each solution.

1. $\frac{1}{x} = \frac{x}{9}$

2. $\frac{4}{x} = \frac{x}{4}$

3. $\frac{3x}{4} = \frac{5x + 1}{3}$

4. $-\frac{4}{x + 1} = \frac{5}{3x + 1}$

5. $\frac{3}{2x - 3} = \frac{1}{5 - 2x}$

6. $\frac{x - 4}{3} = \frac{x - 2}{2}$

7. $\frac{3}{1 - x} = \frac{2}{1 + x}$

8. $\frac{2x - 3}{4} = \frac{2x - 5}{6}$

9. $\frac{1}{x} = \frac{2}{x + 3}$

10. $\frac{x - 1}{6} = \frac{x}{4}$

11. $\frac{3 - x}{6} = \frac{6 - x}{12}$

12. $\frac{4}{x + 3} = \frac{10}{2x - 1}$

13. $\frac{x - 2}{10} = \frac{x - 7}{5}$

14. $\frac{3}{3 - x} = \frac{4}{2 - x}$

15. $\frac{1}{4 - 5x} = \frac{3}{x + 9}$

16. $x + \frac{10}{x - 2} = \frac{x^2 + 3x}{x - 2}$

17. $\frac{2}{x + 3} + \frac{5}{3 - x} = \frac{6}{x^2 - 9}$

18. $\frac{1}{2x + 2} + \frac{5}{x^2 - 1} = \frac{1}{x - 1}$

19. $\frac{2}{6x + 2} = \frac{x}{3x^2 + 11}$

20. $\frac{3}{2x - 4} = \frac{5}{3x + 7}$

21. $\frac{2y}{5} + \frac{2}{6} = \frac{y}{2} - \frac{1}{6}$

22. $\frac{1}{2x + 2} = \frac{1}{x - 1}$

23. $\frac{2}{x + 2} + \frac{5}{x - 2} = \frac{6}{x^2 - 4}$

24. $5 + \frac{5}{x} = \frac{6}{5x}$

25. $\frac{4}{x - 1} = \frac{5}{x - 2}$

26. $\frac{2x - 1}{x + 3} = \frac{5}{3}$

27. $\frac{7}{2} = \frac{7x}{8} - 4$

28. $5 - \frac{4}{x + 1} = 6$

29. $\frac{x}{x + 3} - \frac{x}{x - 3} = \frac{x^2 + 9}{x^2 - 9}$

30. $\frac{x}{3} + \frac{x}{2} = 10$

31. $\frac{2}{3} + \frac{3x - 1}{6} = \frac{5}{2}$

32. $4 + \frac{2y}{y - 5} = \frac{8}{y - 5}$

33. $\frac{4}{x - 3} = \frac{2}{x + 1} + \frac{16}{x^2 - 2x - 3}$

34. $\frac{7}{x^2 - 5x} + \frac{2}{x} = \frac{3}{2x - 10}$

35. $\frac{x + 3}{x^2 + 3x - 4} = \frac{x + 2}{x^2 - 16}$

36. $\frac{3y}{5} + \frac{1}{2} = \frac{y}{10}$

37. A round trip flight took 3.9 h flying time. The plane traveled the 510 mi to the city at 255 mi/h with no wind. How strong was the wind on the return flight? Was the wind a head wind or a tail wind?

38. A round trip flight took 5 h flying time. The plane traveled the 720 mi to the city at 295 mi/h with no wind. How strong was the wind on the return flight? Was the wind a head wind or a tail wind?

39. If one student can complete the decorations for the prom in 5 days working alone, another student could do it in 3 days, and a third could do it in 4 days, how long would it take them working together?

40. Tom and Huck start a business painting fences. They paint Aunt Polly's fence and find that they can paint a 200-ft² fence in 40 min if they work together. If Huck works four times faster than Tom, how long would it take each of them to paint a 500-ft² fence working alone?

Algebra 2 Chapter 9

Reteaching 9-7

OBJECTIVE: Finding probabilities of multiple events

MATERIALS: Colored pencils

Example

Find the probability. A cage at the pet store contains ten white mice. Out of the ten, there are four females and six males. There are also ten black mice, of which six are female and four are male. Suppose you reach into the cage and randomly pick one mouse. What is the probability that the one you selected is female or black?

Step 1: Make a table of possibilities. These are events that can happen at the same time. The events are not mutually exclusive.

Step 2: Find P(female) by putting a circle around each female mouse.

$$P\text{(female)} = \frac{10}{20} = \frac{1}{2}$$

Step 3: Find P(black) by putting an "X" through each black mouse.

$$P\text{(black)} = \frac{10}{20} = \frac{1}{2}$$

ⓕ w	ⓕ w	ⓕ w	ⓕ w
m w	m w	m w	m w
m w	m w	ⓕ ✗	ⓕ ✗
ⓕ ✗	ⓕ ✗	ⓕ ✗	ⓕ ✗
m ✗	m ✗	m ✗	m ✗

Step 4: Find the events that have both a circle and an "X."

$$P\text{(female and black)} = \frac{6}{20} = \frac{3}{10}$$

Step 5: Use the formula $P(A \text{ or } B) = P(A) + P(B) - P(A \text{ and } B)$ to find P(female or black).

$$\frac{10}{20} + \frac{10}{20} - \frac{6}{20} = \frac{14}{20} = \frac{7}{10}, \text{ or } 70\%$$

The probability that you select a mouse that is female or black is 70%.

Exercises

Find the probability of each event.

1. Use the information from the example above to find the probability of selecting a mouse that is either white or male. Use the same table, but use a pencil of a different color.

2. A bag of marbles contains 13 marbles that are opaque and 32 marbles that are translucent. Of the opaque marbles, 3 are red, 5 are blue, and 5 are green. Of the translucent marbles, 8 are red, 12 are blue and 12 are green. What is the probability that you randomly pick a marble that is red or opaque?

3. Use the table you constructed for Exercise 2 and a different color marker to find the probability that you randomly pick a marble that is green or translucent.

Practice 9-7

Integers from 1 to 100 are randomly selected. State whether the events are mutually exclusive.

1. Even integers and multiples of 3

2. Integers less than 40 and integers greater than 50

3. Odd integers and multiples of 4

4. Integers less than 50 and integers greater than 40

Classify each pair of events as *dependent* or *independent*.

5. A member of the junior class and a second member of the same class are randomly selected.

6. A member of the junior class and a member of another class are randomly chosen.

7. An odd-numbered problem is assigned for homework, and an even-numbered problem is picked for a test.

8. The sum and the product of two rolls of a number cube

Find each probability.

9. A flavored-water company wants to know how many people prefer its new lemon-flavored water over two competitors' brands. The company hires you to survey 1000 people and ask them to rank the three drinks in order of preference. After conducting the survey, you find that 35% prefer the lemon-flavored water over Competitor A, 38% prefer the lemon-flavored water over Competitor B, and 47% did not prefer the lemon-flavored water over either competitor's brand. What is the probability that someone prefers the lemon-flavored water over both competitors' brands?

10. A natural number from 1 to 10 is randomly chosen.
   a. $P(\text{even or } 7)$
   b. $P(\text{even or odd})$
   c. $P(\text{multiple of 2 or multiple of 3})$
   d. $P(\text{odd or less than 3})$

11. A standard number cube is tossed.
   a. $P(\text{even or } 3)$
   b. $P(\text{less than 2 or even})$
   c. $P(\text{prime or } 4)$
   d. $P(2 \text{ or greater than } 6)$

12. Only 93% of the airplane parts Salome is examining pass inspection. What is the probability that all of the next five parts pass inspection?

13. There is a 50% chance of thunderstorms the next three days. What is the probability that there will be thunderstorms each of the next three days?

***Q* and *R* are independent events. Find *P(Q and R)*.**

14. $P(Q) = \frac{1}{8}, P(R) = \frac{2}{5}$

15. $P(Q) = 0.8, P(R) = 0.2$

16. $P(Q) = \frac{1}{4}, P(R) = \frac{1}{5}$

***M* and *N* are mutually exclusive events. Find *P(M or N)*.**

17. $P(M) = \frac{3}{4}, P(N) = \frac{1}{6}$

18. $P(M) = 10\%, P(N) = 45\%$

19. $P(M) = \frac{1}{5}, P(N) = 18\%$

Reteaching 10-1

OBJECTIVE: Graphing conic sections	**MATERIALS:** Graph paper

- To graph a conic section, make a table of values, and plot the points associated with those values.

- In the case of a circle or ellipse, connect the points with a smooth curve.

- In the case of hyperbola, connect the points with two smooth curves.

- Determine the lines of symmetry, the domain, and the range from the graph.

Example

Graph the equation $4x^2 + 9y^2 = 36$. Identify the conic section and its lines of symmetry. Then find the domain and range.

Make a table of values.

x	-3	-2	-1	0	1	2	3
y	0	±1.5	±1.9	±2	±1.9	±1.5	0

← Substitute each x-value into the equation. Solve for y.

Plot the points, and connect them with a smooth curve.

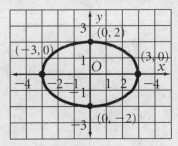

← **The graph should be symmetric.**

The graph shows that the equation is an ellipse. It has two lines of symmetry: the x-axis and the y-axis.

The domain is $\{x \mid -3 \le x \le 3\}$. The range is $\{y \mid -2 \le y \le 2\}$.

Exercises

Graph each equation. Identify the conic section and its lines of symmetry. Then find the domain and range.

1. $25x^2 + 4y^2 = 100$ **2.** $x^2 + y^2 = 36$ **3.** $4x^2 - y^2 = 16$

4. $3x^2 + 3y^2 = 27$ **5.** $9x^2 + 4y^2 = 36$ **6.** $5x^2 - 4y^2 = 80$

Practice 10-1

Exploring Conic Sections

Identify the center and intercepts of each conic section. Give the domain and range of each graph.

1.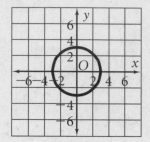

2.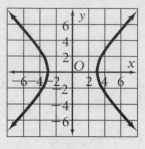

3.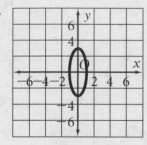

4.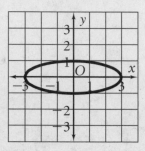

5.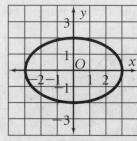

6.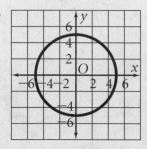

Graph each equation. Identify the conic section and its lines of symmetry. Then find the domain and range.

7. $x^2 + 4y^2 = 4$

8. $4x^2 + y^2 - 4 = 0$

9. $9x^2 + 4y^2 = 36$

10. $x^2 - y^2 = 4$

11. $x^2 - y^2 - 9 = 0$

12. $4x^2 - 9y^2 - 36 = 0$

13. $5x^2 + 5y^2 = 45$

14. $2x^2 + 2y^2 - 4 = 0$

15. $8x^2 + 8y^2 = 40$

16. $3x^2 + 6y^2 - 6 = 0$

17. $3x^2 - 6y^2 = 6$

18. $6y^2 - 3x^2 - 6 = 0$

19. $5x^2 - 5y^2 = 25$

20. $5x^2 + 5y^2 = 125$

21. $9x^2 + 16y^2 = 144$

22. $16y^2 - 9x^2 = 144$

23. $9x^2 - 16y^2 = 144$

24. $9x^2 + 9y^2 = 1$

25. $x^2 - y^2 = 49$

26. $2x^2 + 2y^2 - 32 = 0$

27. $2x^2 + 8y^2 = 32$

28. $y^2 - x^2 + 4 = 0$

29. $49x^2 - y^2 - 48 = 1$

30. $x^2 + y^2 - 40 = 9$

31. $5x^2 - 5y^2 - 45 = 0$

32. $25x^2 + y^2 = 25$

33. $9x^2 + 36y^2 = 36$

34. $25x^2 - y^2 - 25 = 0$

35. $y^2 - x^2 = 9$

36. $4y^2 - 9x^2 = 36$

37. $x^2 + y^2 = 4$

38. $x^2 + y^2 = 36$

39. $3x^2 + 3y^2 - 9 = 0$

40. $4x^2 + 9y^2 - 36 = 0$

41. $6x^2 + y^2 - 12 = 0$

42. $9x^2 + y^2 = 9$

Reteaching 10-2

OBJECTIVE: Graphing parabolas	**MATERIALS:** Graph paper

Example

Graph the equation $y = -\frac{1}{2}x^2$. Include the vertex, focus, and directrix on your graph.

Step 1:

Identify information from the given equation.

$y = -\frac{1}{2}x^2$

$a < 0$ ⟵ ***a* is negative.**
opens downward   ⟵ **When *a* is**
focus: $(0, -c)$ **negative, the**
directrix: $y = c$ **parabola has these**
  characteristics.

Step 2:

Find *c*.

$|a| = \frac{1}{4c}$ ⟵ **True for all parabolas.**

$\left|-\frac{1}{2}\right| = \frac{1}{4c}$ ⟵ **Substitute $-\frac{1}{2}$ for *a*.**

$(2c)\left|-\frac{1}{2}\right| = (2c)\frac{1}{4c} = \frac{1}{2}$ ⟵ **Solve for *c*.**

Step 3:

Find the vertex, the focus, and the equation of the directrix.

$(0, 0)$ ⟵ **The parabola is of the form $y = ax^2$, so the vertex is at the origin.**

$\left(0, -\frac{1}{2}\right)$ ⟵ **The focus is always $(0, -c)$.**

$y = \frac{1}{2}$ ⟵ **The directrix is at $y = c$.**

Step 4:

Locate two more points on the parabola.

$y = -\frac{1}{2}(1)^2$
$y = -\frac{1}{2}$ ⟵ **Substitute 1 for *x*.**
$\left(1, -\frac{1}{2}\right)$ ⟵ **Solve for *y*.**
$y = -\frac{1}{2}(-1)^2$
$y = -\frac{1}{2}$ ⟵ **Substitute –1 for *x*.**
$\left(-1, -\frac{1}{2}\right)$ ⟵ **Solve for *y*.**

Step 5:

Graph the parabola using the information you found.

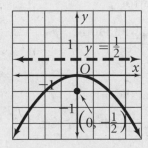

Exercises

Graph each equation. Include the vertex, focus, and directrix on each graph.

1. $y = \frac{1}{4}x^2$ **2.** $y = -\frac{1}{6}x^2$ **3.** $x = -\frac{1}{3}y^2$

4. $x = \frac{3}{4}y^2$ **5.** $y = x^2$ **6.** $x = \frac{1}{2}y^2$

Practice 10-2
.... **Parabolas**

Determine whether each parabola opens upward, downward, to the left, or to the right.

1. $x = -2y^2$ **2.** $y = -6x^2$ **3.** $-8x = y^2$ **4.** $-2y = -3x^2$

5. $-2y + x^2 = 0$ **6.** $2x + 6y^2 = 0$ **7.** $-3x + 4y^2 = 0$ **8.** $y + 12x^2 = 0$

Identify the focus and the directrix of the graph of each equation.

9. $y = -\frac{1}{32}x^2$ **10.** $y = -8x^2$ **11.** $x = \frac{1}{3}y^2$ **12.** $x = 12y^2$

13. $y + 3x^2 = 0$ **14.** $x - 5y^2 = 0$ **15.** $-y + x^2 = 3$ **16.** $-x - 3y^2 = 0$

17. $8x = y^2 + 6y + 9$ **18.** $\frac{1}{8}x = y^2$ **19.** $-8y = -x^2$ **20.** $-\frac{1}{8}y = -x^2$

Write an equation of a parabola with vertex at the origin.

21. focus at $(-2, 0)$ **22.** focus at $(0, 4)$ **23.** directrix at $x = 3$ **24.** directrix at $y = 4$

25. focus at $(0, -3)$ **26.** directrix at $x = -2$ **27.** directrix at $y = -3$ **28.** focus at $(3, 0)$

29. directrix at $x = 6$ **30.** focus at $(-5, 0)$ **31.** focus at $(0, 5)$ **32.** directrix at $y = -7$

Write the equation whose graph is the set of all points in the plane equidistant from the given point and the given line.

33. $F(0, 8)$ and $y = -8$ **34.** $F(1, 0)$ and $x = -1$ **35.** $F(6, 0)$ and $x = -6$

36. $F(0, -4)$ and $y = 4$ **37.** $F(0, 1)$ and $y = -1$ **38.** $F(-3, 0)$ and $x = 3$

39. $F(-1, 0)$ and $x = 1$ **40.** $F(-10, 0)$ and $x = 10$ **41.** $F(0, -3)$ and $y = 3$

42. $F(5, 0)$ and $x = -5$ **43.** $F(0, 5)$ and $y = -5$ **44.** $F(3, 0)$ and $x = -3$

45. A pipe with a diameter of 0.5 in. is located 10 in. from a mirror used as a parabolic solar collector. The pipe is at the focus of the parabola.

   a. Write an equation to model the cross section of the mirror.

   b. The pipe receives 25 times more sunlight than it would without the mirror. The amount of light collected by the mirror is directly proportional to its diameter. Find the width of the mirror.

Write an equation of a parabola opening upward with a vertex at the origin.

46. focus 2 units from vertex   **47.** focus $\frac{1}{4}$ unit from vertex

Identify the vertex, focus, and directrix of the graph of each equation. Then sketch the graph.

48. $y + 1 = -\frac{1}{4}(x - 3)^2$ **49.** $x = 2y^2$ **50.** $y^2 - 4x - 2y = 3$

Reteaching 10-3

OBJECTIVE: Finding the center and radius of a circle   **MATERIALS:** None

- When working with circles, begin by writing the equation in standard form:

$$(x - h)^2 + (y - k)^2 = r^2$$

- Unlike equations of parabolas, which include either x^2 or y^2, the equation of a circle will include both x^2 and y^2.

Example

Find the radius and center of the circle with equation $(x - 2)^2 + (x + 3)^2 = 16$.

$(x - 2)^2 + (y + 3)^2 = 16$	← **The given equation is in standard form.**
$(x - 2)^2 + (y - (-3))^2 = 16$	← **Because standard form has $(y - k)$, change the addition to subtraction.**
$h = 2, k = -3$	← **Find h and k.**
$(2, -3)$	← **The center is (h, k).**
$r^2 = 16$	← **Find r.**
$r = 4$	← **Take the square root of each side. Since radius is a distance, ignore the negative value.**

The center is $(2, -3)$ and the radius is 4.

Exercises

Find the radius and center of each circle.

1. $(x - 5)^2 + (y - 2)^2 = 9$ **2.** $(x + 8)^2 + (y - 4)^2 = 8$

3. $(x - 4)^2 + (y + 3)^2 = 20$ **4.** $(x - 3)^2 + y^2 = 6$

5. $x^2 + (y - 5)^2 = 25$ **6.** $(x + 6)^2 + (y + 7)^2 = 1$

7. $(x + 1)^2 + (y + 2)^2 = 36$ **8.** $(x - 2)^2 + (y - 5)^2 = 4$

9. $x^2 + y^2 = 4$ **10.** $(x - 1)^2 + (y + 3)^2 = 9$

11. $(x - 2)^2 + (y - 3)^2 = 12$ **12.** $(x + 1)^2 + (y - 3)^2 = 25$

13. $x^2 + (y + 3)^2 = 45$ **14.** $(x + 4)^2 + y^2 = 63$

15. $(x + 2)^2 + (y - 6)^2 = 75$ **16.** $(x - 7)^2 + (y + 3)^2 = 18$

17. $(x - 4)^2 + (y + 1)^2 = 24$ **18.** $(x + 9)^2 + (y - 9)^2 = 81$

Practice 10-3

Circles

Write an equation in standard form for each circle.

1.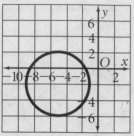

2.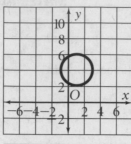

3.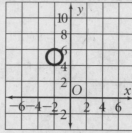

4.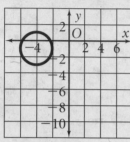

5.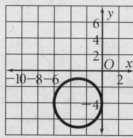

6.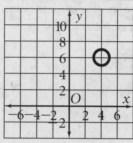

Write an equation of a circle with the given center and radius. Check your answers.

7. center $(0, 0)$, radius 3

8. center $(0, 1)$, radius 2

9. center $(-1, 0)$, radius 6

10. center $(2, 0)$, radius 1

11. center $(0, -3)$, radius 5

12. center $(4, -4)$, radius 1.5

13. center $(-2, 6)$, radius 4

14. center $(5, -1)$, radius 1.1

15. center $(1, -5)$, radius 2.5

16. center $(2, 3)$, diameter 1

Write an equation for each translation.

17. $x^2 + y^2 = 9$; right 4 and down 2

18. $x^2 + y^2 = 12$; left 2 and up 5

19. $x^2 + y^2 = 49$; right 1 and up 7

20. $x^2 + y^2 = 1$; right 5 and up 5

21. $x^2 + y^2 = 25$; up 10

22. $x^2 + y^2 = 36$; left 8 and down 6

Find the center and radius of each circle.

23. $(x + 1)^2 + (y - 8)^2 = 1$

24. $x^2 + (y + 3)^2 = 9$

25. $(x + 3)^2 + (y + 1)^2 = 2$

26. $(x - 6)^2 + y^2 = 5$

27. $(x - 6)^2 + (y - 9)^2 = 4$

28. $x^2 + y^2 = 144$

Use the center and radius to graph each circle.

29. $(x + 9)^2 + (y - 2)^2 = 81$

30. $x^2 + (y + 3)^2 = 121$

31. $(x - 8)^2 + (y + 9)^2 = 64$

32. $(x + 8)^2 + y^2 = 49$

33. $(x - 6)^2 + (y - 3)^2 = 75$

34. $(x + 9)^2 + (y + 9)^2 = 36$

35. $(x + 7)^2 + (y + 2)^2 = 80$

36. $(x - 5)^2 + (y + 7)^2 = 25$

Algebra 2 Chapter 10

Reteaching 10-4

Ellipses

> **OBJECTIVE:** Writing the equation of an ellipse   **MATERIALS:** None

To find the standard form of the equation of an ellipse with center at $(0, 0)$, major axis of length $2a$, and minor axis of length $2b$, where $a > b$, use the following:

- When the width is greater than the height, use $\dfrac{x^2}{a^2} + \dfrac{y^2}{b^2} = 1$.
- When the height is greater than the width, use $\dfrac{x^2}{b^2} + \dfrac{y^2}{a^2} = 1$.

Example

Find the equation of an ellipse that is 10 units wide and 8 units high. Assume that the center is $(0, 0)$.

$\dfrac{x^2}{a^2} + \dfrac{y^2}{b^2} = 1$ ⟵ **Since the width is greater than the height, use the standard form of a horizontal ellipse.**

$2a = 10 \qquad 2b = 8$ ⟵ **Find a and b.**

$a = 5 \qquad\quad b = 4$

$a^2 = 25 \qquad b^2 = 16$ ⟵ **Find a^2 and b^2.**

$\dfrac{x^2}{25} + \dfrac{y^2}{16} = 1$ ⟵ **Substitute 25 for a^2 and 16 for b^2.**

Exercises

Find the equation of the ellipse given the height and width. Assume that the center of the ellipse is $(0, 0)$.

1. height 26 ft, width 24 ft   **2.** height 12 ft, width 4 ft   **3.** height 10 ft, width 6 ft

4. height 6 ft, width 18 ft   **5.** height 20 m, width 50 m   **6.** height 10 ft, width 22 ft

7. height 16 m, width 18 m   **8.** height 20 ft, width 3 ft   **9.** height 3 cm, width 6 cm

10. height 14 m, width 30 m   **11.** height 12 ft, width 9 ft   **12.** height 12 in., width 4 in.

13. height 7 m, width 8 m   **14.** height 2 in., width 10 in.   **15.** height 16 cm, width 9 cm

16. Australian Rules Football is played on an elliptical field. One of the fields used for this sport is 174 meters long and 148 meters wide. Find an equation of the ellipse.

Practice 10-4

Find the foci for each equation of an ellipse. Then graph the ellipse.

1. $\dfrac{x^2}{36} + \dfrac{y^2}{81} = 1$

2. $x^2 + \dfrac{y^2}{36} = 1$

3. $\dfrac{x^2}{9} + \dfrac{y^2}{100} = 1$

4. $16x^2 + 25y^2 = 1600$

5. $4x^2 + y^2 = 49$

6. $\dfrac{x^2}{64} + \dfrac{y^2}{144} = 1$

7. $9x^2 + 25y^2 = 225$

8. $25x^2 + 4y^2 = 100$

9. $\dfrac{x^2}{81} + \dfrac{y^2}{9} = 1$

10. $\dfrac{x^2}{121} + \dfrac{y^2}{4} = 1$

11. $49x^2 + y^2 = 49$

12. $4x^2 + 9y^2 = 36$

13. $\dfrac{x^2}{4} + \dfrac{y^2}{9} = 1$

14. $\dfrac{x^2}{9} + \dfrac{y^2}{4} = 1$

15. $\dfrac{x^2}{16} + y^2 = 1$

16. $\dfrac{x^2}{25} + \dfrac{y^2}{36} = 1$

17. $\dfrac{x^2}{81} + \dfrac{y^2}{16} = 1$

18. $x^2 + \dfrac{y^2}{25} = 1$

19. $3x^2 + 9y^2 = 9$

20. $4x^2 + 8y^2 = 16$

21. $12x^2 + 4y^2 = 48$

Write an equation of each ellipse in standard form with center at the origin and with the given characteristics.

22. height 8; width 18

23. vertices $(\pm 4, 0)$; co-vertices $(0, \pm 2)$

24. foci $(\pm 5, 0)$; co-vertices $(0, \pm 2)$

25. foci $(0, \pm 2)$; co-vertices $(\pm 1, 0)$

26. foci $(\pm 3, 0)$; co-vertices $(0, \pm 1)$

27. height 10; width 8

28. height 3; width 1

29. vertices $(\pm 2, 0)$; co-vertices $(0, \pm 1)$

30. foci $(\pm 1, 0)$; co-vertices $(0, \pm 2)$

31. foci $(0, \pm 3)$; co-vertices $(\pm 3, 0)$

32. vertex $(6, 0)$; co-vertex $(0, -5)$

33. vertex $(0, 10)$; co-vertex $(-7, 0)$

34. height 28 ft; width 20 ft

35. height 20 ft; width 28 ft

36. height 50 ft; width 40 ft

37. height 9 cm; width 12 cm

38. vertex $(0, 2)$; co-vertex $(-1, 0)$

39. vertex $(4, 0)$; co-vertex $(0, 2)$

40. foci $(0, \pm 4)$; co-vertices $(\pm 4, 0)$

41. foci $(\pm 4, 0)$; co-vertices (0 ± 2)

42. vertex $(9, 0)$; co-vertex $(0, -6)$

43. vertex $(11, 0)$; co-vertex $(0, -10)$

44. foci $(\pm 2, 0)$; co-vertices $(0, \pm 4)$

45. foci $(\pm 1, 0)$; co-vertices $(0, \pm 5)$

46. foci $(\pm 3, 0)$; co-vertices $(0, \pm 3)$

47. foci $(0, \pm 2)$; co-vertices $(\pm 1, 0)$

48. vertex $(-7, 0)$; co-vertex $(0, -5)$

49. vertex $(-2, 0)$; co-vertex $(0, -1)$

50. Blinn College is building a new track for cycling teams. The track is to be elliptical. The available land is 200 yd long and 100 yd wide. Find the equation of the ellipse.

Name _____ Class _____ Date _____

Reteaching 10-5

OBJECTIVE: Graphing hyperbolas	**MATERIALS:** Graph paper

- Because the equation of a hyperbola involves subtraction, there are two possibilities for standard form. Put the positive variable first, and the result is either $\frac{x^2}{a^2} - \frac{y^2}{b^2} = 1$ or $\frac{y^2}{a^2} - \frac{x^2}{b^2} = 1$. Note that the a^2 is always the denominator of the first term.

- When the x^2-term is positive, the hyperbola opens to the left and to the right. When the y^2-term is positive, the hyperbola opens upward and downward.

Example

Graph $16y^2 - 9x^2 = 144$.

$\frac{y^2}{9} - \frac{x^2}{16} = 1$ ⟵ **Divide by 144 on each side of the equation.**

$\frac{y^2}{3^2} - \frac{x^2}{4^2} = 1$ ⟵ **Convert to standard form $\frac{y^2}{a^2} - \frac{x^2}{b^2} = 1$.**

$a = 3$ and $b = 4$ ⟵ **Find a and b.**

   ⟵ **Put points at ± 3 on the y-axis and at ± 4 on the x-axis. Use these to draw a central rectangle and the asymptotes.**

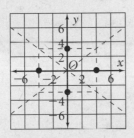

$3^2 + 4^2 = c^2$ ⟵ **Use $a^2 + b^2 = c^2$ to find c. Simplify.**

$c = \pm 5$

The foci are $(0, 5)$ and $(0, -5)$.   ⟵ **Find the foci using $(0, c)$ and $(0, -c)$.**

   ⟵ **Sketch the hyperbola using the vertices $(0, \pm 3)$.**

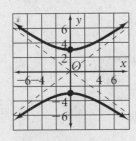

Exercises

Find the foci of each hyperbola. Then draw the graph.

1. $\frac{x^2}{9} - \frac{y^2}{1} = 1$ **2.** $\frac{y^2}{16} - \frac{x^2}{4} = 1$ **3.** $4x^2 - y^2 = 4$

4. $y^2 - 4x^2 = 4$ **5.** $x^2 - y^2 = 3$ **6.** $9y^2 - 25x^2 = 225$

Name _____ Class _____ Date _____

Practice 10-5

Hyperbolas

Find the foci of each graph. Then draw the graph.

1. $\frac{x^2}{4} - \frac{y^2}{4} = 1$

2. $\frac{y^2}{9} - \frac{x^2}{25} = 1$

3. $\frac{x^2}{49} - \frac{y^2}{36} = 1$

4. $4y^2 - 36x^2 = 144$

5. $x^2 - 9y^2 = 9$

6. $16x^2 - y^2 = 64$

7. $9y^2 - 16x^2 = 144$

8. $4x^2 - 9y^2 = 36$

9. $121y^2 - 4x^2 = 121$

10. $\frac{y^2}{16} - \frac{x^2}{9} = 1$

11. $\frac{x^2}{64} - \frac{y^2}{9} = 1$

12. $\frac{y^2}{100} - \frac{x^2}{4} = 1$

13. $25y^2 - 4x^2 = 100$

14. $49y^2 - x^2 = 49$

15. $4x^2 - 100y^2 = 100$

16. $\frac{x^2}{25} - \frac{y^2}{4} = 1$

17. $y^2 - \frac{x^2}{9} = 1$

18. $\frac{y^2}{25} - \frac{x^2}{16} = 1$

19. $\frac{y^2}{4} - \frac{x^2}{9} = 1$

20. $x^2 - \frac{y^2}{16} = 1$

21. $\frac{x^2}{4} - \frac{y^2}{16} = 1$

22. $\frac{x^2}{36} - y^2 = 1$

23. $\frac{x^2}{64} - \frac{y^2}{16} = 1$

24. $y^2 - x^2 = 16$

25. $y^2 - 4x^2 = 16$

26. $4x^2 - 4y^2 = 100$

27. $25x^2 - 4y^2 = 100$

28. $16y^2 - 4x^2 = 80$

29. $9y^2 - 4x^2 = 36$

30. $4x^2 - 36y^2 = 36$

31. $x^2 - 25y^2 = 25$

32. $4x^2 - y^2 = 16$

33. $9y^2 - 16x^2 = 225$

34. $16y^2 - 9x^2 = 225$

35. $4x^2 - 9y^2 = 36$

36. $9x^2 - 4y^2 = 36$

37. $\frac{y^2}{9} - x^2 = 1$

38. $\frac{x^2}{9} - \frac{y^2}{16} = 1$

39. $\frac{y^2}{4} - \frac{x^2}{16} = 1$

40. $\frac{x^2}{25} - \frac{y^2}{16} = 1$

41. $y^2 - \frac{x^2}{16} = 1$

42. $\frac{x^2}{9} - \frac{y^2}{36} = 1$

43. $4y^2 - 25x^2 = 100$

44. $y^2 - 4x^2 = 16$

45. $16x^2 - y^2 = 64$

Find the equation of a hyperbola with the given a and c values. Assume that the transverse axis is horizontal.

46. $a = 432{,}356, c = 1{,}984{,}576$

47. $a = 176{,}398, c = 1{,}984{,}576$

48. $a - 7, c = 9$

49. $a = 292{,}954, c = 365{,}987$

50. $a = 5, c = 15$

51. $a = 7654, c = 8675$

52. $a = 67, c = 92$

53. $a = 75, c = 180$

54. $a = 8, c = 20$

55. $a = 6, c - 9$

56. $a = 6, c = 10$

57. $a = 6, c = 8$

58. $a = 1, c = 9$

59. $a = 3, c = 7$

60. $a = 8, c = 10$

61. $a = 9, c = 12$

Algebra 2 Chapter 10

Reteaching 10-6

OBJECTIVE: Writing and identifying the equation of a translated conic section

MATERIALS: Graph paper

Example

Identify the conic section $4x^2 + 4y^2 + 20x - 16y + 37 = 0$.
Rewrite the equation in standard form. Then sketch the graph.

$$4x^2 + 4y^2 + 20x - 16y + 37 = 0$$

$$4x^2 + 20x + 4y^2 - 16y + 37 = 0 \qquad \longleftarrow \text{ Group the } x\text{- and } y\text{-terms.}$$

$$4x^2 + 20x + 4y^2 - 16y = -37 \qquad \longleftarrow \text{ Subtract 37 from each side.}$$

$$4(x^2 + 5x) + 4(y^2 - 4y) = -37 \qquad \longleftarrow \text{ Factor out coefficients of the } x^2\text{- and the } y^2\text{-terms.}$$

$$4\left(x^2 + 5x + \frac{25}{4}\right) + 4(y^2 - 4y + 4) = -37 + 25 + 16 \qquad \longleftarrow \text{ Complete the square.}$$

$$4\left(x + \frac{5}{2}\right)^2 + 4(y - 2)^2 = 4 \qquad \longleftarrow \text{ Simplify.}$$

$$\left(x + \frac{5}{2}\right)^2 + (y - 2)^2 = 1 \qquad \longleftarrow \text{ Divide each side by 4.}$$

There are no denominators, and both x and y have squared terms.
The equation fits the standard form of a circle. The center of the circle is
$\left(-\frac{5}{2}, 2\right)$ and the radius of the circle is 1.

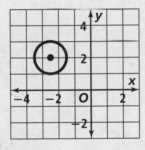

$\longleftarrow$ **Graph the center. Plot points 1 unit upward, downward, to the right and to the left from the center. Connect with a smooth curve.**

Exercises

Identify the conic section represented by each equation by writing the equation in standard form. Then sketch the graph.

1. $x^2 - 2x + 4y - 3 = 0$

2. $x^2 + 4y^2 + 6x - 8y + 9 = 0$

3. $9x^2 - 4y^2 + 18x + 16y - 43 = 0$

4. $x^2 + y^2 + 10x - 6y + 18 = 0$

5. $y^2 - 8x - 6y + 9 = 0$

6. $4x^2 + y^2 + 64x - 12y + 288 = 0$

7. $y^2 - 4x - 4y + 16 = 0$

8. $x^2 - 4y^2 - 2x - 8y - 7 = 0$

Practice 10-6

Identify the conic section represented by each equation by writing the equation in standard form. For a parabola, give the vertex. For a circle, give its center and radius. For an ellipse or hyperbola, give its center and foci. Sketch the graph.

1. $3x^2 + 6x + 5y^2 - 20y - 13 = 0$

2. $x^2 - 9y^2 + 36y - 45 = 0$

3. $x^2 + 4y^2 + 8x - 48 = 0$

4. $x^2 + y^2 - 8x - 4y + 19 = 0$

5. $x^2 + y^2 + 6y - 27 = 0$

6. $x^2 - 10x - 4y^2 + 24y - 15 = 0$

7. $16x^2 - 96x - 9y^2 + 36y - 36 = 0$

8. $10x^2 + 10y^2 - 70 = 0$

9. $x^2 + 2x + y^2 + 14y - 31 = 0$

10. $25x^2 + 50x - 9y^2 - 18y - 209 = 0$

11. $4x^2 - 16x + 4y^2 - 16y - 4 = 0$

12. $x^2 + 4y^2 - 4x + 8y = 0$

13. $x^2 - 10x + y^2 + 4y - 7 = 0$

14. $x^2 + 2x + y^2 - 10y - 38 = 0$

15. $x^2 - 2x - y + 3 = 0$

16. $x^2 + 6x - y + 7 = 0$

17. $x^2 + 8x + y^2 + 2y + 1 = 0$

18. $x^2 - y^2 - 4 = 0$

19. $y^2 + 2y - x + 3 = 0$

20. $x^2 - 4x + 3 - y = 0$

Write an equation of a conic section with the given characteristics.

21. circle with center $(-4, 5)$, radius 6

22. hyperbola with center $(-4, 5)$, one vertex $(-4, 7)$, one focus $(-4, 8)$

23. Points on the hyperbola are 96 units closer to one focus than to the other. The foci are located at $(0, 0)$ and $(100, 0)$.

24. parabola with vertex $(1, -2)$, x-intercept 3, and opens to the right

25. ellipse with center $(0, 2)$, horizontal major axis of length 6, minor axis of length 4

26. ellipse with center $(-4, -5)$, endpoints of major and minor axes $(-4, -7), (-4, -3), (-1, -5), (-7, -5)$

27. circle with center $(-1, 2)$, diameter 12

28. parabola with vertex $(-1, 5)$, y-intercept 4, and opens downward

29. hyperbola with vertices $(0, 2)$ and $(4, 2)$, foci $(-1, 2)$ and $(5, 2)$

30. ellipse with center $(2, -5)$, one end of each axis $(2, -9)$ and $(-3, -5)$

31. Points on the hyperbola are 12 units closer to one focus than to the other. The foci are located at $(0, 0)$ and $(250, 0)$.

32. ellipse with center $(0, -2)$, vertical major axis of length 5, minor axis of length 3

Reteaching 11-1

Mathematical Patterns

OBJECTIVE: Finding the nth term in a sequence	**MATERIALS:** None

Some patterns are much easier to determine than others. Here are some tips that can help with unfamiliar patterns.

- If the terms become progressively smaller, subtraction or division may be involved.

- If the terms become progressively larger, addition or multiplication may be involved.

Example

Find the next term in this sequence: 6, 8, 11, 15, 20, . . .

6   8   11   15   20   ⟵ **Spread the numbers in the sequence apart, leaving space between numbers.**

   +2   +3   +4   +5   ⟵ **Beneath each space, write what can be done to get the next number in the sequence.**

In each term, the number that is added   ⟵ **Find a pattern.**
to the previous term increases by one.

If the pattern is continued, the next term is 20 + 6, or 26.

Exercises

Describe the pattern that is formed. Find the next three terms.

  1. 38, 33, 28, 23, . . .   **2.** 7, 14, 28, 56, . . .   **3.** −5, −7, −9, −11, . . .

  4. 2, 6, 18, 54, . . .   **5.** 4.5, 5, 5.5, 6, . . .   **6.** 17, 19, 23, 29, . . .

Match each sequence on the left with a statement on the right.

  7. 9, 15, 21, 27, . . .   **A.** The next term in the sequence is −2.

  8. 9, 10.5, 13.5, 19.5, . . .   **B.** The sixth term is 39.

  9. 3, 2.5, 1.5, 0, . . .   **C.** Each term is one half of the previous term.

10. −4, 4, 12, 20, . . .   **D.** Each term is two times the previous term.

11. 32, 16, 8, 4, . . .   **E.** The fifth term is 31.5.

12. 2, 4, 8, 16, . . .   **F.** The eighth term is 52.

Practice 11-1

Write a recursive formula for each sequence. Then find the next term.

1. $-14, -8, -2, 4, 10, \ldots$

2. $6, 5.7, 5.4, 5.1, 4.8, \ldots$

3. $1, -2, 4, -8, 16, \ldots$

4. $1, 3, 9, 27, \ldots$

5. $1, \frac{1}{2}, \frac{1}{4}, \frac{1}{8}, \frac{1}{16}, \ldots$

6. $\frac{2}{3}, 1, 1\frac{1}{3}, 1\frac{2}{3}, 2, \ldots$

7. $36, 39, 42, 45, 48, \ldots$

8. $36, 30, 24, 18, 12, \ldots$

9. $9.6, 4.8, 2.4, 1.2, 0.6, \ldots$

Write an explicit formula for each sequence. Then find a_{20}.

10. $7, 14, 21, 28, 35, \ldots$

11. $2, 8, 14, 20, 26, \ldots$

12. $5, 6, 7, 8, 9, \ldots$

13. $-1, 0, 1, 2, 3, \ldots$

14. $3, 5, 7, 9, 11, \ldots$

15. $0.8, 1.6, 2.4, 3.2, 4, \ldots$

16. $\frac{1}{4}, \frac{1}{2}, \frac{3}{4}, 1, \frac{5}{4}, \ldots$

17. $\frac{1}{2}, \frac{1}{4}, \frac{1}{6}, \frac{1}{8}, \frac{1}{10}, \ldots$

18. $\frac{2}{3}, 1\frac{2}{3}, 2\frac{2}{3}, 3\frac{2}{3}, 4\frac{2}{3}, \ldots$

Describe each pattern formed. Find the next three terms.

19. $1, 2, 4, 8, 16, \ldots$

20. $44, 39, 34, 29, 24, \ldots$

21. $0.7, 0.8, 0.9, 1.0, 1.1, \ldots$

22. $4, 11, 18, 25, 32, \ldots$

23. $1\frac{1}{4}, 2\frac{1}{2}, 5, 10, 20, \ldots$

24. $-6, -9, -12, -15, -18, \ldots$

Decide whether each formula is *explicit* or *recursive*. Then find the first five terms of each sequence.

25. $a_n = \frac{1}{3}n$

26. $a_n = n^2 - 6$

27. $a_1 = 5, a_n = 3a_{n-1} - 7$

28. $a_n = \frac{1}{2}(n - 1)$

29. $a_1 = 5, a_n = 3 - a_{n-1}$

30. $a_1 = -4, a_n = 2a_{n-1}$

31. The first figure of a fractal contains one segment. For each successive figure, six segments replace each segment.

    a. How many segments are in each of the first four figures of the sequence?

    b. Write a recursive formula for the sequence.

32. The sum of the measures of the exterior angles of any polygon is 360. All the angles have the same measure in a regular polygon.

    a. Find the measure of one exterior angle in a regular hexagon (six angles).

    b. Write an explicit formula for the measure of one exterior angle in a regular polygon with n angles.

    c. Why would this formula not be meaningful for $n = 1$ or $n = 2$?

Reteaching 11-2

OBJECTIVE: Finding the nth term of an arithmetic sequence

MATERIALS: None

Example

Find the 15th term of an arithmetic sequence whose first three terms are 20, 16.5, and 13.

$20 - 16.5 = 3.5$ $16.5 - 13 = 3.5$	← **First, find the common difference. The difference between consecutive terms is 3.5. The sequence decreases. The common difference is −3.5.**
$a_n = a_1 + (n - 1)\,d$	← **Use the explicit formula.**
$a_{15} = 20 + (15 - 1)(-3.5)$	← **Substitute $a_1 = 20$, $n = 15$, and $d = -3.5$.**
$= 20 + (14)(-3.5)$	← **Subtract within parentheses.**
$= 20 + -49$	← **Multiply.**
$= -29$	← **The 15th term is −29.**

Check the answer. Write $a_1, a_2, \ldots, a_{15}$ down the left side of your paper. Start with $a_1 = 20$. Subtract 3.5 and record 16.5 next to a_2. Continue until you find a_{15}.

Exercises

Find the 25th term of each sequence.

1. $20, 18, 16, 14, \ldots$

2. $0.0057, 0.0060, 0.0063, \ldots$

3. $4, 0, -4, -8, \ldots$

4. $0.2, 0.7, 1.2, 1.7, \ldots$

5. $-10, -8.8, -7.6, -6.4, \ldots$

6. $22, 26, 30, 34, \ldots$

7. Suppose you begin to work selling ads for a newspaper. You will be paid $50.00/wk plus a minimum of $7.50 for each potential customer you contact. What is the least amount of money you earn after contacting eight businesses in 1 wk?

8. In March, Jaime starts a savings account for a mountain bike. He initially deposits $15.00. He decides to increase each deposit by $8.00. How much is his seventeenth deposit?

9. Sue is knitting a blanket for her infant niece. Each day, she knits four more rows than the day before. She knitted seven rows on Sunday. How many rows did she knit on the following Saturday?

Practice 11-2

Arithmetic Sequences

Find the 43rd term of each sequence.

1. $12, 14, 16, 18, \ldots$

2. $13.1, 3.1, -6.9, -16.9, \ldots$

3. $19.5, 19.9, 20.3, 20.7, \ldots$

4. $27, 24, 21, 18, \ldots$

5. $2, 13, 24, 35, \ldots$

6. $21, 15, 9, 3, \ldots$

7. $1.3, 1.4, 1.5, 1.6, \ldots$

8. $-2.1, -2.3, -2.5, -2.7, \ldots$

9. $45, 48, 51, 54, \ldots$

Is the given sequence arithmetic? If so, identify the common difference.

10. $2, 3, 5, 8, \ldots$

11. $0, -3, -6, -9, \ldots$

12. $0.9, 0.5, 0.1, -0.3, \ldots$

13. $3, 8, 13, 18, \ldots$

14. $14, -15, -44, -73, \ldots$

15. $3.2, 3.5, 3.8, 4.1, \ldots$

16. $-34, -28, -22, -16, \ldots$

17. $2.3, 2.5, 2.7, 2.9, \ldots$

18. $127, 140, 153, 166, \ldots$

Find the missing term of each arithmetic sequence.

19. $\ldots 23, \blacksquare, 49, \ldots$

20. $14, \blacksquare, 28, \ldots$

21. $\ldots 29, \blacksquare, 33, \ldots$

22. $\ldots 14, \blacksquare, 15, \ldots$

23. $\ldots -45, \blacksquare, -39, \ldots$

24. $\ldots -5, \blacksquare, -2, \ldots$

25. $-2, \blacksquare, 2, \ldots$

26. $\ldots -6, \blacksquare, 2, \ldots$

27. $-34, \blacksquare, 77, \ldots$

28. $\ldots -45, \blacksquare, -12, \ldots$

29. $-2, \blacksquare, 456, \ldots$

30. $\ldots 34, \blacksquare, 345, \ldots$

Find the arithmetic mean a_n of the given terms.

31. $a_{n-1} = 2, a_{n+1} = 7$

32. $a_{n-1} = 13.2, a_{n+1} = 15.8$

33. $a_{n-1} = 29, a_{n+1} = -11$

34. $a_{n-1} = \frac{2}{5}, a_{n+1} = \frac{4}{5}$

35. $a_{n-1} = 15, a_{n+1} = -17$

36. $a_{n-1} = -6, a_{n+1} = -7$

37. Each year, a volunteer organization expects to add 5 more people to the number of shut-ins for whom the group provides home maintenance services. This year, the organization provides the service for 32 people.

    a. Write a recursive formula for the number of people the organization expects to serve each year.

    b. Write the first five terms of the sequence.

    c. Write an explicit formula for the number of people the organization expects to serve each year.

    d. How many people would the organization expect to serve in the 20th year?

Reteaching 11-3

Geometric Sequences

••

OBJECTIVE: Finding the nth term of a geometric sequence	**MATERIALS:** None

- A geometric sequence has a constant ratio between consecutive terms. This ratio is the common ratio.

- A geometric sequence formula can be written as a recursive formula, $a_n = a_{n-1} \cdot r$, or as an explicit formula, $a_n = a_1 \cdot r^{n-1}$.

Example

Find the 12th term of the geometric sequence $5, 15, 45, \ldots$.

$5, 15, 45, \ldots$

$r = \dfrac{15}{5} = \dfrac{45}{15} = 3$ ⟵ **Find r by calculating the common ratio between consecutive terms. This is a geometric sequence because there is a common ratio between consecutive terms.**

$a_n = 5(3)^{n-1}$ ⟵ **Substitute $a_1 = 5$ and $r = 3$ into the explicit formula to find a formula for the nth term of the sequence.**

$a_{12} = 5(3)^{11}$ ⟵ **Substitute $n = 12$ to find the 12th term of the sequence.**

$a_{12} = 885{,}735$ ⟵ **Remember to first calculate 3^{11}, then multiply by 5.**

Exercises

Find the indicated term of the geometric sequence.

1. $4, 2, 1, \ldots$ Find a_{10}.

2. $5, \dfrac{15}{2}, \dfrac{45}{4}, \ldots$ Find a_8.

3. $6, -2, \dfrac{2}{3}, \ldots$ Find a_{12}.

4. $1, -\dfrac{2}{3}, \dfrac{4}{9}, \ldots$ Find a_7.

5. $100, 200, 400, \ldots$ Find a_9.

6. $8, 32, 128, \ldots$ Find a_4.

Write the explicit formula for each sequence. Then generate the first five terms.

7. $a_1 = 1, r = \dfrac{1}{2}$

8. $a_1 = 2, r = 3$

9. $a_1 = 12, r = 3$

10. $a_1 = 1, r = \dfrac{1}{4}$

11. $a_1 = 5, r = \dfrac{1}{10}$

12. $a_1 = 1, r = \dfrac{1}{3}$

13. $a_1 = 5, r = 2$

14. $a_1 = 1, r = 3$

15. $a_1 = 3, r = 6$

16. $a_1 = 3, r = 3$

17. $a_1 = 2, r = 2$

18. $a_1 = 2, r = \dfrac{1}{2}$

19. $a_1 = 1, r = \dfrac{1}{5}$

20. $a_1 = 3, r = 4$

21. $a_1 = 5, r = \dfrac{1}{4}$

Practice 11-3

Find the missing term of each geometric sequence.

1. $4, \blacksquare, 16, \ldots$

2. $9, \blacksquare, 16, \ldots$

3. $2, \blacksquare, 8, \ldots$

4. $3, \blacksquare, 12, \ldots$

5. $2, \blacksquare, 50, \ldots$

6. $4, \blacksquare, 5.76, \ldots$

Is the given sequence geometric? If so, identify the common ratio and find the next two terms.

7. $3, 9, 27, 81, \ldots$

8. $4, 8, 16, 32, \ldots$

9. $4, 8, 12, 16, \ldots$

10. $4, -8, 16, -32, \ldots$

11. $1, 0.5, 0.25, 0.125, \ldots$

12. $100, 30, 9, 2.7, \ldots$

13. $-5, 0, 5, 10, \ldots$

14. $64, -32, 16, -8, \ldots$

15. $1, 4, 9, 16, \ldots$

Identify each sequence as *arithmetic, geometric,* or *neither.* Then find the next two terms.

16. $9, 3, 1, \frac{1}{3}, \ldots$

17. $1, 0, -2, -5, \ldots$

18. $2, -2, 2, -2, \ldots$

19. $-3, 2, 7, 12, \ldots$

20. $1, -2, -5, -8, \ldots$

21. $1, -2, 3, -4, \ldots$

Write the explicit formula for each sequence. Then generate the first five terms.

22. $a_1 = 3, r = -2$

23. $a_1 = 5, r = 3$

24. $a_1 = -1, r = 4$

25. $a_1 = -2, r = -3$

26. $a_1 = 32, r = -0.5$

27. $a_1 = 2187, r = \frac{1}{3}$

28. $a_1 = 9, r = 2$

29. $a_1 = -4, r = 4$

30. $a_1 = 0.1, r = -2$

31. When a pendulum swings freely, the length of its arc decreases geometrically. Find each missing arc length.

   a. 20th arc is 20 in.; 22nd arc is 18.5 in.

   b. 8th arc is 27 mm; 10th arc is 3 mm

32. The deer population in an area is increasing. This year, the population was 1.025 times last year's population of 2537.

   a. Assuming that the population increases at the same rate for the next few years, write an explicit formula for the sequence.

   b. Find the expected deer population for the fourth year of the sequence.

33. You enlarge a picture to 150% of its size several times. After the first increase, the picture is 1 in. wide.

   a. Write an explicit formula to model the size after each increase.

   b. How wide is the photo after the 2nd increase?

   c. How wide is the photo after the 3rd increase?

   d. How wide is the photo after the 12th increase?

Reteaching 11-4

Arithmetic Series

OBJECTIVE: Finding the sum of a given number of terms of a series	**MATERIALS:** None

Example

Evaluate the series $\sum_{n=2}^{4} (5 - 2n)$.

$$\sum_{n=2}^{4} (5 - 2n)$$

← Circle the upper and lower limits. Box the explicit formula.

$(n = 2)$ $(n = 3)$ $(n = 4)$

← In circles, write all possible values of n, beginning with the lower limit and ending with the upper limit.

$(n = 2)$ $(n = 3)$ $(n = 4)$

$5 - 2(2)$ $5 - 2(3)$ $5 - 2(4)$

← Under each circle, draw a box; copy the explicit formula, substituting the value in the circle above the box for the value of n.

$(n = 2)$ $(n = 3)$ $(n = 4)$

$\sum_{n=2}^{4} (5 - 2n) = 5 - 2(2) + 5 - 2(3) + 5 - 2(4)$

← The value of the series is the sum of the values in the boxes.

$= 1 + (-1) + (-3)$

← Evaluate each expression.

$= -3$

← Find the sum of the terms.

The sum of the series is -3.

Exercises

Evaluate each series.

1. $\sum_{n=1}^{3} (n - 4)$

2. $\sum_{n=1}^{4} \frac{1}{3}n$

3. $\sum_{n=3}^{8} (3n - 1)$

4. $\sum_{n=3}^{8} \frac{2n}{3}$

5. $\sum_{n=3}^{9} (4 - 2n)$

6. $\sum_{n=1}^{5} 8n$

7. $\sum_{n=2}^{7} 4n$

8. $\sum_{n=1}^{7} (3 - 2n)$

9. $\sum_{n=2}^{5} (5n + 1)$

10. An outdoor amphitheater has 45 rows of seats. The first row has 89 seats. The last row has 177 seats. Each row has 2 more seats than the previous row. Write an explicit formula representing the number of seats in the nth row. Then find the sum of the 45 rows of seats.

Practice 11-4

For each sum, find the number of terms, the first term, and the last term. Then evaluate the series.

1. $\sum_{n=1}^{4} (n-1)$

2. $\sum_{n=2}^{6} (2n-1)$

3. $\sum_{n=3}^{8} (n+25)$

4. $\sum_{n=2}^{5} (5n+3)$

5. $\sum_{n=1}^{4} (2n+0.5)$

6. $\sum_{n=1}^{6} (3-n)$

7. $\sum_{n=5}^{10} n$

8. $\sum_{n=1}^{4} (-n-3)$

9. $\sum_{n=3}^{6} (3n+2)$

Write the related series for each finite sequence. Then evaluate each series.

10. $1, 3, 5, \ldots, 15$

11. $5, 8, 11, \ldots, 26$

12. $4, 9, 14, 19, \ldots, 44$

13. $10, 25, 40, 55, 70, 85$

14. $17, 25, 33, 41, 49, 57, 65$

15. $125, 126, 127, \ldots, 131$

Use summation notation to write each arithmetic series for the specified number of terms.

16. $1 + 3 + 5 + \ldots; n = 7$

17. $2.3 + 2.6 + 2.9 + \ldots; n = 5$

18. $4 + 8 + 12 + \ldots; n = 4$

19. $10 + 7 + 4 + \ldots; n = 6$

20. $3 + 7 + 11 + \ldots; n = 8$

21. $15 + 25 + 35 + \ldots; n = 7$

Tell whether each list is a *series* or a *sequence*. Then tell whether it is *finite* or *infinite*.

22. $7, 12, 17, 22, 27$

23. $3 + 5 + 7 + 9 + \ldots$

24. $8, 8.2, 8.4, 8.6, 8.8, 9.0, \ldots$

25. $1 + 5 + 9 + 13 + 17$

26. $40, 20, 10, 5, 2.5, 1.25, \ldots$

27. $10 + 20 + 30 + 40 + 50$

Each sequence has six terms. Evaluate each related series.

28. $1, 0, -1, \ldots, -4$

29. $4, 5, 6, \ldots, 9$

30. $-7, -9, -11, \ldots, -17$

31. $-6, -7, -8, \ldots, -11$

32. $0, 0.3, 0.6, \ldots, 1.5$

33. $5, 7, 9, \ldots, 15$

34. An embroidery pattern calls for 5 stitches in the first row and for three more stitches in each successive row. The 25th row, which is the last row, has 77 stitches. Find the total number of stitches in the pattern.

35. A marching band formation consists of 6 rows. The first row has 9 musicians, the second has 11, the third has 13 and so on. How many musicians are in the last row and how many musicians are there in all?

Name _____ Class _____ Date _____

Reteaching 11-5

Geometric Series

OBJECTIVE: Finding the sum of a finite and of an infinite geometric series	**MATERIALS:** None

- The sum of a finite geometric series is the sum of the terms of a geometric sequence. This sum can be found by using the formula

  $S_n = \dfrac{a_1(1 - r^n)}{1 - r}$, where a_1 is the first term, r is the common ratio, and n is the number of terms.

- The sum of an infinite geometric series with $|r| < 1$ is found by using the formula $S = \dfrac{a_1}{1 - r}$, where a_1 is the first term and r is the common ratio. If $|r| \geq 1$, then the series has no sum.

Example

Find the sum of the first ten terms of the series
$8 + 16 + 32 + 64 + 128 + \ldots$

$a_1 = 8$ ⟵ a_1 **is the first term in the series.**

$r = \dfrac{16}{8} = \dfrac{32}{16} = \dfrac{64}{32} = \dfrac{128}{64} = 2$ ⟵ **Simplify the ratio formed by any two consecutive terms to find** r.

$n = 10$ ⟵ n **is the number of terms in the series to be added together.**

$S_{10} = \dfrac{8(1 - 2^{10})}{1 - 2}$ ⟵ **Substitute** $a_1 = 8$, $r = 2$, **and** $n = 10$ **into the formula for the sum of a finite geometric series.**

$= \dfrac{8(-1023)}{-1}$ ⟵ **Simplify inside the parentheses.**

$= 8184$ ⟵ **Simplify.**

Exercises

Evaluate the series to the given term.

1. $3 + 12 + 48 + 192 + \ldots; S_6$

2. $8 + 2 + \dfrac{1}{2} + \dfrac{1}{8} + \ldots; S_5$

3. $-10 - 5 - 2.5 - 1.25 - \ldots; S_7$

4. $10 + (-5) + \dfrac{5}{2} + \left(-\dfrac{5}{4}\right) + \ldots; S_{11}$

Evaluate each infinite geometric series.

5. $10 + 5 + 2.5 + \ldots$

6. $-1 + \dfrac{2}{11} - \dfrac{4}{121} + \ldots$

7. $\dfrac{1}{4} + \dfrac{7}{32} + \dfrac{49}{256} + \ldots$

8. $\dfrac{1}{2} - \dfrac{1}{5} + \dfrac{2}{25} - \ldots$

9. $-\dfrac{1}{6} + \dfrac{1}{12} - \dfrac{1}{24} + \ldots$

10. $20 + 16 + \dfrac{64}{5} + \ldots$

11. $12 + 4 + \dfrac{4}{3} + \ldots$

12. $\dfrac{1}{4} - \dfrac{1}{8} + \dfrac{1}{16} - \ldots$

13. $\dfrac{2}{3} + \dfrac{2}{15} + \dfrac{2}{75} + \ldots$

Practice 11-5

Decide whether each infinite geometric series *diverges* or *converges*. State whether each series has a sum.

1. $3 + \frac{3}{2} + \frac{3}{4} + \ldots$

2. $4 + 2 + 1 + \ldots$

3. $17 + 15.3 + 13.77 + \ldots$

4. $6 + 11.4 + 21.66 + \ldots$

5. $-20 - 8 - 3.2 - \ldots$

6. $50 + 70 + 98 + \ldots$

Evaluate each infinite series that has a sum.

7. $\sum_{n=1}^{\infty} 5\left(\frac{2}{3}\right)^{n-1}$

8. $\sum_{n=1}^{\infty} (-2.1)^{n-1}$

9. $\sum_{n=1}^{\infty} \left(-\frac{1}{2}\right)^{n-1}$

10. $\sum_{n=1}^{\infty} 2\left(\frac{5}{3}\right)^{n-1}$

Evaluate each infinite geometric series.

11. $8 + 4 + 2 + 1 + \ldots$

12. $1 + \frac{1}{3} + \frac{1}{9} + \frac{1}{27} + \ldots$

13. $120 + 96 + 76.8 + 61.44 + \ldots$

14. $1000 + 750 + 562.5 + 421.875 + \ldots$

Determine whether each series is *arithmetic* or *geometric*. Then evaluate the series to the given term.

15. $2 + 5 + 8 + 11 + \ldots; S_9$

16. $\frac{1}{8} + \frac{1}{16} + \frac{1}{32} + \frac{1}{64} + \ldots; S_8$

17. $-3 + 6 - 12 + 24 - \ldots; S_{10}$

18. $-2 + 2 + 6 + 10 + \ldots; S_{12}$

Evaluate the series to the given term.

19. $40 + 20 + 10 + \ldots; S_{10}$

20. $4 + 12 + 36 + \ldots; S_{15}$

21. $15 + 12 + 9.6 + \ldots; S_{40}$

22. $27 + 9 + 3 + \ldots; S_{100}$

23. $0.2 + 0.02 + 0.002 + \ldots; S_8$

24. $100 + 200 + 400 + \ldots; S_6$

25. This month, Julia deposits $400 to save for a vacation. She plans to deposit 10% more each successive month for the next 11 months. How much will she have saved after the 12 deposits?

26. Suppose your business made a profit of $5500 the first year. If the profit increases 20% per year, find the total profit over the first 5 yr.

27. The end of a pendulum travels 50 cm on its first swing. Each swing after the first travels 99% as far as the preceding one. How far will the pendulum travel before it stops?

28. A seashell has chambers that are each 0.82 times the length of the next chamber. The outer chamber is 32 mm around. Find the total length of the shell's spiraled chambers.

29. The first year a toy manufacturer introduces a new toy, its sales total $495,000. The company expects its sales to drop 10% each succeeding year. Find the total expected sales in the first 6 yr. Find the total expected sales if the company offers the toy for sale for as long as anyone buys it.

Reteaching 11-6

Area Under a Curve

• •

> **OBJECTIVE:** Developing area under a curve as a series
>
> **MATERIALS:** Graph paper, colored pencils

You can use rectangles to approximate the area under the curve $f(x)$. You can use summation notation to represent the sum of the areas of these rectangles.

$$A = \sum_{n=1}^{b} (w)f(a_n)$$ ← number of rectangles

width of each rectangle   function value at a_n

Example

Graph $f(x) = x^2 + 2$. Use inscribed rectangles 0.5 units wide to approximate the area under the curve for $0 \le x \le 2$.

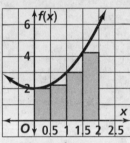

← **Draw the curve on the grid.**

← **Determine and label the interval endpoints. Counting from 0 to 2 by 0.5 units, we get 4 intervals with endpoints at 0, 0.5, 1, 1.5, and 2.**

← **Draw segments from these endpoints on the x-axis to the graph of f. When using inscribed rectangles, the shortest of each consecutive pair of segments represents the height of the rectangle. Draw and shade these 4 rectangles.**

$A = \sum_{n=1}^{b} (w)f(a_n)$ ← **Write the formula.**

$= \sum_{n=1}^{4} (0.5)f(a_n)$ ← **Substitute $b = 4$ since there are 4 rectangles, and $w = 0.5$ since each rectangle is 0.5 units wide.**

$= (0.5)f(a_1) + (0.5)f(a_2) + (0.5)f(a_3) + (0.5)f(a_4)$ ← **Expand the summation.**

$= (0.5)(2) + (0.5)(2.25) + (0.5)(3) + (0.5)(4.25)$ ← **$f(a_1)$ is the height of the first rectangle. This corresponds to $f(0)$ which is 2. Similarly determine the heights of the remaining rectangles: $f(0.5) = 2.25$, $f(1) = 3$, and $f(1.5) = 4.25$.**

$= 0.5(2 + 2.25 + 3 + 4.25)$ ← **Use the Distributive Property.**

$= 5.75$ ← **Simplify.**

The area is approximately 5.75 units^2.

Exercises

Use the method shown in the Example to approximate the area under each curve for the interval $0 \le x \le 2$. Use inscribed rectangles 0.5 unit wide.

1. $f(x) = 2x^2$

2. $f(x) = -x^2 + 4$

3. $y = 2x + 3$

4. $y = -x + 2$

5. $f(x) = x^2 + 1$

6. $f(x) = -x^2 + 6$

• •

Practice 11-6

Write and evaluate a sum to approximate the area under each curve for the domain $0 \leq x \leq 2$.
   a. Use inscribed rectangles 0.5 unit wide.
   b. Use circumscribed rectangles 0.5 unit wide.

1. $y = -x^2 + 4$ **2.** $f(x) = -2x^2 + 16$ **3.** $g(x) = -0.5x^2 + 2$

4. $f(x) = x^2 + 4$ **5.** $y = 2x^2 + 6$ **6.** $h(g) = 0.5x^2 + 2$

7. $y = -3x^2 + 15$ **8.** $f(x) = 3x^2 + 2$ **9.** $f(x) = 10 - x^2$

10. a. Graph the curve $y = 2x^2 + 1$.

     b. Use inscribed rectangles to approximate the area under the curve
        for the interval $0 \leq x \leq 2$ and rectangle width of 0.5 unit.

     c. Repeat part b using circumscribed rectangles.

     d. Find the mean of the areas you found in parts b and c. Of the three
        estimates, which best approximates the area for the interval?

Use your graphing calculator to find the area under each curve for the domain $-2 \leq x \leq 1$.

11. $y = -x^3 + 1$ **12.** $f(x) = -2x^3 + 3$ **13.** $f(x) = 2x^2 + 1$

14. $g(x) = 3x^2 + 1$ **15.** $y = -\frac{1}{4}x^2 + 1$ **16.** $f(x) = 4x^2 + 2$

17. $y = -x^2 + 4$ **18.** $f(x) = x^2 + 1$ **19.** $y = \sqrt{x + 3}$

Given each set of axes, what does the area under the curve represent?

20. y-axis: feet per second, x-axis: seconds

21. y-axis: computers produced per day, x-axis: days

22. y-axis: miles per hour, x-axis: hours

23. y-axis: gallons per minute, x-axis: minutes

24. y-axis: molecules per second, x-axis: seconds

25. y-axis: price per pound of apples, x-axis: pounds of apples

Graph each curve. Use inscribed rectangles to approximate the area under the curve for the interval and rectangle width given.

26. $y = \frac{1}{4}x^2, 2 \leq x \leq 4, 1$ **27.** $y = x^3 + 1, 0 \leq x \leq 2, 0.5$

Reteaching 12-1

Probability Distributions

OBJECTIVE: Making a probability distribution	**MATERIALS:** None

Example

Create a frequency table and a probability distribution to report the probability that a student in a class carries more than $1 in coins.

Step 1:

Ask each student to find the dollar amount of coins that they are carrying and record the data.

Student #	1	2	3	4	5	6	7	8	9	10	11	12	13	14	15
Amount	0.00	0.25	0.50	1.25	0.00	0.78	0.80	1.49	0.50	0.00	0.75	1.00	0.00	1.05	0.00

Step 2:
Organize the data into a frequency table.

Dollar amount of coins carried by students

Amount	No. of students
Less than $1.00	11
Exactly $1.00	1
More than $1.00	3
Total	15

Step 3:
Give the probability for each possibility.

P(less than $1.00) $= \frac{11}{15}$

P(exactly $1.00) $= \frac{1}{15}$

P(more than $1.00) $= \frac{3}{15}$

Check that the sum of the probabilities is 1.

$\frac{11}{15} + \frac{1}{15} + \frac{3}{15} = \frac{15}{15} = 1$

The probability that a student carries more than $1.00 in change is $\frac{3}{15}$ or $\frac{1}{5}$.

Exercises

Create a frequency table. Find the probability distribution for the following.

1. Average rainfall in inches for the month of April over the past 13 years in a city is as follows:
   1.7 1.7 1.0 2.1 2.7 0.2 2.4 1.9 0.4 0.8 1.4 2.5 1.2
   Report the probability that this city will have less than 1 in. of rain in April.

2. The status of professors in a university math department is as follows:
   tenured, nontenured, nontenured, tenured, beginning, nontenured, tenured, nontenured, nontenured, beginning, tenured, nontenured, beginning, nontenured, tenured
   Report the probability that a professor in this department is tenured.

Practice 12-1

1. Use the frequency table to find each probability.

   a. What is the probability that a person living alone is 45 or older?

   b. In a sample of 100 persons living alone, predict how many are age 35 and older.

   c. Find P(15 to 24 years of age)

   d. Find P(35 to 44 years of age)

   e. Find P(65 years and older)

   Persons Living Alone in 1999 (in thousands)

15 to 24 years of age	1,313
25 to 34 years of age	3,714
35 to 44 years of age	4,074
45 to 64 years of age	7,757
65 years and older	9,747

   Source: *www.infoplease.com*

2. You roll two number cubes. Make a table to show the probability distribution for each sample space.

   a. {the sum of the cubes is 5 or less, the sum is greater than 5}

   b. {the sum of the cubes is prime, the sum is composite}

   c. {only one cube shows 2, both cubes show the same number, the cubes show different numbers and neither is a 2}

3. A survey of student pizza preferences showed that 43 students preferred cheese, 56 preferred sausage, 39 preferred pepperoni, 28 preferred supreme, 31 preferred another kind, and 19 did not like any type of pizza.

   a. Organize this data in a frequency table.

   b. Find the experimental probability for each outcome in the table. Round to the nearest tenth of a percent. What is the sum of the experimental probabilities? Explain.

   c. Graph the probability distribution for {pizza, no pizza}.

   d. Graph the probability distribution for {cheese, sausage or pepperoni, supreme or other, no pizza}.

   e. How are the probability distributions related?

4. Visitors to the game preserve see up to eight species of large mammals as they drive through. A survey shows that the number of species seen varies according to the distribution below.

   Probability Distribution for Number of Species Seen

s	0	1	2	3	4	5	6	7	8
$P(s)$	0.08	0.12	0.21	0.18	0.12	0.11	0.09	0.08	0.01

   a. Use random numbers to simulate the number of species seen in each of 20 visits to the preserve. What is the average per visit?

   b. You donate $5 to the preserve for upkeep of each species you see. On the basis of your simulation, how much would you donate in 20 visits?

Reteaching 12-2

Conditional Probability

| **OBJECTIVE:** Finding conditional probabilities | **MATERIALS:** None |

Example

A college computer lab has 100 computers. Some of these computers are personal computers (PCs), and others are Macintoshes (Macs). Some of the computers are new, and others are used. A student enters the lab and picks a computer at random. Find each probability.

Types of Computers in Lab

	PCs	Macs	Total
New	40	30	70
Used	20	10	30
Total	60	40	100

$P(\text{computer is new}) = \dfrac{70}{100}$ ← **Write the probability as a ratio.**

$= \dfrac{7}{10}$ ← **Reduce.**

$P(\text{computer is a PC}) = \dfrac{60}{100}$ ← **Write P as a ratio.**

$= \dfrac{3}{5}$ ← **Reduce.**

$P(\text{computer is new and a PC}) = \dfrac{40}{100}$ ← **Write P as a ratio.**

$= \dfrac{2}{5}$ ← **Reduce.**

Given that the computer is new, what is the probability that it is a Mac?

$P(\text{Mac} \mid \text{new}) = \dfrac{30}{70}$ ← **Write P as a ratio.**

$= \dfrac{3}{7}$ ← **Reduce.**

Given that the computer is used, what is the probability that it is a PC?

$P(\text{PC} \mid \text{used}) = \dfrac{20}{30}$ ← **Write P as a ratio.**

$= \dfrac{2}{3}$ ← **Reduce.**

Exercises

A bag contains 20 red balls with a blue dot and 15 red balls without the dot. In addition, the bag contains 30 white balls with a blue dot and 25 white balls without the dot. Use a table similar to the one above to find each probability.

1. $P(\text{red})$ **2.** $P(\text{white})$ **3.** $P(\text{with a dot})$

4. $P(\text{no dot})$ **5.** $P(\text{red and with a dot})$ **6.** $P(\text{white and no dot})$

7. $P(\text{red} \mid \text{with a dot})$ **8.** $P(\text{white} \mid \text{no dot})$ **9.** $P(\text{no dot} \mid \text{white})$

Practice 12-2

1. The table contains information about the 1205 employees at one business. Find each probability. Round to the nearest tenth of a percent.

   Education and Salary of Employees

	Under $20,000	$20,000 to $30,000	Over $30,000
Less than high school	69	36	2
High school	112	98	14
Some college	102	193	143
College degree	13	178	245

   a. P(employee has less than a high school education)

   b. P(employee earns under $20,000)

   c. P(employee earns over $30,000 and has less than a high school education)

   d. P(employee earns under $20,000 and has a college degree)

   e. given that the employee has only a high school education, the probability that the employee earns over $30,000

   f. given that the employee earns over $30,000, the probability that the employee has only a high school education or less

2. High school students in one school chose their favorite leisure activity. Find each probability. Round to the nearest tenth of a percent.

   Favorite Leisure Activities

	Sports	Hiking	Reading	Phoning	Shopping	Other
Female	39	48	85	62	71	29
Male	67	58	76	54	68	39

   a. P(sports | female) b. P(female | sports) c. P(reading | male) d. P(male | reading)
   e. P(hiking | female) f. P(hiking | male) g. P(male | shopping) h. P(female | shopping)

3. The senior class is 55% female, and 32% are females who play a competitive sport. Find the probability that a student plays a competitive sport, given that the student is female.

Draw a tree diagram. Find each probability.

4. A softball game has an 80% chance of being canceled for a light drizzle and a 30% chance of being canceled for a heavy fog when there is no drizzle. There is a 70% chance of heavy fog and a 30% chance of light drizzle.

   a. Find the probability that the game will be canceled.

   b. Find the probability there will be a light drizzle and the game will not be canceled.

5. The students of a high school are 51% males; 45% of the males and 49% of the females attend concerts.

   a. Find the probability that a student attends concerts.

   b. Find the probability that a student is a female and does not attend concerts.

Reteaching 12-3

OBJECTIVE: Analyzing statistical data	**MATERIALS:** Number cube, two different-colored pencils

- When finding central tendencies, use these clues: The <u>mo</u>de is the number that occurs <u>mo</u>st often. The <u>med</u>ian is the number that occurs in the <u>mid</u>dle. The mean is the average of data values.

Example

Find the mean, median, and mode for the values below.
2 2 5 5 1 4 6 6 3 5 3 4 3 2 4 4 5 2 4 1
3 5 4 3 5 3 4 4 3 5 3 3 1 5 6 3 1 1 4 4 1

Step 1: To find the mode, rewrite the data in numerical order from least to greatest. Draw circles around like data using one colored pencil. Record the frequency of each.
1 1 1 1 1 1 2 2 2 2 3 3 3 3 3 3 3 3 3 3 4 4 4 4 4 4 4 4 4
5 5 5 5 5 5 5 5 6 6 6
The mode is 3 because it occurs most often.

Step 2: To find the median, put a box around the middle value(s) with a different colored pencil.
1 1 1 1 1 1 2 2 2 2 3 3 3 3 3 3 3 3 3 3 4 4 4 4 4 4 4 4 4
5 5 5 5 5 5 5 5 6 6 6
Since there are two middle values, find their mean, or average.

$$\frac{(3 + 4)}{2} = \frac{7}{2} = 3.5$$

The median is 3.5.

Step 3: To find the mean, add all values and divide by the number of values.
138 ÷ 40 = 3.45.
The mean is 3.45.

Exercises

Find the mean, median, and mode for each set of values.

1. 872 888 895 870 882 878 891 890 888

2. 0.5 0.5 0.4 1.2 0.0 0.9 1.4 1.0 2.1 0.7 0.5 1.7

3. 2020 2040 2068 2120 2015 2301 2254

4. 322 101 245 289 135 409 375 185 340

5. 25 27 26 33 28 26 24 30 26 28 24 27

6. 8 9 21 12 7 24 14 21 10 14 18 21 16

7. 4.4 5.6 1.5 2.1 3.8 1.9 4.7 2.5 4.7 2.8

8. 6371 6378 6372 6371 6379 6380 6374

9. 194 502 413 768 986 616 259 351 825

10. 85 84 81 81 85 82 86 84 83 86 90 81

Practice 12-3

Analyzing Data

Identify the outliers of each set of values.

1. 23 76 79 76 77 74 75

2. 43 46 49 50 52 54 78 47

3. 32 35 3 36 37 35 38 40 42 34

4. 153 156 176 156 165 110 159 169 172

Find the mean, median, and mode of each set of values.

5. 98 87 79 82 101 99 97 97 102 91 93

6. 41 41 45 46 54 52 53 50 49 47 49 48 44

7. 2.3 2.4 2.5 2.8 2.4 2.4 2.9 2.6 2.4 2.9

8. 15.2 15.3 15.9 16.1 16.3 15.4 15.5 15.6 15.8

9. 245 345 365 566 442 476 423 495 412

10. 1002 1005 1023 1034 1012 1054 1023

11. 0.019 0.021 0.018 0.019 0.018 0.020

12. 23 29 31 32 29 27 21 19 25 26 28 29 24

13. 45 49 41 45 51 39 42 46 49 48 42 40

14. 3 5 31 35 41 49 50 51 52 53 54 69 81 99

15. 14 15 19 15 15 16 19 20 21 29 16 17

16. 1.8 1.3 1.9 1.5 1.6 1.5 1.8 1.5 1.3 1.4 1.3

17. 8.7 8.8 8.9 9.4 10.2 9.8 9.0 8.1 9.5

18. 101 114 128 106 125 122 120 114 116

19. 4.25 4.46 4.19 4.23 4.25 4.28 4.27 4.35

20. 11 15 18 22 25 29 32 36 39 41 42 45 48 51

Make a box-and-whisker plot for each set of values.

21. 2 8 3 7 3 6 4 9 10 15 21 29 32 30 5 7 32 4 11 13 11 14 10 12 13 15

22. 1054 1165 1287 1385 1456 1398 1298 1109 1067 1384 1499 1032 1222 1045

23. 43.4 46.5 47.9 51.0 50.2 49.5 42.5 41.6 46.8 50.0

24. 19 20 21 22 23 25 27 12 19 31 53 52 48 41 29 33 48 46 44 42

Find the values at the 20th and 80th percentiles for each set of values.

25. 188 168 174 198 186 178 184 190 176 172 170 180 182 186 176

26. 376 324 346 348 350 352 356 368 345 360

27. 98 99 96 94 95 96 97 99 95 94 93 96 97 98 99 97 96 94 92 97

28. 2 12 17 20 22 28 32 37 38 41 44 51 53 59 62 78 86 92 102 112

29. The data shows the average temperatures in January for several cities in the mid-South.
49.1 50.8 42.9 44.0 44.2 51.4 45.7 39.9 50.8 46.7 52.4 50.4

a. Find the mean of the temperatures.

b. Find the median of the temperatures.

c. Find the mode of the temperatures.

d. Find the quartiles of the data. Sketch a box-and-whisker plot, and label the quartiles.

Reteaching 12-4

> **OBJECTIVE:** Determining standard deviation **MATERIALS:** None

The standard deviation of a collection of numbers $(x_1, x_2, x_3, \ldots, x_n)$,

$$\sigma = \sqrt{\frac{(x_1 - \overline{x})^2 + (x_2 - \overline{x})^2 + \ldots + \ldots + (x_n - \overline{x})^2}{n}},$$ where $\overline{x}$ is the mean of $x_1, x_2, \ldots, x_n$.

Example

Find the standard deviation for 100, 158, 170, 192.

$$\overline{x} = \frac{100 + 158 + 170 + 192}{4} \longleftarrow \textbf{Find the mean.}$$

$$\overline{x} = 155$$

$(100 - 155)^2 = 3025$ $\longleftarrow$ **Subtract the mean from each value in**
$(158 - 155)^2 = 9$ **the data set. Square each difference.**
$(170 - 155)^2 = 225$
$(192 - 155)^2 = 1369$

$$\sigma = \sqrt{\frac{3025 + 9 + 255 + 1369}{4}} \longleftarrow \textbf{Find the standard deviation.}$$

$$= \sqrt{1157}$$

$$\approx 34$$

Exercises

Find the standard deviation of each set of values.

1. 6.5 7.0 9.0 8.0 7.5

2. 5.6 5.8 5.9 6.1

3. 201 203 208 210 211

4. 12 14 15 17 19

A family goes grocery shopping every week. In a month the costs of the groceries are $72.42, $91.50, $58.99, and $69.02.

5. What is the mean?

6. What is the standard deviation?

7. Within how many standard deviations of the mean is a cost of $50.00?

8. Within how many standard deviations of the mean is a cost of $102.00?

The distances driven by eight different vehicles using 12 gal of gasoline were 174 mi, 271 mi, 208 mi, 196 mi, 340 mi, 214 mi, 236 mi, and 385 mi.

9. Find the mean and the standard deviation for the distances traveled.

10. How many items in the data set fall within one standard deviation of the mean? Within two standard deviations?

Practice 12-4

Find the mean and the standard deviation for each set of values. Round to the nearest tenth.

1. 232 254 264 274 287 298 312 342 398

2. 26 27 28 28 28 29 30 30 32 35 35 36

3. 2.2 2.2 2.3 2.4 2.4 2.4 2.5 2.5 2.5 2.6

4. 75 73 77 79 79 74 81 74 70 68 70 72

5. 87 21 90 43 54 23 123 110 90 44 50

Find the range, mean, and interquartile range of each set of values.

6. 10 12 13 10 9 5 6 11

7. 23 56 59 60 123 164 180 212

8. 524 526 532 531 534 539 530 535

9. 1.4 1.6 1.9 2.2 2.6 2.7 2.9 3.1

10. 45 48 46 47 45 48 46 49 46 47

11. 97 102 99 105 100 101 99 101

Determine the number of standard deviations that includes all data values.

12. The mean test score on a standardized test is 216; the standard deviation is 52.
127 98 236 192 267 335 217 365 472 177

13. The mean age of students in a school is 16.4 years; the standard deviation is 1.5.
13 17 18 15 16 14 15 18 17 16 15 16 13

14. The average rainfall for the month of April for several Eastern cities is as follows:
3.0 3.4 4.3 3.6 3.6 2.9 2.8 3.9 2.8 2.9 4.5 3.8 4.2 3.6 4.0 2.9 3.1

  a. Find the mean of the data.

  b. Find the standard deviation of the data.

  c. Find the range of the data.

  d. Within how many standard deviations is a rainfall of 2.8 in.? 4.0 in.?

15. The test scores on a college algebra test are as follows:
67 69 71 75 78 78 83 85 85 85 85 86 87 89 92 95 98 98 98 100
100 100 100 100 100

  a. Find the range of the data.

  b. Find the interquartile range.

  c. Find the mean of the data.

  d. Find the standard deviation.

  e. Within how many standard deviations of the mean is a score of 65?

  f. Within how many standard deviations of the mean is a score of 100?

16. A set of values has a mean of 67 and a standard deviation of 8. Find the *z*-score of the value 70.

17. A set of values has a mean of 102 and a standard deviation of 12. Find the *z*-score of the value 135.

Reteaching 12-5

OBJECTIVE: Finding the margin of error	**MATERIALS:** None

- A random sample cannot be entirely accurate. The margin of error allows you to find the likely range for the true population proportion. The margin of error is $\pm\dfrac{1}{\sqrt{n}}$ for a sample of size n.

Example

A random sample of 784 high school students reports that 38% of them choose math as their favorite subject. Find the margin of error. Use it to find the likely range for the true population proportion.

$$\text{The margin of error} = \pm\dfrac{1}{\sqrt{784}} \quad \longleftarrow \quad \textbf{Use the margin of error formula.}$$

$$= \pm\dfrac{1}{28} \quad \longleftarrow \quad \textbf{Simplify.}$$

$$\approx \pm0.036 \quad \longleftarrow \quad \textbf{Convert the fraction to a decimal.}$$

$$= \pm3.6\% \quad \longleftarrow \quad \textbf{Convert the decimal to a percent.}$$

$$38\% + 3.6\% = 41.6\% \quad \longleftarrow \quad \textbf{Use the result from the sample. Add and subtract the margin of error.}$$

$$38\% - 3.6\% = 34.4\%$$

The proportion of students who say math is their favorite subject is likely to be between 34.4% and 41.6%.

Exercises

Find the margin of error. Find an interval that is likely to contain the true population proportion for the following. Round to the nearest tenth of a percent.

1. In a random sample of 1296 high school football players, 72% have purchased a brand of shoes based on the type worn by their favorite NFL player.

2. In a survey of 576 math students, 86% report having used up the eraser of their pencil before the pencil is half gone.

3. In a certain part of the country, only 12% of the 324 dogs sampled suffered from fleas.

4. In a poll of 1460 voters, 54% voted for the Republican candidate.

5. In a survey of 2891 high school students, 78% report having seen the music video made for a song before they purchased a recording of the song.

Practice 12-5

1. In a survey, participants were asked their opinion of a new government program. The response scale ranged from 1 to 4, with 4 being a favorable response to the program. Which sample was largest? Explain.

Sample	Score	Standard Deviation
A	3.0	1.1
B	2.8	1.3
C	2.9	0.8

Identify any bias in each sampling method. When appropriate, suggest a sampling method that is more likely to produce a random sample.

2. A committee wants to find how much time students spend reading each week. They ask the students as they enter the library.

3. The students planning the junior class party want to know what kinds of pizza to buy. They ask the pizza restaurant what kinds sell the most.

4. The county road department wants to know which roads cause the most concern among the residents of the county. They ask the local restaurant to hand out survey forms.

5. A politician wants to know what issues are most important to the voters in his district. He spends all day Tuesday talking to people as they enter the grocery store.

6 A politician wants to know the voters' views on an important issue. She has her campaign workers call people randomly from the phone book.

Find the sample size that produces each margin of error.

7. ±15%
8. ±2%
9. ±0.9%
10. ±0.6%

For each sample find the sample proportion, the margin of error, and an interval likely to contain the true population proportion. Round to the nearest percent.

11. In a survey of 38 parents of preschool children, 20 would like to have their local school district provide play group sessions at least one evening a month.

12. In a random sample of 526 visitors to the craft center, 378 want the craft center to be open later in the evenings.

13. In a survey of 165 visitors to the library, 102 want the library to have more novels available.

14. In one lake, 98 of the last 323 fish caught have a certain chemical present in their body.

15. In a traffic survey, 537 of the 1287 drivers passing through the checkpoint were traveling more than 100 miles from home.

Reteaching 12-6

Binomial Distributions

| **OBJECTIVE:** Finding binomial probabilities | **MATERIALS:** None |

- Suppose you have repeated independent trials, each with a probability of success p and a probability of failure q (with $p + q = 1$). Then the probability of x successes in n trials is $_nC_x p^x q^{n-x}$.

Example

Find the probability of two successes in five trials with a probability of success of 0.2 for each trial.

$$q = 1 - p \qquad \longleftarrow \textbf{Find } q.$$

$$q = 0.8$$

$$_nC_x = \frac{5!}{2!(5-2)!} \qquad \longleftarrow \textbf{Find } _nC_x.$$

$$= 10$$

$$_nC_x p^x q^{n-x} = {_5C_2}(0.2)^2(0.8)^{5-2} \qquad \longleftarrow \textbf{Substitute } x, n, p, \textbf{ and } q \textbf{ values.}$$

$$= 10(0.2)^2(0.8)^3 \qquad \longleftarrow \textbf{Substitute 10 for } _nC_x.$$

$$= 10(0.04)(0.512) \qquad \longleftarrow \textbf{Simplify.}$$

$$= 0.2048$$

The probability is about 20%.

Exercises

Find the probability of x successes in n trials for the given probability of success p on each trial. Round to the nearest tenth of a percent.

1. $x = 3, n = 4, p = 0.3$ 　　　　**2.** $x = 4, n = 6, p = 0.1$

3. $x = 7, n = 9, p = 0.4$ 　　　　**4.** $x = 5, n = 6, p = 0.3$

5. A light fixture contains six light bulbs. With normal use, each bulb has a 95% chance of lasting for 2 yr. What is the probability that all six bulbs last for 2 yr?

6. Use the information from Exercise 5. What is the probability that five of the six bulbs will last for 2 yr?

7. Suppose the bulbs have an 80% chance of lasting for 2 yr. Find the probability that three of the six bulbs will last for 2 yr.

Practice 12-6

1. The probability that a baby is a male is 50%. Use a tree diagram to find each probability.

   a. P(at least 1 baby in a family with 3 children is a male)

   b. P(at least 2 babies in a family of 3 children are male)

   c. P(exactly 2 of 3 babies born in the hospital on any day are male)

For each situation, describe a trial and a success. Then design and run a simulation to find the probability.

2. The probability that the weather will be acceptable for a launch of the space shuttle over the next 3 days is 70% each day. Find the probability that the weather will be acceptable at least one of the next three days.

3. A poll shows that 30% of the voters favor an earlier curfew. Find the probability that all of five people chosen at random favor an earlier curfew.

4. The probability that a machine part is defective is 10%. Find the probability that exactly one part is defective in a sample of five parts.

Find the probability of x successes in n trials for the given probability of success p on each trial.

5. $x = 5, n = 5, p = 0.4$ 6. $x = 2, n = 8, p = 0.9$

7. $x = 3, n = 10, p = 0.25$ 8. $x = 1, n = 3, p = 0.2$

Use the binomial expansion of $(p + q)^n$ to calculate and graph each binomial distribution.

9. $n = 5, p = 0.6$ 10. $n = 3, p = 0.7$

11. $n = 3, p = 0.1$ 12. $n = 4, p = 0.8$

13. There is a 60% probability of rain each of the next 5 days. Find each probability. Round to the nearest percent.

   a. P(rain at least 3 of the next 5 days)   **b.** P(rain at least 1 of the next 5 days)

   c. P(rain at least 1 of the next 4 days)   **d.** P(rain at least 1 of the next 2 days)

14. In one area the probability of a power outage during a rainstorm is 4%. Find each probability. Round to the nearest percent.

   a. P(at least 1 outage in the next 5 rainstorms)

   b. P(at least 2 outages in the next 10 rainstorms)

   c. P(at least 1 outage in the next 20 rainstorms)

Reteaching 12-7

OBJECTIVE: Using a normal curve to describe data distribution

MATERIALS: None

- The standard deviation tells how each data value in the set differs from the mean.

- Because normal curves contain the same probability distribution, they can easily be used to make predictions on a set of data.

Example

The length of life of a particular battery is normally distributed with the mean equal to 500 h. The standard deviation is equal to 50 h. Out of 250 batteries tested, find the number of batteries that are still working after 550 h.

Step 1: Sketch the normal curve. Label the mean 500. Label the standard deviations using intervals of 50.

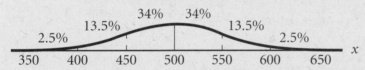

Step 2: A battery that is still going after 550 h falls more than one standard deviation above the mean. Calculate the percent of batteries at least one standard deviation above the mean.

$$13.5\% + 2.5\% = 16\%$$ ⟵ **Add the percentages that fall more that one standard deviation above the mean.**

$$0.16(250) = 40$$ ⟵ **Find 16% of the 250 original batteries.**

About 40 of the 250 batteries are still working after 550 h.

Exercises

Sketch and label the normal curve for the following data. Make a prediction based on the curve.

1. A light bulb lasts an average of 219 h. Out of 1000 bulbs, how many will not last 79 h if the standard deviation is 70 h?

2. In a math class of 26 students, a series of 100 multiplication problems can be completed in a mean time of 4 min. The standard deviation is 1 min. How many math students will still be working after 5 min?

3. A group of 71 frogs had a mean hopping distance of 66 in. and a standard deviation of 3 in. How many frogs will hop more than 72 in.?

Practice 12-7

A set of data with a mean of 45 and a standard deviation of 8.3 is normally distributed. Find each value, given its distance from the mean.

1. +1 standard deviation from the mean

2. +3 standard deviations from the mean

3. −1 standard deviation from the mean

4. −2 standard deviations from the mean

Sketch a normal curve for each distribution. Label the *x*-axis at one, two, and three standard deviations from the mean.

5. mean = 95; standard deviation = 12

6. mean = 100; standard deviation = 15

7. mean = 60; standard deviation = 6

8. mean = 23.8; standard deviation = 5.2

9. mean = 676; standard deviation = 60

10. mean = 54.2; standard deviation = 12.3

A set of data has a normal distribution with a mean of 5.1 and a standard deviation of 0.9. Find the percent of data within each interval.

11. between 4.2 and 5.1

12. between 6.0 and 6.9

13. greater than 6.9

14. between 4.2 and 6.0

15. less than 4.2

16. less than 5.1

17. Scores on an exam are normally distributed with a mean of 76 and a standard deviation of 10.

   a. In a group of 230 tests, how many students score above 96?

   b. In a group of 230 tests, how many students score below 66?

   c. In a group of 230 tests, how many students score within one standard deviation of the mean?

18. The number of nails of a given length is normally distributed with a mean length of 5.00 in. and a standard deviation of 0.03 in.

   a. Find the number of nails in a bag of 120 that are less than 4.94 in. long.

   b. Find the number of nails in a bag of 120 that are between 4.97 and 5.03 in. long.

   c. Find the number of nails in a bag of 120 that are over 5.03 in. long.

19. The actual weights of bags of pet food are normally distributed. The mean of the weights is 50.0 lb, with a standard deviation of 0.2 lb. Use the graph for a–c.

   a. About what percent of bags of pet food weigh less than 49.8 lb?

   b. In a group of 250 bags, how many would you expect to weigh more than 50.4 lb?

   c. In a group of 50 bags, how many would you expect to be within 1.5 standard deviations of the mean?

Reteaching 13-1

Exploring Periodic Data

OBJECTIVE: Recognizing periodic graphs and their features	**MATERIALS:** Yellow, pink, and green highlighting markers

- The Graph of a *periodic function* shows a repeating pattern. The distance from one point on the graph to the point where the pattern begins repeating is called the *period*.

- To find the amplitude, use A $= \frac{1}{2}$ (maximum value – minimum value).

Example

Determine if the graph represents a periodic function. If it is periodic, calculate the period and amplitude of the function.

The repeating pattern determines that the function is periodic.

Draw a vertical line on the graph with the yellow marker. Draw another vertical line at the point where the graph completes one cycle of the pattern.

Draw a horizontal line with a green marker from the *y*-axis to the highest points on the graph.

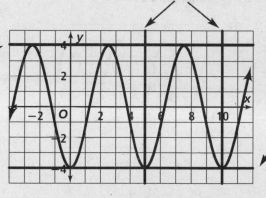

Draw a horizontal line with the pink marker from the *y*-axis to the lowest points on the graph.

Period = 10 − 5 = 5 ← **Calculate the period by determining the distance from one yellow line to the other.**

Amplitude $= \frac{1}{2}(4 - (-4)) = \frac{1}{2}(8) = 4$ ← **Calculate the amplitude using the formula with the maximum being the *y*-value at the green marker and the minimum value the *y*-value at the pink marker.**

Exercises

For each graph of a periodic function, calculate the period and amplitude of the function.

1.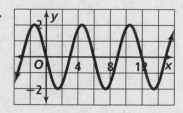

2.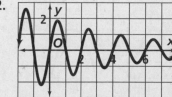

3.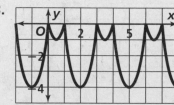

Practice 13-1

Exploring Periodic Data

Determine whether each function *is* or *is not* periodic. If it is, find the period.

1.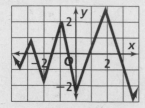

2.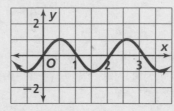

3.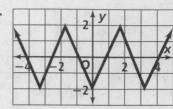

For each function, identify one cycle in two different ways. Then determine the period of the function.

4.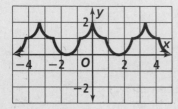

5.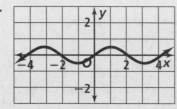

6.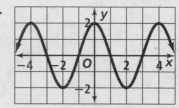

Find the period and amplitude of each periodic function.

7.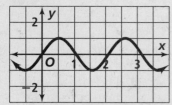

8.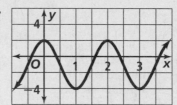

9.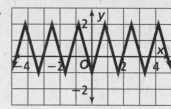

10.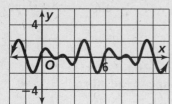

11.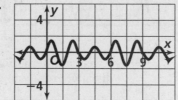

12.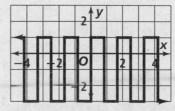

13.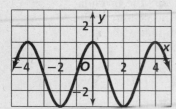

14.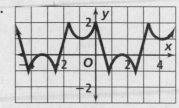

15.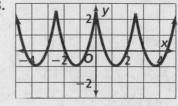

16.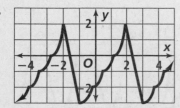

17.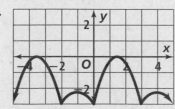

18.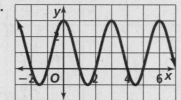

Reteaching 13-2

OBJECTIVE: Finding the coordinates of points on the unit circle

MATERIALS: Ruler, protractor, compass, and calculator

Example

Find the coordinates of the point where the terminal side of a 315° angle intersects the unit circle.

Step 1: Use a compass to draw a unit circle. Use a protractor to sketch the angle. Have the terminal side of the angle intersect the circle.

Step 2: Since the terminal side is in the fourth quadrant, x is positive and y is negative.

Step 3: Use a ruler to draw the horizontal leg of the right triangle. The terminal side of the angle is its hypotenuse. The negative y-axis is the other leg.

Step 4: Since $360 - 315 = 45$, you can label the acute angles of the triangle as 45°. Use properties of special right triangles. The length of the hypotenuse is $\sqrt{2}$ times the length of a leg. Label each leg s.

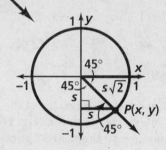

hypotenuse $= 1$

Step 5: The unit circle has a radius of 1 unit.

$s\sqrt{2} = 1$

Substitute $s\sqrt{2}$ **for the length of the hypotenuse.**

$s = \dfrac{1}{\sqrt{2}}$

Divide both sides by $\sqrt{2}$.

$s = \dfrac{\sqrt{2}}{2}$

Rationalize the denominator by multiplying the fraction by $\dfrac{\sqrt{2}}{\sqrt{2}}$.

each leg $= \dfrac{\sqrt{2}}{2}$

The coordinates of the point of intersection are $\left(\dfrac{\sqrt{2}}{2}, -\dfrac{\sqrt{2}}{2}\right)$.

Exercises

Find the coordinates of the point where the terminal side of each angle intersects the unit circle.

1. $-150°$ **2.** $30°$ **3.** $-330°$ **4.** $-45°$ **5.** $120°$ **6.** $225°$

Practice 13-2

Angles and the Unit Circle

Sketch each angle in standard position.

1. 30°   **2.** 60°   **3.** 100°   **4.** 135°   **5.** 210°

6. 270°   **7.** 330°   **8.** −30°   **9.** −90°   **10.** −190°

11. −150°   **12.** −330°   **13.** −45°   **14.** 315°   **15.** −180°

16. 120°   **17.** −120°   **18.** 145°   **19.** −145°   **20.** −355°

Find the measure of an angle between 0° and 360° coterminal with each given angle.

21. −100°   **22.** −60°   **23.** −225°   **24.** −145°   **25.** 372°

26. −15°   **27.** 482°   **28.** 484°   **29.** −20°   **30.** 421°

31. 409°   **32.** −38°   **33.** 376°   **34.** −210°   **35.** 387°

36. 390°   **37.** 660°   **38.** 440°   **39.** −170°   **40.** 370°

41. −700°   **42.** 458°   **43.** 480°   **44.** 406°   **45.** −120°

46. 460°   **47.** −222°   **48.** −330°   **49.** −127°   **50.** 377°

Find the exact coordinates of the point where the terminal side of the given angle intersects the unit circle. Then find the decimal equivalents. Round your answers to the nearest hundredth.

51. 45°   **52.** 225°   **53.** −225°   **54.** −45°   **55.** 330°

56. −330°   **57.** 150°   **58.** −150°   **59.** 300°   **60.** −300°

61. 240°   **62.** 120°   **63.** −90°   **64.** 360°   **65.** 720°

66.
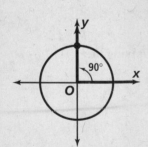

67.
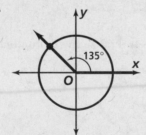

68.
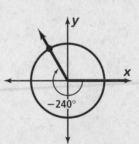

Find the measure of each angle in standard position.

69.
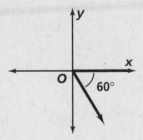

70.
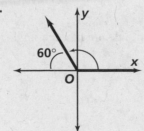

71.
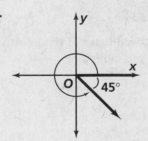

Reteaching 13-3

OBJECTIVE: Using radian measure for angles **MATERIALS:** None

- When converting radians to degrees or degrees to radians, use the proportion
$\dfrac{\text{degree measure}}{360} = \dfrac{\text{radian measure}}{2\pi}$.

Example

Write the measure of 225° in radians.

$\dfrac{225}{360} = \dfrac{x}{2\pi}$ ⟵ **Substitute 225 for degree measure and a variable for radian measure.**

$360x = 450\pi$ ⟵ **Cross multiply.**

$x = \dfrac{450\pi}{360}$ ⟵ **Divide each side by 360.**

$x = \dfrac{5\pi}{4}$ ⟵ **Simplify.**

$x \approx 3.93$ ⟵ **Use a calculator.**

$\dfrac{\theta}{360} = \dfrac{\frac{5}{4}\pi}{2\pi}$ ⟵ **Check by substituting the radians into the proportion and solving for degrees.**

$\dfrac{\theta}{360} = \dfrac{\frac{5}{4}\cancel{\pi}}{2\cancel{\pi}}$ ⟵ **Cancel π since it is in the numerator and denominator.**

$2\theta = 450$ ⟵ **Cross multiply.**

$\theta = 225$ ⟵ **Divide each side by 2. This gives the degree measure.**

An angle of 225° measures about 3.93 radians.

Exercises

Write each measure in radians and check.

1. 20° **2.** 150° **3.** 45°

4. −110° **5.** 315° **6.** 320°

Write each measure in degrees and check.

7. $-\dfrac{3\pi}{2}$ **8.** $\dfrac{5\pi}{3}$ **9.** $\dfrac{\pi}{12}$

10. $\dfrac{8\pi}{5}$ **11.** $-\dfrac{7\pi}{6}$ **12.** $\dfrac{9\pi}{2}$

Practice 13-3

Radian Measure

Write each measure in radians. Express your answer in terms of π.

1. 45° **2.** 90° **3.** 30° **4.** 150° **5.** 180°

6. 240° **7.** 270° **8.** 300° **9.** 360° **10.** 40°

11. 80° **12.** 110° **13.** 160° **14.** 200° **15.** 220°

Write each measure in degrees. Round your answer to the nearest degree, if necessary.

16. π **17.** 2π **18.** $\frac{5\pi}{6}$ **19.** $\frac{3\pi}{4}$ **20.** $\frac{3\pi}{2}$

21. $\frac{\pi}{6}$ **22.** $\frac{7\pi}{6}$ **23.** $\frac{11\pi}{6}$ **24.** $\frac{\pi}{3}$ **25.** $\frac{4\pi}{3}$

26. $\frac{5\pi}{4}$ **27.** $\frac{7\pi}{4}$ **28.** $\frac{2\pi}{3}$ **29.** $\frac{\pi}{9}$ **30.** $\frac{2\pi}{9}$

The measure θ of an angle in standard position is given. Find the exact values of $\cos\theta$ and $\sin\theta$ for each angle measure.

31. $\frac{\pi}{6}$ radians **32.** $\frac{\pi}{3}$ radians **33.** $-\frac{3\pi}{4}$ radians **34.** $\frac{7\pi}{4}$ radians

35. $\frac{5\pi}{6}$ radians **36.** $\frac{4\pi}{3}$ radians **37.** $\frac{11\pi}{6}$ radians **38.** $\frac{2\pi}{3}$ radians

Use each circle to find the length of the indicated arc. Round your answer to the nearest tenth.

39.
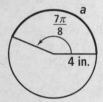

40.
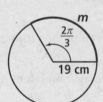

41.
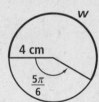

42.
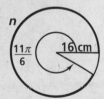

43.
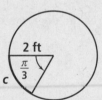

44.
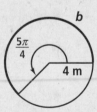

45. A pendulum swings through an angle of 1.8 radians. The distance the tip of the pendulum travels is 32 in. How long is the pendulum?

46. A 0.8 m pendulum swings through an angle of 1.5 radians. What distance does the tip of the pendulum travel?

Reteaching 13-4

OBJECTIVE: Graphing sine curves	**MATERIALS:** Graph paper, colored pencils, and string

Example

Graph at least two cycles of the function $y = 2 \sin \frac{1}{2} \theta$.

$|a| = 2$ **Step 1:** **Find the amplitude.**

$b = \frac{1}{2}$ **Find the number of cycles in the interval from 0 to 2π.**

$\dfrac{2\pi}{b} = \dfrac{2\pi}{\frac{1}{2}}$ **Find the period of the curve.**

$= 4\pi$

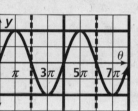

Step 2: **Draw a horizontal and vertical axis. Label π, 2π, 3π ..., 8π. Draw a red solid vertical line at 0, 4π, and 8π to denote the end of each cycle. Draw a blue dotted vertical line at 2π and 6π to denote one-half cycle. Draw a green solid horizontal line at $y = 2$ and $y = -2$ to denote the amplitude.**

Step 3: **Use string to form the graph. Then draw the graph.**

Exercises

Graph each function.

1. $y = \sin \frac{1}{2}\theta$ **2.** $y = 2 \sin 3\theta$ **3.** $y = 5 \sin \theta$

4. $y = 2 \sin 2\theta$ **5.** $y = \sin \frac{1}{3}\theta$ **6.** $y = \frac{1}{2} \sin \theta$

7. $y = -2 \sin \frac{1}{2}\theta$ **8.** $y = -\sin 3\theta$ **9.** $y = -\frac{1}{4} \sin \theta$

Practice 13-4

The Sine Function

Find the amplitude and period of each sine curve. Then write an equation for each curve.

1.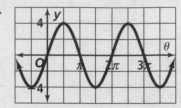

2.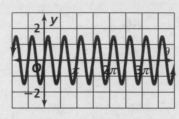

3.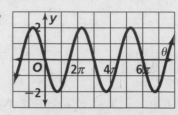

4.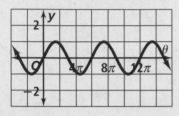

5.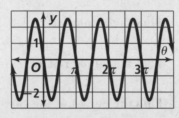

6.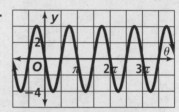

Sketch one cycle of each sine curve. Assume $a > 0$. Write an equation for each graph.

7. amplitude = 2; period = π

8. amplitude = 3; period = 2π

9. amplitude = 2; period = $\frac{\pi}{2}$

10. amplitude = 2; period = $\frac{\pi}{4}$

11. amplitude = 1.5; period = $\frac{\pi}{3}$

12. amplitude = 2.5; period = 2π

Sketch one cycle of the graph of each sine function.

13. $y = 2 \sin \theta$

14. $y = -2 \sin 4\theta$

15. $y = \sin 2\theta$

16. $y = 3 \sin \frac{\theta}{2}$

17. $y = -\sin 2\theta$

18. $y = -5 \sin 3\theta$

19. $y = -3 \sin 2\theta$

20. $y = 4 \sin 5\theta$

21. $y = -4 \sin \frac{\theta}{2}$

Use the graph at the right to find the value of $y = 0.3 \sin \theta$ for each value of θ.

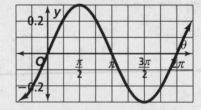

22. 6 radians

23. $\frac{\pi}{4}$ radians

24. $\frac{3\pi}{4}$ radians

25. $\frac{\pi}{2}$ radian

Use the graph at the right to find the value of $y = 0.3 \sin \theta$ for each value of θ.

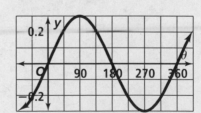

26. 160°

27. 135°

28. 270°

29. 225°

Reteaching 13-5

The Cosine Function

> **OBJECTIVE:** Graphing cosine curves   **MATERIALS:** None

- The basic equation for a cosine function is $y = a \cos b\theta$. The amplitude is $|a|$ and the period is $\frac{2\pi}{b}$.

Example

Identify the amplitude and period for the function
$y = 4 \cos 2\pi\theta$. Graph the function.

$y = 4 \cos 2\pi\theta$

$|a| = |4| = 4$ $\longleftarrow$ **Find the amplitude of the function.**

$\frac{2\pi}{b} = \frac{2\pi}{2\pi} = 1$ $\longleftarrow$ **Calculate the period of the function.**

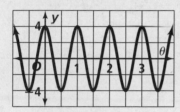 $\longleftarrow$ **Since the amplitude is 4, start the graph at (0, 4). Complete one cycle between 0 and 1 since the period is 1.**

Exercises

Identify the amplitude and period. Graph each function.

1. $y = \frac{1}{2} \cos 2\theta$ **2.** $y = 3 \cos \frac{1}{2}\theta$ **3.** $y = \cos 3\theta$

4. $y = \frac{1}{4} \cos \pi\theta$ **5.** $y = -2 \cos \frac{1}{2}\theta$ **6.** $y = 2 \cos 6\pi\theta$

7. $y = -2 \cos \theta$ **8.** $y = \cos \frac{1}{5}\theta$ **9.** $y = 2 \cos 2\theta$

Practice 13-5

The Cosine Function

Sketch the graph of each function in the interval from 0 to 2π.

1. $y = \cos \theta$

2. $y = 2 \cos \pi\theta$

3. $y = 5 \cos \theta$

4. $y = -\cos \theta$

5. $y = -5 \cos \theta$

6. $y = \cos 2\pi\theta$

7. $y = -2 \cos 2\theta$

8. $y = 3 \cos 4\theta$

9. $y = \cos \frac{\theta}{2}$

10. $y = 3 \cos 8\theta$

11. $y = -4 \cos \pi\theta$

12. $y = 0.5 \cos \pi\theta$

13. $y = -\cos 2\theta$

14. $y = -3 \cos \frac{\pi}{2}\theta$

15. $y = 4 \cos \pi\theta$

16. Suppose 12 in. waves occur every 5 s. Write an equation using a cosine function that models the height of a water particle as it moves from crest to crest.

Write the equation of a cosine function for each graph.

17.

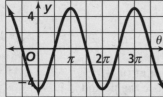

18.

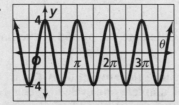

19.

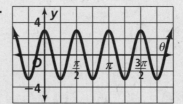

Find the period and amplitude of each cosine function. Identify where the maximum value, minimum value, and zeros occur in the interval from 0 to 2π.

20.

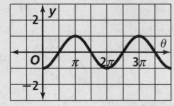

21.

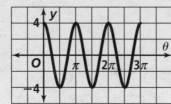

22.

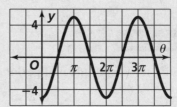

Solve each equation in the interval from 0 to 2π. Round to the nearest hundredth.

23. $2 \cos 3\theta = 1.5$

24. $\cot \frac{t}{3} = 1$

25. $1.5 \cos \pi\theta = -1.5$

26. $3 \cos \frac{\pi}{5} \theta = 2$

27. $3 \cos t = 2$

28. $0.5 \cos \frac{\theta}{2} = 0.5$

29. $4 \cos \frac{\pi}{4} \theta = -2$

30. $3 \cos \frac{\theta}{4} = 1.5$

31. $3 \cos \theta = -3$

Write a cosine function for each description. Assume that $a > 0$.

32. amplitude $= 2\pi$, period $= 1$

33. amplitude $= \frac{1}{2}$, period $= \pi$

Reteaching 13-6

OBJECTIVE: Graphing tangent curves	**MATERIALS:** None

The tangent function is a discontinuous periodic function. Its equation in standard form is $y = \tan b\theta$. For the tangent function, b, represents the number of cycles from 0 to π, and its period is $\frac{\pi}{b}$. One cycle occurs in the interval from $-\frac{\pi}{2b}$ to $\frac{\pi}{2b}$, and vertical asymptotes occur at the end of each cycle.

Example

Graph the function $y = 3 \tan \pi\theta$.

$\frac{\pi}{b} = \frac{\pi}{\pi} = 1$ ⟵   **Calculate the period of the function. One cycle occurs in the interval $-\frac{1}{2}$ to $\frac{1}{2}$.**

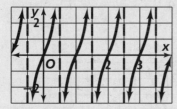   ⟵   **Because the period is 1, asymptotes occur every 1 unit— at . . . , $-\frac{1}{2}, \frac{1}{2}, \frac{3}{2}, \frac{5}{2}, \frac{7}{2}, \ldots$.**

Plot three points in each cycle. Sketch the curve.

Exercises

Identify the period and tell where the asymptotes occur between 0 and 2π. Graph each function.

1. $y = 3 \tan 2\theta$ **2.** $y = -2 \tan \frac{1}{2}\theta$ **3.** $y = -2 \tan \theta$

4. $y = 2 \tan 2\theta$ **5.** $y = -\tan \frac{\pi}{2}\theta$ **6.** $y = \frac{1}{2} \tan \theta$

7. $y = \tan 3\theta$ **8.** $y = -2 \tan \frac{1}{2}\pi\theta$ **9.** $y = 2 \tan \frac{\pi}{4}\theta$

Practice 13-6

The Tangent Function

Identify the period and tell where the asymptotes occur, in the interval from 0 to 2π, for each function.

1. $y = \tan \theta$

2. $y = 2 \tan \frac{\theta}{2}$

3. $y = 3 \tan \frac{\theta}{4}$

4. $y = 4 \tan 2\theta$

5. $y = -\tan \frac{\pi}{2}\theta$

6. $y = -2 \tan \pi\theta$

7. $y = -3 \tan 2\theta$

8. $y = -4 \tan \theta$

9. $y = 0.5 \tan \pi\theta$

Sketch two cycles of the graph of each function.

10. $y = \tan \theta$

11. $y = 2 \tan \theta$

12. $y = -\tan \theta$

13. $y = -2 \tan \theta$

14. $y = -0.5 \tan 2\theta$

15. $y = 3 \tan \theta$

16. $y = -3 \tan 2\theta$

17. $y = 5 \tan \frac{\pi}{2}\theta$

18. $y = 2 \tan 3\theta$

19. $y = 0.5 \tan 2\theta$

20. $y = -2.5 \tan \frac{\pi}{2}\theta$

21. $y = -5 \tan 2\pi\theta$

22. $y = -2 \tan 4\theta$

23. $y = -0.25 \tan 3\theta$

24. $y = -4 \tan 4\pi\theta$

25. $y = -2.25 \tan \theta$

26. $y = -0.25 \tan \frac{\pi}{3}\theta$

27. $y = 0.75 \tan 4\theta$

Identify the period of each tangent function.

28.
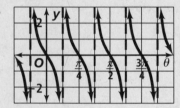

29.
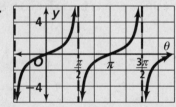

30.
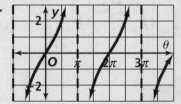

Use the graph of $y = \tan \theta$ to find each value. If the tangent is undefined at that point, write *undefined*.

31. $\tan \frac{\pi}{2}$

32. $\tan \left(-\frac{3\pi}{4}\right)$

33. $\tan \left(-\frac{\pi}{4}\right)$

34. $\tan \frac{3\pi}{2}$

Using your graphing calculator, graph each function on the interval $0° < x < 470°$ and $-300 < y < 300$. Evaluate the function at $x = 45°, 90°$, and $135°$.

35. $y = 200 \tan x$

36. $y = -75 \tan \left(\frac{1}{4}x\right)$

37. $y = -50 \tan x$

Reteaching 13-7

OBJECTIVE: Graphing translations of trigonometric curves	**MATERIALS:** None

A horizontal translation of a periodic function is a phase shift.
When $g(x) = f(x-h)$, the value of h is the amount of the shift left or right.
If $h > 0$, the shift is to the right. If $h < 0$, the shift is to the left.

A vertical translation can occur as well. When $g(x) = f(x) + k$, the value
of k is the amount of the shift up or down. If $k > 0$, the shift is up. If $k < 0$,
the shift is down.

Example

Sketch the graph of $y = 2 \sin 3\left(x - \dfrac{\pi}{3}\right) + 1$ in the interval from 0 to 2π.

Since $a = 2$ and $b = 3$, the graph is a translation of $y = 2 \sin 3x$.

Step 1: **Sketch one cycle of $y = 2 \sin 3x$.**
Use five points in the pattern
zero–max–zero–min–zero.

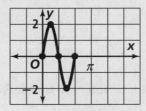

Step 2: **Since $h = \dfrac{\pi}{3}$ and $k = 1$, translate**
the graph $\dfrac{\pi}{3}$ units to the right and 1 unit up.
Extend the periodic pattern throughout
the interval from 0 to 2π. Sketch the graph.

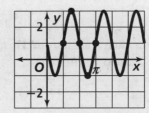

Exercises

Sketch each graph in the interval from 0 to 2π.

1. $y = \cos 3\left(x + \dfrac{\pi}{2}\right)$ **2.** $y = -2 \sin \dfrac{1}{2}x - 1$ **3.** $y = -2 \cos (x + \pi) - 2$

4. $y = \dfrac{1}{2} \sin 2(x - 2)$ **5.** $y = -\sin 2x + 3$ **6.** $y = \dfrac{1}{2} \cos \left(x - \dfrac{\pi}{3}\right)$

7. $y = \sin 3x + \dfrac{1}{2}$ **8.** $y = -2 \cos \dfrac{1}{2}(x + \pi)$ **9.** $y = 2 \cos \dfrac{\pi}{4}x + 2.5$

Practice 13-7

Translating Sine and Cosine Functions

Graph each function in the interval from 0 to 2π.

1. $y = -\sin\left(x + \frac{\pi}{2}\right)$

2. $y = 3\sin\left(x - \frac{\pi}{4}\right) + 2$

3. $y = \cos\frac{1}{2}x + 1$

4. $y = 3\cos(x - 2)$

5. $y = \sin 3(x - \pi)$

6. $y = \cos(x + 4)$

7. $y = \cos x + 3$

8. $y = -2\sin x + 1$

9. $y = -\cos 2\left(x + \frac{\pi}{4}\right)$

10. $y = \frac{1}{2}\cos x + 3$

11. $y = \sin\frac{1}{2}(x + \pi)$

12. $y = \cos\left(x + \frac{\pi}{6}\right)$

13. $y = -2\cos x + 3$

14. $y = \sin 2x + 1$

15. $y = \sin 2\left(x - \frac{\pi}{3}\right)$

Write an equation for each translation.

16. $y = \sin x$, 2 units down

17. $y = \cos x$, π units left

18. $y = \cos x$, $\frac{\pi}{4}$ units up

19. $y = \sin x$, 3.2 units to the right

Find the amplitude and period of each function. Describe any phase shift and vertical shift in the graph.

20. $y = 3\cos x + 2$

21. $y = -2\sin\left(x + \frac{\pi}{2}\right)$

22. $y = \cos 2x + 1$

23. $y = -\sin\left(x - \frac{\pi}{3}\right)$

24. $y = \frac{1}{2}\cos x - 3$

25. $y = \cos\frac{1}{2}x - 2$

Use the function $f(x)$ at the right. Graph each translation.

26. $f(x) + 3$

27. $f(x + 1)$

28. $f(x) - 5$

29. $f(x + 3)$

30. $f(x + 2) - 1$

31. $f(x) - 4$

What is the value of h in each translation? Describe each phase shift (use a phrase like *3 units to the left*).

32. $g(x) = f(x + 2)$

33. $g(x) = f(x - 1)$

34. $h(t) = f(t + 1.5)$

35. $f(x) = g(x - 1)$

36. $y = \cos\left(x - \frac{\pi}{2}\right)$

37. $y = \cos(x + \pi)$

Reteaching 13-8

Reciprocal Trigonometric Functions

· ·

OBJECTIVE: Graphing reciprocal trigonometric functions	**MATERIALS:** None

The cosecant (csc), secant (sec), and cotangent (cot) functions are defined as reciprocals of the sine (sin), cosine (cos), and tangent (tan) functions, respectively. Their domains include all real numbers except those that make a denominator zero.

$$\csc \theta = \frac{1}{\sin \theta} \qquad \sec \theta = \frac{1}{\cos \theta} \qquad \cot \theta = \frac{1}{\tan \theta}$$

Example

Sketch the graph of $y = \cos \theta$ and $y = \sec \theta$ in the interval from 0 to 2π.

Step 1: **Make a table of values. The graph of $y = \sec \theta$ has asymptotes where $\cos \theta$ is equal to zero.**

θ	0	$\frac{\pi}{4}$	$\frac{\pi}{2}$	$\frac{3\pi}{4}$	π	$\frac{5\pi}{4}$	$\frac{3\pi}{2}$	$\frac{7\pi}{4}$	2π
$\cos \theta$	1	0.71	0	-0.71	-1	-0.71	0	0.71	1
$\sec \theta$	1	1.41	—	-1.41	-1	-1.41	—	1.41	1

Step 2: **Plot the points and sketch the graphs.**

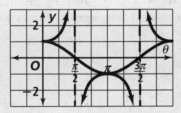

Exercises

Sketch each graph in the interval from 0 to 2π.

1. $y = \cot 3\theta$

2. $y = -2 \sec \frac{1}{2}\theta$

3. $y = -2 \csc (\theta + \pi) - 2$

4. $y = \frac{1}{2} \csc 2(\theta - 2)$

5. $y = -\sec 2\theta$

6. $y = \frac{1}{2} \cot \left(\theta - \frac{\pi}{2}\right)$

7. $y = \cot 3\theta + \frac{1}{2}$

8. $y = -2 \csc \frac{1}{2}\theta$

9. $y = 2 \cot \frac{\pi}{4}\theta$

· ·

Practice 13-8

Reciprocal Trigonometric Functions

Evaluate each expression. Each angle is given in radians. Round to the nearest thousandth, if necessary.

1. $\cot 4$

2. $\csc \frac{\pi}{6}$

3. $\csc(-2)$

4. $\sec \pi$

5. $\cot(-\pi)$

6. $\sec(-3.5)$

7. $\cot \frac{\pi}{3}$

8. $\sec 1.5$

9. $\csc(-1.5)$

10. $\cot \pi$

11. $\sec 3$

12. $\csc \frac{\pi}{4}$

Evaluate each expression. Write your answer in exact form. If appropriate, also state it as a decimal rounded to the nearest hundredth. If the expression is undefined, write *undefined*.

13. $\sec 45°$

14. $\cot 180°$

15. $\sec 30°$

16. $\csc 30°$

17. $\cot(-180°)$

18. $\csc(-45°)$

19. $\csc 180°$

20. $\cot 45°$

21. $\sec 90°$

22. $\sec(-30°)$

23. $\csc(-60°)$

24. $\sec 60°$

25. Suppose $\tan \theta = \frac{6}{9}$. Find $\cot \theta$

26. Suppose $\sin \theta = \frac{2}{5}$. Find $\csc \theta$

27. Suppose $\cos \theta = \frac{14}{20}$. Find $\sec \theta$

28. Suppose $\tan \theta = -\frac{2}{3}$. Find $\cot \theta$

Graph each function in the interval from 0 to 2π.

29. $y = \cot 2\theta$

30. $y = -\cot \frac{1}{2}\theta$

31. $y = \sec\left(\theta - \frac{\pi}{2}\right)$

32. $y = \csc 2\theta + 1$

33. $y = -\csc 3\theta$

34. $y = \sec \theta + 2$

35. $y = \cot(\theta + \pi)$

36. $y = \sec \frac{1}{4}\theta$

37. $y = \csc \theta - 1$

Use the graph of the appropriate reciprocal trigonometric function to find each value. Round to the nearest thousandth, if necessary.

38. $\cot 30°$

39. $\csc 180°$

40. $\cot 70°$

41. $\sec 100°$

42. $\sec 50°$

43. $\csc 100°$

44. $\cot 20°$

45. $\sec 120°$

46. A fire truck is parked on the shoulder of a freeway next to a long wall. The red light on the top of the truck rotates through one complete revolution every 2 seconds. The function $y = 10 \sec \pi t$ models the length of the beam in feet to a point on the wall in terms of time t.

  a. Graph the function.

  b. Find the length at time 1.75 seconds.

  c. Find the length at time 2 seconds.

Reteaching 14-1   Trigonometric Identities

OBJECTIVE: Verifying trigonometric identities   **MATERIALS:** None

To verify an identity, you should transform one side of the equation until it is the same as the other side. It is sometimes helpful to write all the functions in terms of sine and cosine.

Example

Verify the identity $1 + \cot^2 \theta = \csc^2 \theta$.

$$1 + \cot^2 \theta = 1 + \left(\frac{\cos \theta}{\sin \theta}\right)^2 \qquad \longleftarrow \textbf{Cotangent identity}$$

$$= 1 + \frac{\cos^2 \theta}{\sin^2 \theta} \qquad \longleftarrow \textbf{Simplify.}$$

$$= \frac{\sin^2 \theta}{\sin^2 \theta} + \frac{\cos^2 \theta}{\sin^2 \theta} \qquad \longleftarrow \textbf{Write the fractions with common denominators.}$$

$$= \frac{\sin^2 \theta + \cos^2 \theta}{\sin^2 \theta} \qquad \longleftarrow \textbf{Add.}$$

$$= \frac{1}{\sin^2 \theta} \qquad \longleftarrow \textbf{Pythagorean identity}$$

$$= \csc^2 \theta \qquad \longleftarrow \textbf{Reciprocal identity}$$

Exercises

Verify each identity.

1. $\cot \theta \tan \theta = 1$

2. $\cos \theta \sec \theta = 1$

3. $\csc \theta \tan \theta + \cot^2 \theta = \csc^2 \theta$

4. $\sin \theta (1 + \cot^2 \theta) = \csc \theta$

5. $\sec \theta \cot \theta = \csc \theta$

6. $\sec^2 \theta - \sec^2 \theta \cos^2 \theta = \tan^2 \theta$

7. $\cot \theta \tan \theta + \tan^2 \theta = \sec^2 \theta$

8. $\csc^2 \theta - \cot^2 \theta = 1$

9. $\sin \theta + \cos \theta \cot \theta = \csc \theta$

10. $\frac{\sec \theta - \cos \theta}{\sec \theta} = \sin^2 \theta$

11. $\cot \theta \sec \theta \sin \theta = 1$

12. $\tan \theta (\sin \theta - \csc \theta) = -\cos \theta$

Practice 14-1

Verify each identity.

1. $\sin \theta \sec \theta \cot \theta = 1$

2. $\csc \theta = \cot \theta \sec \theta$

3. $\dfrac{\sin \theta}{\csc \theta} = \sin^2 \theta$

4. $\cos \theta \csc \theta \tan \theta = 1$

5. $\sin \theta \tan \theta + \cos \theta = \sec \theta$

6. $\dfrac{\csc \theta}{\cot \theta} = \sec \theta$

7. $\sec \theta = \tan \theta \csc \theta$

8. $\tan \theta + \cot \theta = \sec \theta \csc \theta$

9. $\tan^2 \theta + 1 = \sec^2 \theta$

10. $\cos \theta \cot \theta + \sin \theta = \csc \theta$

11. $\dfrac{\sec \theta}{\csc \theta} = \tan \theta$

12. $\sec \theta \cot \theta = \csc \theta$

13. $\sec^2 \theta - \tan^2 \theta = 1$

14. $\sec \theta = \csc \theta \tan \theta$

15. $\dfrac{\sin \theta + \cos \theta}{\sin \theta} = 1 + \cot \theta$

16. $\cos \theta (\sec \theta - \cos \theta) = \sin^2 \theta$

17. $\cot \theta \sec \theta = \csc \theta$

18. $(1 - \sin \theta)(1 + \sin \theta) = \cos^2 \theta$

Simplify each trigonometric expression.

19. $1 - \sec^2 \theta$

20. $\dfrac{\sec \theta}{\tan \theta}$

21. $\csc \theta \tan \theta$

22. $\sec \theta \cos^2 \theta$

23. $\csc^2 \theta - \cot^2 \theta$

24. $1 - \sin^2 \theta$

25. $\tan \theta \cot \theta$

26. $\cos \theta \cot \theta + \sin \theta$

27. $\cos \theta \tan \theta$

28. $\dfrac{\sin \theta \cot \theta}{\cos \theta}$

29. $\sec \theta \tan \theta \csc \theta$

30. $\sec \theta \cot \theta$

31. $\dfrac{\sin \theta}{\csc \theta} + \dfrac{\cos \theta}{\sec \theta}$

32. $\dfrac{\tan \theta \csc \theta}{\sec \theta}$

33. $\cot^2 \theta - \csc^2 \theta$

34. $\dfrac{\cot \theta}{\csc \theta}$

Reteaching 14-2

Solving Trigonometric Equations Using Inverses

• •

OBJECTIVE: Solving trigonometric equations using inverses

MATERIALS: Calculator

Example

Solve $4 \sin \theta - \sqrt{3} = 2 \sin \theta$ for $0 \le \theta < 2\pi$.

$4 \sin \theta - \sqrt{3} = 2 \sin \theta$

$2 \sin \theta - \sqrt{3} = 0$ ⟵ **Subtract $2 \sin \theta$ from each side.**

$2 \sin \theta = \sqrt{3}$ ⟵ **Add $\sqrt{3}$ to each side.**

$\sin \theta = \dfrac{\sqrt{3}}{2}$ ⟵ **Divide each side by 2.**

$\sin^{-1} \dfrac{\sqrt{3}}{2} = \dfrac{\pi}{3}$ ⟵ **Use the inverse function to find one value of θ.**

The sine function is also positive in Quadrant II. So another value of θ is

$\pi - \dfrac{\pi}{3} = \dfrac{2\pi}{3}$.

The two solutions between 0 and 2π are $\dfrac{\pi}{3}$ and $\dfrac{2\pi}{3}$.

Exercises

Solve each equation for $0 \le \theta < 2\pi$.

1. $\sin \theta + 2 \sin \theta \cos \theta = 0$

2. $2 \sin \theta - 4 = -2 \sin \theta$

3. $2 \cos^2 \theta + \cos \theta - 1 = 0$

4. $\cos \theta - 2 \sin \theta \cos \theta = 0$

5. $\sqrt{3} + 5 \sin \theta = 3 \sin \theta$

6. $3 \sin \theta = 1$

7. $2 \tan \theta - 4 = 0$

8. $4 \sin^2 \theta - 1 = 0$

9. $2 \sin^2 \theta + 3 \sin \theta = -1$

10. $\tan \theta(\sin \theta - 1) = 0$

11. $3 \tan \theta = -\sqrt{3}$

12. $-5 \cos \theta = \cos \theta - 3\sqrt{3}$

Practice 14-2

Solving Trigonometric Equations Using Inverses

Solve each equation for $0 \leq \theta < 2\pi$.

1. $2 \tan \theta + 2 = 0$

2. $2 \cos \theta = 1$

3. $2 \cos \theta + \sqrt{3} = 0$

4. $\sqrt{3} \cot \theta - 1 = 0$

5. $4 \sin \theta - 3 = 0$

6. $4 \sin \theta + 3 = 0$

7. $\left(2 \cos \theta + \sqrt{3}\right)(2 \cos \theta + 1) = 0$

8. $\sqrt{3} \tan \theta - 2 \sin \theta \tan \theta = 0$

9. $2 \cos^2 \theta + \cos \theta = 0$

10. $5 \cos \theta - 3 = 0$

11. $\tan \theta - 2 \cos \theta \tan \theta = 0$

12. $\tan \theta (\tan \theta + 1) = 0$

13. $(\cos \theta - 1)(2 \cos \theta - 1) = 0$

14. $\tan^2 \theta - \tan \theta = 0$

15. If a projectile is fired into the air with an initial velocity v at an angle of elevation θ, then the height h of the projectile at time t is given by $h = -16t^2 + vt \sin \theta$.

    a. Find the angle of elevation θ of a rifle barrel, to the nearest tenth of a degree, if a bullet fired at 1500 ft/s takes 2 s to reach a height of 750 ft.

    b. Find the angle of elevation of a rifle, to the nearest tenth of a degree, if a bullet fired at 1500 ft/s takes 3 s to reach a height of 750 ft.

Use a calculator and inverse functions to find the radian measures of the angles.

16. angles whose tangent is 2.5

17. angles whose sine is 0.75

18. angles whose cosine is (-0.24)

19. angles whose cosine is 0.45

Use a unit circle and 45°–45°–90° triangles to find the degree measures of the angles.

20. angles whose sine is $\dfrac{\sqrt{2}}{2}$

21. angles whose tangent is 1

22. angles whose cosine is $\dfrac{\sqrt{2}}{2}$

23. angle whose sine is 1

Use the graph of the inverse of $y = \cos \theta$ at the right.

24. Find the measures of the angles whose cosine is -1.

25. Find the measures of the angles whose cosine is 0.

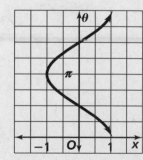

Reteaching 14-3

OBJECTIVE: Using trigonometric ratios to find missing measures of right triangles

MATERIALS: Calculator

To apply a trigonometric formula correctly, label the triangle's adjacent leg, opposite leg, and hypotenuse first. Follow these steps:

Step 1: Place an index finger on the right angle. Place your other index finger on the side opposite the right angle. Label it the *hypotenuse*.

Step 2: Place an index finger on the given angle. Place your other index finger on the leg touching the given angle. Label it *adjacent*.

Step 3: Keep the index finger on the given angle. Place your other index finger on the leg opposite the given angle. Label it *opposite*.

Example

In right $\triangle ABC$, $m\angle A = 42°$ and $c = 28$. Find the lengths of a and b. Round to the nearest tenth.

$\sin \theta = \dfrac{\text{opp}}{\text{hyp}}$ ←   **To find *a*, the opposite leg, use sine.**

$\sin 42° = \dfrac{a}{28}$ ←   **Substitute values.**

$28(\sin 42°) = a$ ←   **Multiply each side by 28.**

$28(0.6691) = a$ ←   **Use a calculator.**

$18.7 = a$ ←   **Label *a* = 18.7 on the triangle.**

$\cos \theta = \dfrac{\text{adj}}{\text{hyp}}$ ←   **To find *b*, the adjacent leg, use cosine.**

$\cos 42° = \dfrac{b}{28}$ ←   **Substitute values.**

$28(\cos 42°) = b$ ←   **Multiply each side by 28.**

$28(0.7431) = b$ ←   **Use a calculator.**

$20.8 = b$ ←   **Label *b* = 20.8 on the triangle.**

Exercises

In $\triangle ABC$, $\angle C$ is a right angle. Two measures are given. Find the remaining sides and angles to the nearest tenth.

1. $m\angle B = 20°, a = 6$ **2.** $m\angle B = 60°, c = 14$ **3.** $m\angle A = 10°, a = 10$

4. $b = 7, c = 10$ **5.** $a = 35, b = 21$ **6.** $m\angle A = 36.5°, c = 28.2$

Practice 14-3

Right Triangles and Trigonometric Ratios

Use the triangle at the right to find the exact values of the trigonometric ratios.

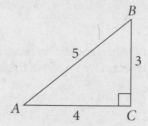

1. $\cos A$

2. $\cos B$

3. $\tan A$

4. $\tan B$

5. $\cot B$

6. $\sec A$

7. $\csc A$

8. $\sin B$

In $\triangle DEF$, $\angle D$ is a right angle. Find the remaining sides and angles. Round answers to the nearest tenth.

9. $f = 8$, $e = 15$ **10.** $f = 1$, $d = 2$ **11.** $f = 1$, $e = 2$ **12.** $f = 2$, $e = 1$

13. $f = 1$, $d = 500$ **14.** $d = 21$, $e = 8$ **15.** $e = 6$, $d = 12$ **16.** $e = 5$, $f = 1$

17. Suppose you are standing on one bank of a river. A tree on the other side of the river is known to be 150 ft tall. A line from the top of the tree to the ground at your feet makes an angle of 11° with the ground. How far from you is the base of the tree?

18. A kite string makes a 62° angle with the horizontal, and 300 ft of string is let out. The string is held 6 ft off the ground. How high is the kite?

19. You are designing several access ramps. What angle would each ramp make with the ground, to the nearest 0.1°?

    a. 20 ft long, rises 16 in.   **b.** 8 ft long, rises 8 in.   **c.** 12 ft long, rises 6 in.

    d. 30 ft long, rises 32 in.   **e.** 4 ft long, rises 6 in.   **f.** 6 ft long, rises 14 in.

20. In $\triangle ABC$, $\angle C$ is a right angle and $\tan A = \frac{2}{3}$. Draw a diagram and find each value in fraction form and in decimal form.

    a. $\cos A$ **b.** $\tan B$ **c.** $\sin A$

    d. $\cot B$ **e.** $\sec A$ **f.** $\csc B$

Find the measure of each angle to the nearest tenth of a degree.

21. $\sin^{-1}\left(\frac{\sqrt{2}}{2}\right)$ **22.** $\cos^{-1}(0.5)$ **23.** $\tan^{-1}\left(\sqrt{3}\right)$ **24.** $\sin^{-1}(0.3232)$

25. $\cos^{-1}(0.8)$ **26.** $\tan^{-1}(1)$ **27.** $\cos^{-1}(0.4)$ **28.** $\tan^{-1}(3.2678)$

29. $\sin^{-1}(0.75)$ **30.** $\tan^{-1}(0.5)$ **31.** $\tan^{-1}(12.0001)$ **32.** $\sin^{-1}(0.1044)$

Reteaching 14-4

Area and The Law of Sines

OBJECTIVE: Using the Law of Sines to find the measures of the sides or angles of a triangle	**MATERIALS:** None

Law of Sines: $\frac{\sin A}{a} = \frac{\sin B}{b} = \frac{\sin C}{c}$

Use the Law of Sines when you are given the measure of two angles of a triangle and the length of any side or the measure of two sides and the measure of the angle opposite one of them.

Example

Based on the given information, use the Law of Sines to find side b in the triangle.

$A = 30°, B = 70°, a = 8$ ⟵ **Because we know two angles and a side, use the Law of Sines.**

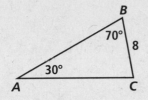

⟵ **Draw a triangle, and label A, B, and a.**

$\frac{\sin 30°}{8} = \frac{\sin 70°}{b}$ ⟵ **Substitute values into the Law of Sines formula.**

$\frac{0.5}{8} = \frac{0.9397}{b}$ ⟵ **Use a calculator to find sin 30° and sin 70°.**

$0.5b = 7.52$ ⟵ **Multiply each side by 8b.**

$b = 15.04$ ⟵ **Solve for b.**

Exercises

Find the unknown side measure or angle for each triangle. Round to the nearest tenth.

1. Find a if $A = 18°, B = 28°$, and $b = 100$.

2. Find c if $B = 18°, C = 152°$, and $b = 4$.

3. Find a if $C = 16°, A = 92°$, and $c = 32$.

4. Find B if $C = 95°, b = 5$, and $c = 6$.

5. Find B if $A = 40°, b = 6$, and $a = 12$.

6. Find c if $A = 50°, C = 60°$, and $a = 36$.

7. Find c if $B = 110°, C = 40°$, and $b = 18$.

8. Find a if $A = 5°, C = 125°$, and $c = 510$.

Practice 14-4

Area and the Law of Sines

Use the Law of Sines. Find the measure of the indicated part of each triangle. Round answers to the nearest tenth.

1. Find $m\angle X$ if $x = 10$, $y = 12$, and $m\angle Y = 18°$.

2. Find x if $y = 21$, $m\angle X = 31°$, and $m\angle Y = 43°$.

3. Find z if $y = 15$, $m\angle Y = 79°$, and $m\angle Z = 79°$.

4. Find $m\angle Z$ if $y = 23$, $z = 19$, and $m\angle Y = 123°$.

5. Find y if $z = 54$, $m\angle Y = 65°$, and $m\angle Z = 21°$.

6. Find $m\angle Y$ if $y = 36$, $z = 42$, and $m\angle Z = 39°$.

7. Find $m\angle X$ if $x = 54$, $z = 63$, and $m\angle Z = 33°$.

8. Find x if $z = 18$, $m\angle X = 25°$, and $m\angle Z = 31°$.

9. Find x if $y = 20$, $m\angle X = 30°$, and $m\angle Y = 60°$.

10. Find $m\angle X$ if $x = 63$, $y = 72$, and $m\angle Y = 45°$.

11. Find $m\angle Z$ if $y = 7$, $z = 3$, and $m\angle Y = 31°$.

12. Find x if $y = 35$, $m\angle X = 118°$, and $m\angle Y = 20°$.

13. Find $m\angle X$ if $x = 9$, $y = 15$, and $m\angle Y = 62°$.

14. Find y if $z = 70$, $m\angle Y = 25°$, and $m\angle Z = 100°$.

Find the area of each triangle.

15.

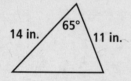

14 in.   65°   11 in.

16.

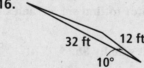

32 ft   12 ft   10°

17.

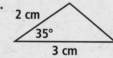

2 cm   35°   3 cm

18. A triangle has sides of lengths 15 in. and 22 in., and the measure of the angle between them is 95°. Find the area of the triangle.

19. A hot-air balloon is observed from two points, A and B, on the ground 800 ft apart as shown in the diagram. The angle of elevation of the balloon is 65° from point A and 37° from point B. Find the distance from point A to the balloon.

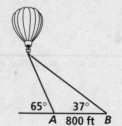

65°   37°
A   800 ft   B

20. Two searchlights on the shore of a lake are located 3020 yd apart as shown in the diagram. A ship in distress is spotted from each searchlight. The beam from the first searchlight makes an angle of 38° with the baseline. The beam from the second light makes an angle of 57° with the baseline. Find the ship's distance from each searchlight.

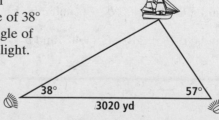

38°   57°
3020 yd

Reteaching 14-5

The Law of Cosines

• •

OBJECTIVE: Using the Law of Cosines to find the measures of the sides or angles of a triangle

MATERIALS: None

- To determine whether to use the Law of Sines or the Law of Cosines, look at the given information.

- If given the measure of two sides for a triangle and the angle between them or the measure of all three sides, use the Law of Cosines.

- If given the measure of two angles of a triangle and the length of any side or the measure of two sides and the measure of the angle opposite one of them, use the Law of Sines.

Example

Based on the given information, use the Law of Cosines to find the third side of the triangle.

$B = 20°, a = 120, c = 100$
⟵ **Because B is between a and c, use the Law of Cosines.**

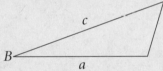

⟵ **Draw a triangle and label a, c, and B.**

$b^2 = 120^2 + 100^2 - 2(120)(100)\cos 20°$
⟵ **Insert the values into the Law of Cosines formula. Note that the side you are finding the length of and that side's opposite angle are on opposite ends of the equation.**

$b^2 = 14400 + 10000 - (24000)(0.93969)$
⟵ **Use a calculator to find cos 20°.**

$b^2 = 1847.4$
⟵ **Simplify.**

$b = 42.98$
⟵ **Find the square root of each side.**

Exercises

Find the unknown side measure or angle for each triangle. Round to the nearest tenth.

1. Find a if $A = 18°, c = 72$, and $b = 100$.

2. Find c if $a = 15, C = 152°$, and $b = 4$.

3. Find A if $B = 45°, a = 9$, and $c = 19$.

4. Find a if $A = 16°, b = 92$, and $c = 32$.

5. Find B if $a = 9, b = 3$, and $c = 11$.

6. Find c if $C = 30°, a = 15$, and $b = 15$.

7. Find C if $B = 95°, a = 5$, and $c = 6$.

8. Find B if $a = 18, b = 26$, and $c = 15$.

• •

Practice 14-5

The Law of Cosines

Use the Law of Cosines. Find the measure of the indicated part of each triangle. Round answers to the nearest tenth.

1. Find x if $y = 4$, $z = 9$, and $m\angle X = 16°$.

2. Find y if $x = 8$, $z = 5$, and $m\angle Y = 8°$.

3. Find $m\angle Y$ if $x = 17.2$, $y = 22.1$, and $z = 31.3$.

4. Find z if $x = 32$, $y = 25$, and $m\angle Z = 21°$.

5. Find $m\angle Y$ if $x = 14$, $y = 6$, and $z = 10$.

6. Find $m\angle X$ if $x = 24.9$, $y = 32.0$, and $z = 42.3$.

7. Find x if $y = 16$, $z = 4$, and $m\angle X = 123°$.

8. Find $m\angle Z$ if $x = 6.2$, $y = 5.9$, and $z = 3.4$.

9. Find z if $x = 321$, $y = 543$, and $m\angle Z = 54°$.

10. Find $m\angle Z$ if $x = 235$, $y = 154$, and $z = 239$.

11. Find x if $y = 10$, $z = 12$, and $m\angle X = 29°$.

12. Find y if $x = 3$, $z = 6$, and $m\angle Y = 15°$.

13. Find x if $y = 8$, $z = 7$, and $m\angle X = 149°$.

14. Find z if $x = 7$, $y = 22$, and $m\angle Z = 12°$.

15. Find z if $x = 46$, $y = 67$, and $m\angle Z = 85°$.

16. Find $m\angle X$ if $x = 4$, $y = 7$, and $z = 10$.

17. Find $m\angle Y$ if $x = 32$, $y = 79$, and $z = 86$.

18. Find $m\angle Z$ if $x = 3$, $y = 2.9$, and $z = 4.6$.

19. Find $m\angle Y$ if $x = 34.7$, $y = 18.9$, and $z = 21.5$.

20. Find $m\angle Z$ if $x = 14$, $y = 16$, and $z = 18$.

21. The sides of a triangular lot are 158 ft, 173 ft, and 191 ft. Find the measure of the angle opposite the longest side to the nearest tenth of a degree.

22. A car travels 50 miles due west from point A. At point B, the car turns and travels at an angle of 35° north of due east. The car travels in this direction for 40 miles, to point C. How far is point C from point A?

Reteaching 14-6

Angle Identities

OBJECTIVE: Finding exact trigonometric values using angle sum and difference identities	**MATERIALS:** None

We can use the following identities to find exact values for some trigonometric functions.

Angle Difference Identities

$\sin (A - B) = \sin A \cos B - \cos A \sin B$
$\cos (A - B) = \cos A \cos B + \sin A \sin B$

$\tan (A - B) = \dfrac{\tan A - \tan B}{1 + \tan A \tan B}$

Angle Sum Identities

$\sin (A + B) = \sin A \cos B + \cos A \sin B$
$\cos (A + B) = \cos A \cos B - \sin A \sin B$

$\tan (A + B) = \dfrac{\tan A + \tan B}{1 - \tan A \tan B}$

Example

Find the exact value of $\sin 75°$.

$$75° = 45° + 30°$$

⟵ **We know exact values for the trigonometric functions at 45° and 30°, so we can use the sum identity for sine.**

$\sin (A + B) - \sin A \cos B + \cos A \sin B$ ⟵ **Sine Angle Sum Identity**

$\sin (45° + 30°) = \sin 45° \cos 30° + \cos 45° \sin 30°$ ⟵ **Substitute 45° for A and 30° for B.**

$$= \frac{\sqrt{2}}{2} \cdot \frac{\sqrt{3}}{2} + \frac{\sqrt{2}}{2} \cdot \frac{1}{2}$$ ⟵ **Replace with exact values.**

$$= \frac{\sqrt{6}}{4} + \frac{\sqrt{2}}{4}$$ ⟵ **Simplify.**

$$= \frac{\sqrt{6} + \sqrt{2}}{4}$$

So $\sin 75° = \dfrac{\sqrt{6} + \sqrt{2}}{4}$.

Exercises

Find each exact value. Use a sum or difference identity if needed.

1. $\sin 150°$ **2.** $\cos 195°$ **3.** $\cos 150°$

4. $\sin 165°$ **5.** $\cos (-75°)$ **6.** $\sin (-75°)$

7. $\tan (-300°)$ **8.** $\tan 120°$ **9.** $\sin (-45°)$

Practice 14-6

Angle Identities

Find each exact value. Use a sum or difference identity.

1. $\sin 240°$

2. $\tan(-300°)$

3. $\sin(-105°)$

4. $\cos 15°$

5. $\sin 15°$

6. $\sin 135°$

7. $\cos 225°$

8. $\tan 225°$

9. $\tan 240°$

10. $\cos 390°$

11. $\sin(-300°)$

12. $\tan(-75°)$

Verify each identity.

13. $\cot\left(\theta - \dfrac{\pi}{2}\right) = -\tan\theta$

14. $\sin\left(\theta - \dfrac{\pi}{2}\right) = -\cos\theta$

15. $\cos\left(\theta - \dfrac{\pi}{2}\right) = \sin\theta$

16. $\sec\left(\theta - \dfrac{\pi}{2}\right) = \csc\theta$

Use the definitions of the trigonometric ratios for a right triangle to derive each cofunction identity.

17. A cofunction identity for $\tan(90° - A)$

18. A cofunction identity for $\cos(90° - A)$

Solve each trigonometric equation for $0 \le \theta < 2\pi$.

19. $2\sin\left(\dfrac{\pi}{2} - \theta\right)\tan\theta = 1$

20. $\cos\left(\dfrac{\pi}{2} - \theta\right)\tan\theta - \sec(-\theta) = 1$

21. $\sin^2\theta + \cos^2\theta = \tan\theta$

22. $2\sin^2\theta = \sin(-\theta)$

23. $\sqrt{3}\cos\left(\dfrac{\pi}{2} - \theta\right) = \cos(-\theta)$

24. $\cot\left(\dfrac{\pi}{2} - \theta\right) = \sin\theta$

25. $\csc\left(\dfrac{\pi}{2} - \theta\right) = \tan\theta$

26. $2\cos\left(\dfrac{\pi}{2} - \theta\right) = \tan(-\theta)$

27. $\csc^2\theta - \cot^2\theta = 2\cos\theta$

28. $\sin\left(\theta - \dfrac{\pi}{2}\right)\cos\theta = 0$

Use mental math to find the value of each trigonometric expression.

29. $\sin 10° \cos 80° + \cos 10° \sin 80°$

30. $\cos 110° \cos 70° - \sin 110° \sin 70°$

31. $\sin 310° \cos 130° - \cos 310° \sin 130°$

32. $\cos 95° \cos 50° + \sin 95° \sin 50°$

Reteaching 14-7

Double-Angle and Half-Angle Identities

OBJECTIVE: Using double-angle and half-angle identities to verify other identities

MATERIALS: None

Double-Angle Identities

$\cos 2\theta = \cos^2 \theta - \sin^2 \theta$

$\cos 2\theta = 2\cos^2 \theta - 1$

$\cos 2\theta = 1 - 2\sin^2 \theta$

$\sin 2\theta = 2\sin \theta \cos \theta$

$\tan 2\theta = \dfrac{2\tan \theta}{1 - \tan^2 \theta}$

Half-Angle Identities

$\sin \dfrac{\theta}{2} = \pm\sqrt{\dfrac{1 - \cos \theta}{2}}$

$\cos \dfrac{\theta}{2} = \pm\sqrt{\dfrac{1 + \cos \theta}{2}}$

$\tan \dfrac{\theta}{2} = \pm\sqrt{\dfrac{1 - \cos \theta}{1 + \cos \theta}}$

You can use the double-angle and half-angle identities to verify other identities.

Example

Verify the identity $\sin^2 \theta = \dfrac{1 - \cos 2\theta}{2}$

$\sin^2 \theta = \dfrac{1 - \cos 2\theta}{2}$

$\sin^2 \theta = \dfrac{1 - (1 - 2\sin^2 \theta)}{2}$ ⟵ **Use the double-angle identity for cos 2θ.**

$\sin^2 \theta = \dfrac{2\sin^2 \theta}{2}$ ⟵ **Simplify.**

$\sin^2 \theta = \sin^2 \theta$ ⟵ **Simplify.**

Exercises

Verify each identity.

1. $2\cot 2\theta = \cot \theta - \tan \theta$

2. $\cos^2 \theta = \dfrac{1 + \cos 2\theta}{2}$

3. $\csc \theta - 2\sin \theta = \dfrac{\cos 2\theta}{\sin \theta}$

4. $\sin^2 \dfrac{\theta}{2} = \dfrac{\csc \theta - \cot \theta}{2\csc \theta}$

5. $\cot \theta = \dfrac{\sin 2\theta}{1 - \cos 2\theta}$

6. $\sin^2 \dfrac{\theta}{2} = \dfrac{\tan \theta - \sin \theta}{2\tan \theta}$

Practice 14-7

Double-Angle and Half-Angle Identities

Given $\sin \theta = \frac{7}{25}$ and $90° < \theta < 180°$, find the exact value of each expression.

1. $\cos \frac{\theta}{2}$ **2.** $\sin \frac{\theta}{2}$ **3.** $\tan \frac{\theta}{2}$

4. $\sec \frac{\theta}{2}$ **5.** $\csc \frac{\theta}{2}$ **6.** $\cot \frac{\theta}{2}$

Given $\cos \theta = -\frac{8}{17}$ and $180° < \theta < 270°$, find the exact value of each expression.

7. $\sin \frac{\theta}{2}$ **8.** $\cos \frac{\theta}{2}$ **9.** $\cot \frac{\theta}{2}$

10. $\tan \frac{\theta}{2}$ **11.** $\csc \frac{\theta}{2}$ **12.** $\sec \frac{\theta}{2}$

Use an angle sum identity to verify each identity.

13. $\cos 2\theta = \cos^2 \theta - \sin^2 \theta$ **14.** $\cos 2\theta = 2 \cos^2 \theta - 1$

15. $\cos 2\theta = 1 - 2 \sin^2 \theta$ **16.** $\sin 2\theta = 2 \sin \theta \cos \theta$

Verify each identity.

17. $\cos^2 \theta = \frac{1 + \cos 2\theta}{2}$ **18.** $\cot \theta = \frac{\sin 2\theta}{1 - \cos 2\theta}$

19. $\tan \theta + \cot \theta = 2 \csc 2\theta$ **20.** $\frac{\cos 2\theta}{\sin \theta \cos \theta} = \cot \theta - \tan \theta$

Use a double-angle identity to find the exact value of each expression.

21. $\sin 120°$ **22.** $\tan 600°$ **23.** $\sin 660°$

24. $\cos 660°$ **25.** $\tan 90°$ **26.** $\cos 90°$

27. $\tan 660°$ **28.** $\sin 240°$ **29.** $\tan 120°$

Use a half-angle identity to find the exact value of each expression.

30. $\cos 15°$ **31.** $\cos 7.5°$ **32.** $\tan 7.5°$

33. $\sin 7.5°$ **34.** $\cos 45°$ **35.** $\tan 22.5°$

36. $\cos 22.5°$ **37.** $\sin 90°$ **38.** $\cos 90°$